Supercalc 5

An Active-Learning Approach

PH Bassett

Paul Bassett is a Senior Lecturer at Dudley College, specialising in accounts and information technology.

DP Publications Ltd
Aldine Place
LONDON W12 8AW
1993

A058050

A CIP catalogue record for this book is available from the British Library

ISBN 1 85805 048 0

Printed by The Guernsey Press Co. Ltd.,
Braye Road, Vale, Guernsey, Channel Islands

Preface

This book is designed with two principal objectives in mind:

- firstly, that the user should be able to develop skills in using the various SuperCalc commands and formulae;
- secondly, that the user should develop an awareness of the possible applications that SuperCalc can be used for.

Therefore, each of the lessons in this book covers a variety of SuperCalc commands, and demonstrates how SuperCalc can be used in a practical application. As the book is essentially designed for Computer and Business Studies students the areas selected are all associated with the Accounting function; however, as users get to grips with the commands they should be able to develop applications within other functional areas as well.

It should be particularly useful for students on BTEC and Degree courses as it reinforces subject matter in accounting subjects, and also fulfils the objectives relating to the use of spreadsheets.

Designed as a teach-yourself guide to the SuperCalc spreadsheet program, the book is divided into individual lessons, each of which covers some of the commands and options available when using SuperCalc. Simple exercises are included at the end of each lesson so that the user can practise the commands taught in that lesson. Suggested answers to these exercises can be found at the end of the book.

Each lesson builds upon the work done in the previous lesson, and by the end of the book the user should be capable of using all of the commands offered by the SuperCalc program.

Users are advised to proceed through the book in the correct sequence, as some lessons assume that the user has built up knowledge from the preceding lessons, and a number of lessons use files created in earlier lessons.

To aid users when they are creating their own spreadsheets a full list and explanation of all commands and formulae is provided at the end of the book.

Note re compatibility: The book can be used, as far as the author is aware, on all 'bug free' versions of SuperCalc 5.

Introduction

This section identifies and describes the concepts and terms used in SuperCalc, and defines the term 'spreadsheet'.

Spreadsheets

Originally, in the days before computers were widely available, a spreadsheet was a large sheet of paper divided into rows and columns. These sheets were principally used by engineers and accountants for setting out details of complex calculations.

A spreadsheet program uses the memory of a computer to store the spreadsheet and allows the user to key in whatever headings and entries are required. The advantage over the original manual method lies in the ability of the program to perform calculations automatically, and also the so-called 'what-if' function.

The 'what-if' function is the most important aspect of computerised spreadsheets. It enables the user to set up his or her working data (as in a manual system), but any alterations or adjustments can be made instantly by simply amending any one figure. The spreadsheet program should ensure that the effects of the adjustment are recalculated throughout the entire spreadsheet. In a manual system the user would have to redraft the entire sheet.

Unfortunately, computers do not, generally, have very large screens, which means that only a small proportion of the spreadsheet can be shown at any one time. Like most computer applications it is possible to scroll the screen so that different parts of the spreadsheet can be examined. References are used in order to make it easier for the user to find the required part of the spreadsheet.

Each row is given a number:

```
Row: 1: ..............................
     2: ..............................
     3: ..............................
     4: ..............................
```

and, each column is given a letter:

```
Column:      :  A  :  B  :  C  :  D  :  E  :
             |     |     |     |     |     |
             |     |     |     |     |     |
```

Therefore, the user can move to any row or column simply by entering the appropriate command to move to the desired row number or column letter. The columns and rows overlap like some huge sheet of graph paper, and each 'square' in the spreadsheet is referred to as a **cell**. Each cell can be referred to by its column letter and row number:

```
Column:         :  A  :  B  :  C  :  D  :  E  :
Row:        1:  |     |     |     |     |     |
            2:  |     |-----|     |     |     |
            3:  |     |     |     |     |     |
            4:  |     |     |     |     |     |
```

The cell highlighted is B2; (ie: column B and row 2)

All spreadsheet packages have this same basic layout, and many of them have very similar commands. Consequently, someone who has learnt how to use SuperCalc should be able to use other well known spreadsheet packages, such as Lotus 1-2-3 and Multiplan, without a great deal of additional training.

The size of different packages will vary, and even the different versions of SuperCalc are of different sizes, this is because the size of the spreadsheet is dependent on the amount of memory available on the computer. The size of SuperCalc 5 is 9,999 rows by 255 columns, which gives a total of 2,549,745 cells.

However, the total number of cells available for most computers will be a lot less than this as the actual cells available will be limited by the memory of the computer used. Fortunately not many applications will require over two million cells.

Use of the keyboard

SuperCalc makes extensive use of the special keys, found on most keyboards, to simplify and speed up the process of designing and operating a spreadsheet program. Most of the keys used in SuperCalc have similar functions in other software packages, which means that users can quickly develop skills in other packages. The main keys used in SuperCalc are as follows:

SHIFT There are two shift keys, one on either side of the keyboard. Hold down either of these keys to select a letter or character above the numeric keys, or to produce text in upper case (Capitals).

CAPS LOCK Press this key once and all subsequent letters are produced in upper case. Press it again to return to lower case.

NUM LOCK Press this key once and all keys pressed on the **numeric keypad** will produce numbers only. Press it again the keys will move the cursor in various directions.

SCROLL Locks the cursor in place, pressing the arrow keys will move the rest of the screen rather than the cursor.

TAB Use with the arrow keys to move the cursor to the last occupied cell in the spreadsheet.

ARROW KEYS Moves the cursor right, left, up or down one cell at a time.

HOME Moves the cursor back to the first cell in the spreadsheet (A1).

END When used in conjunction with arrow keys this will move the cursor to the last occupied cell to the right, left, up or down.

PgUp Moves the cursor up one screen (20 lines).

PgDn Moves the cursor down one screen (20 lines).

CTRL When used in conjunction with arrow keys will move the cursor one 'screen' to the right, left, up or down. Also used in conjunction with other keys to clear the entry line (**Ctrl** and **Break**), and perform various functions with multiple spreadsheets (with **function** keys).

ESC Used to remove last operation, usually used to alter a particular command option or return to the spreadsheet after viewing a HELP menu.

= Used as part of formulae, but also used in conjunction with the **GoTo** command to move the cursor across large areas of the spreadsheet.

+ Used in formulae to **add** numbers or cells.

– Used in formulae to **subtract** numbers or cells.

* Used in formulae to **multiply** numbers or cells.

/ Used in formulae to **divide** numbers or cells.

Function keys These are the 'F' keys found either at the top or left hand side of the keyboard, and have for a variety of uses. They are generally used as a quick method of using a standard command, eg: F10 is the quick way of viewing graphs (this operation can also be performed by using the **Graphics** command). F1 is used to examine the various HELP menus – a common use for this key in many other programs.

ALT Used in conjunction with the **function** keys to produce a wider range of 'quick' commands. Most of the Alt and function keys are used for **Macro** commands.

Loading instructions

Instructions for loading SuperCalc have deliberately been left out of this manual as the pathname used is likely to vary depending upon whether the user has a twin drive machine or hard disk machine. The space below has been left blank so that loading instructions can be written in if required.

Contents

Lesson 1 *The basics of SuperCalc*

This lesson concentrates on getting to grips with the basics of SuperCalc. You will learn how to move the cursor and howto enter formulae and text into a spreadsheet.
At the end of this lesson you should be able to:

a) move the cursor using the cursor keys
b) use the GoTo command
c) use formulae to add, subtract, divide, multiply, find averages, maximum, minimum and count the number of cells used.
d) correct errors
e) load and save work
f) display formulae
g) quit SuperCalc

1.1 Getting started

To load SuperCalc follow the instructions given in the SuperCalc manual, or those you have written in at the front of this manual.

When SuperCalc has loaded you will be presented with the following screen:

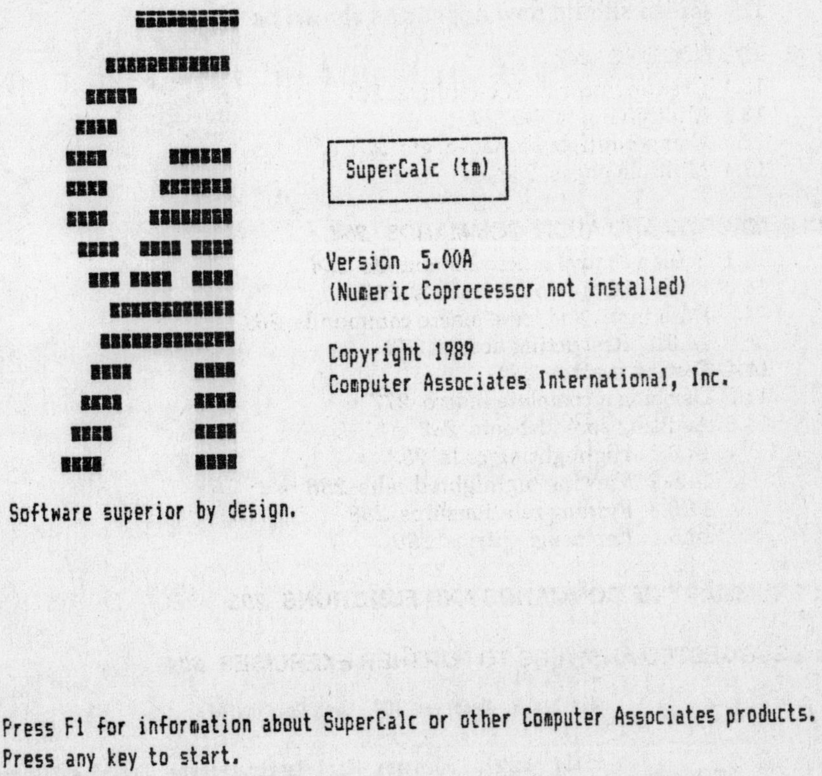

SuperCalc (tm)
Version 5.00A
(Numeric Coprocessor not installed)
Copyright 1989
Computer Associates International, Inc.
Software superior by design.
Press F1 for information about SuperCalc or other Computer Associates products.
Press any key to start.

Fig 1.1

This screen simply shows the details of the version of SuperCalc that you are using and the copyright details from the manufacturers.

The bottom of the screen shows the two options that are available to you: you can either press **F1** to examine the SuperCalc HELP menu or press any key to start.

Press **F1** and the first HELP menu will be displayed. This menu merely contains details of the various services and products offered by Computer Associates. This information is not especially important but does show how you can access the SuperCalc HELP menus by pressing **F1**. HELP menus are designed as *memory-joggers* and are not intended to show the first-time user how to operate SuperCalc.

SuperCalc has a large number of commands, most of which have a number of different options presented in the form of a menu. When you have done a few more lessons you will understand most of the information contained in these menus, and they will then become useful, for example if you are doing an exercise and cannot remember one of the commands, it will be quicker to jog your memory by referring to the HELP menu than by looking back through this manual.

In order to leave the HELP menu and get into SuperCalc you will have to move the cursor onto the item **Esc=Return to SuperCalc** which is shown at the bottom left of the screen. When the phrase is highlighted press **ENTER**. Alternatively, you can simply press the **ESC** key.

1.2 The spreadsheet

The screen should now appear as shown below.

```
      |  A  ||  B  ||  C  ||  D  ||  E  ||  F  ||  G  ||  H  |
 1
 2
 3
 4
 5
 6
 7
 8
 9
10
11
12
13
14
15
16
17
18
19
20
↓TEMP1!A1
Width:  9  Memory:  189  Last Col/Row:A1
  1>
READY F1:Help  F3:Names  Ctrl-Backspace:Undo  Ctrl-Break:Cancel
```

Fig 1.2

Do not touch anything yet!

Before proceeding it is essential that you understand exactly what is on the screen. The present screen is showing only the top left-hand corner of the spreadsheet, consisting of *columns* A to H and *rows* 1 to 20. The spreadsheet cursor will be shown either as a highlighted cell or as < >, depending on the machine that you are using. The cursor should be in cell A1.

If you look at the bottom of the screen under row 20 you should see four additional lines which are very important and need some explanation:

The ***status line*** is the first line and shows:

the name of the file in use, ie ↓TEMP1! *(this is used when no file name has been designated)*

the current cell, ie A1

The ***prompt line*** is the next line down and shows:

the width of the current cell, ie 9 spaces

the memory available, ie 189 kilobytes *(this will vary according to the memory available in different computers)*

the last cell used on the spreadsheet, ie A1

The ***entry line*** is the next line and is used for making entries into the spreadsheet. The purpose of a separate line is that entries can be typed in on this line and checked for accuracy before being transferred to the actual spreadsheet.

The bottom line shows some of the function keys used by SuperCalc. **F1** can be used to call up the HELP menu and the use of the other keys will be explained later.

The full purpose of each of these lines will become apparent shortly, but for the time being you should try to remember what each line is called.

1.3 Moving the cursor

The screen is currently showing only a small proportion of the spreadsheet because it is so large that it cannot all be shown on the screen at any one time. In order to view the rest of the spreadsheet and to move the cursor to other cells it is necessary to use the cursor movement keys.

The cursor can be moved one cell at a time by using the *arrow keys* on the *numeric keypad* or the *cursor movement keypad* If the keys are held down then the cursor will continue to move automatically. See if you can move the cursor into cell E16.

The screen should now show the following:

```
      |   A    ||   B    ||   C    ||   D    ||   E    ||   F    ||   G    ||   H    |
  1
  2
  3
  4
  5
  6
  7
  8
  9
 10
 11
 12
 13
 14
 15
 16
 17
 18
 19
 20
 TEMP1!E16
Width:  9  Memory:  189  Last Col/Row:A1
 1>
READY F1:Help  F3:Names  Ctrl-Backspace:Undo  Ctrl-Break:Cancel
```

Fig 1.3

Note that the entry on the *status line* now shows **E16** as this is the new current cell. The arrow at the beginning of the line shows the direction of movement (this may be down or right) and is the direction in which the cursor will move if the **RETURN** or **ENTER** key is pressed. Now you try, to see if it works.

The arrow keys are the main keys used for moving the cursor but are a bit slow if a very large spreadsheet is being used. There are some other cursor movement keys available if you want to move the cursor a long way.

Firstly, try pressing the **PgUp** key (or number 9 with **NUMLOCK** off) – this will return the cursor to the top of column E (ie: E1). Now try pressing the **PgDn** key (or number 3) – this will move the cursor down the spreadsheet 20 rows at a time. Press **PgDn** a few times see how it works.

Most spreadsheets will start in cell A1 and this cell can be jumped to at any time by pressing the **HOME** key (number 7). Use this to return to cell A1.

Sometimes you will want to go to a specific cell, for example BK589. This would take some time to reach using the normal keys or even with the **PgDn** keys. A quick way of getting to any specific cell is to use the **GoTo** command. Press the = key and the *prompt* and *entry* lines should alter as shown in Fig1.4.

```
    |  A  ||  B  ||  C  ||  D  ||  E  ||  F  ||  G  ||  H  |
1
2
3
4
5
6
7
8
9
10
11
12
13
14
15
16
17
18
19
20
 TEMP1!A1
Enter cell to jump to.
  5>=>A1
POINT F1:Help F2:Edit F3:Names Home:1st End-Arrow:last Ctrl-Break:Cancel
```

Fig 1.4

Note that both the *prompt line* and the *entry line* have changed – the program has assumed that you will want to jump to cell A1 as this is the *current cell.* This is not the cell required and this entry will be removed as soon as you start typing in another cell reference.

Type in bk589. This should appear on the *entry line* for you to check, and if you have typed it in correctly then you can press **ENTER**. The cursor should now move to cell BK589.

Practise moving the cursor using the numeric keypad keys and the **GoTo** command. Note that the function key **F5** can also be used to call up the **GoTo** command. See if you can find the bottom right-hand cell in your spreadsheet.

1.4 Correcting errors

Now that you can move the cursor around the spreadsheet it is time to start making entries in the spreadsheet. As spreadsheets are mainly used for performing complex calculations, we will start by seeing how SuperCalc deals with numbers and calculations.

However, you are bound to make at least one mistake whilst working through this manual, so the first thing to learn is how to remove errors.

Firstly, move the cursor back to cell A1 (press the **HOME** key). Let us suppose that the cell should contain the number 345; type this number and it should appear on the *entry line.*

```
        |  A  ||  B  ||  C  ||  D  ||  E  ||  F  ||  G  ||  H  |
  1
  2
  3
  4
  5
  6
  7
  8
  9
 10
 11
 12
 13
 14
 15
 16
 17
 18
 19
 20
 TEMP1!A1
Width:  9  Memory:  189  Last Col/Row:A1
 4>345
ENTRY F1:Help F2:Edit F3:Names Home:1st End-Arrow:last Ctrl-Break:Cancel
```

Fig 1.5

This number has not yet been entered onto the spreadsheet and amendments can still be made in one of three ways:

Method 1

The *entry line* has its own cursor which is flashing one space to the right of your number. Suppose the number should have been 325 not 345. If you press the **DELETE** or **BACKSPACE** (←) keys (different keyboards have different uses for these keys). You can delete characters from the end of the number. Do this to delete numbers 5 then 4. Now type in the number 2 followed by 5. Now press **ENTER** and the number will be transferred onto the spreadsheet in cell A1.

Method 2

The spreadsheet cursor will now be in either cell A2 or B1 (it doesn't matter which). This is the cell that will be used for the next entry.

Type the number 620 onto the entry line.

This number is incorrect and should be 914. It could be amended by using the **DELETE** key but it will be quicker to start all over again. Press the key marked

Ctrl and hold it down whilst pressing **Z** once. This will clear the entire entry line so that you can start all over again. Type in 914 then press **ENTER**.

The more modern way of deleting or cancelling entries is to use the **Ctrl** key in conjunction with the **Break** key (usually situated on the right-hand side of the keyboard). This combination of keys can be used to stop a wide variety of commands.

Method 3

Sometimes when devising your own spreadsheet you will change your mind as to layout or contents and will want to start all over again. This is easily achieved by the use of the **Zap** command.

All proper SuperCalc commands are called up by the / key. Press this key once and you should get the screen shown below:

```
      |   A   ||   B   ||   C   ||   D   ||   E   ||   F   ||   G   ||   H   |
 1       325
 2       914
 3
 4
 5
 6
 7
 8
 9
10
11
12
13
14
15
16
17
18
19
20
Arrange  Blank  Copy  Delete  Edit  Format  Global  Insert  Justify  Load  Move
Name  Output  Protect  Quit  Save  Title  Unprotect  Window  Zap  1-2-3  /more
  2>/
MENU  Sort spreadsheet (or specified range) by a column or row
```

Fig 1.6

The *prompt line* has altered again and now shows a list of commands – these are just some of the commands available in SuperCalc 5 and you will be using all of these later on in this manual, but for the time being the only one you require is the **Zap** command. Not surprisingly this is obtained by typing the letter **Z**, or by moving the cursor onto the word **Zap** by using the arrow keys and then pressing **ENTER**.

The *prompt line* will then ask you to press **N** for **no**, **Y** for **yes**, **S** for save or **P** for page.

Notice that SuperCalc gives some limited advice relating to each option. If you move the cursor onto each option by using the arrow keys, the bottom line of the screen will briefly explain each option.

These options give you the chance to change your mind as, once the spreadsheet is **zapped,** the data is gone completely and cannot be recovered. However, the data on your existing spreadsheet is not needed so you can press **Y** to **zap** everything. Once again this can be selected by either pressing **Y** or moving the cursor onto **Y** and then pressing **ENTER**. You should now have a completely blank spreadsheet.

1.5 Help menus

You have already seen how to load HELP by pressing **F1**. The HELP menus available once you have loaded SuperCalc are quite detailed and relate to how to use the program.

This section will demonstrate how to load and work through the HELP menus, but you should try and remember that these menus are designed as *memory-joggers* and are not intended to teach you how to use SuperCalc.

The main HELP menu is known as the HELP INDEX and is obtained by pressing **F1**. This is shown on the bottom of the screen at all times. If you press this now you will be presented with a screen similar to the one shown in Fig 1.7 (this menu will vary slightly depending on which version of SuperCalc you are using).

The HELP INDEX is divided into the different function areas of Supercalc, so if you have never used a spreadsheet program before this will probably be fairly meaningless. However, the areas highlighted are the **function areas,** and the items listed underneath refer to those items that can be selected from the **HELP INDEX**.

Help Index — SuperCalc AnswerScreen

SuperCalc Basics:	Entering Data:	Spreadsheet Format:
SuperCalc Startup	Erasing Data	Text Display
Program Defaults	Undo Feature	Number Display
Optimizing SuperCalc	Hiding Data	Date and Time Display
Modes and Indicators	Using Point Mode	Currency Format
Searching for Files	Reference Syntax	Column Width
Optimizing Memory		
Saving, Loading, Quitting		
Creating Reports:	Formulas:	Advanced Topics:
Printing Reports	Functions	Macros
Fonts, Borders & Shade	Cell References	Charting
Creating Lines	Operators	Using a Database
Device Selection	Formula Display	How To Parse Data
Multiple Spreadsheets:	Miscellaneous:	Keys:
Basic Concepts	Transpose Rows to Columns	Keys and Function Keys
Creating	Named Ranges	International Keys
Display Windows	Spreadsheet Auditing	Entering ASCII Chars
Spreadsheet Pages		

RELATED TOPICS: Slash Commands // Commands

ESC=Return to SuperCalc F2 = How to use Help F3 = Help Index

Fig 1.7

You have learned some of the ways to move the cursor around the spreadsheet, but there are many others, the details of which can be found under the function area entitled **Keys:**.Use the arrow keys to select the first item (**Keys and Functions Keys**) under this heading, and then press **ENTER** to select it.

The screen will now change to show the HELP screen relating to **keys and Function keys**. Each item that is prefixed with the word ***see*** has its own subsidiary HELP screen. The problem with using HELP menus is that they can create even more confusion for the inexperienced user – which is probably how you feel right now!

Move the cursor onto the item marked **ENTRY & EDIT Keys**, then press **ENTER**, and you will be presented with the screen below. This explains the use of the cursor movement keys that you have been using so far in this lesson.

SuperCalc AnswerScreen

ENTRY & EDIT Keys

→ ←	{RT}{LT}	ENTRY: Enters data and moves spreadsheet cursor. EDIT: Moves one character right or left.
↑ ↓	{UP}{DN}	ENTRY: Enters data and moves spreadsheet cursor. EDIT: Inserts or Deletes character.
Home	{HOME}	Moves to start of entry line.
End	{END}	Moves to end of entry line.
Tab	{TAB}	Moves between start and end of entry line.
Backspace	{BS}	Moves left and deletes one character.
Esc	{ESC}	Clears entire data entry. Press ALT-F8 or Esc again to recover.
Del	{DEL}	Deletes character at the edit cursor.
Ins	{INS}	Toggles insert mode. Cursor shape indicates mode.

RELATED TOPICS: Function Keys Ready & Point Keys
ESC=Return to SuperCalc F2 = How to use Help F3 = Help Index

Fig 1.8

The cursor should be positioned at the bottom of the screen which shows that there are two **RELATED TOPICS** which could be selected if more HELP is required. The other options are **Return to SuperCalc, How to use Help** or **return to the Help Index**.

Now you have an idea of how the HELP menu system in SuperCalc work, you can ignore the other HELP options and select **ESC** to return to the SuperCalc screen.

1.6 Numbers and formulae

Spreadsheets are mainly used in accounting procedures, and SuperCalc has a number of functions that can be used for performing various calculations.

In order to demonstrate these functions (or formulae) it is first necessary to have some figures to use in calculations. The cursor should be in cell A1. Type in 22 and press **ENTER** to transfer this onto the spreadsheet. Now move the cursor into cell A2 and enter the numbers as shown on the screen below:

```
      |  A  ||  B  ||  C  ||  D  ||  E  ||  F  ||  G  ||  H  |
   1     22
   2     37
   3     12
   4     45
   5     80
   6
   7
   8
   9
  10
  11
  12
  13
  14
  15
  16
  17
  18
  19
  20
 TEMP1!A6
Width:  9  Memory:  189  Last Col/Row:A5
  1>
READY F1:Help  F3:Names  Ctrl-Backspace:Undo  Ctrl-Break:Cancel
```

Fig 1.9

You now have a series of numbers displayed on the spreadsheet, the next step is to use these numbers to perform a series of calculations.

Adding

The obvious thing to do is to add up all the numbers shown on the spreadsheet. This is achieved by the SUM statement. Make sure that the cursor is in cell A6. Type in the following (NB: don't worry if it is in lower case as SuperCalc will accept commands in both upper and lower case):

SUM(A1.A5)

The . between the two cell references can also be written as .. or :. The SUM statement tells the computer it must add some numbers (A1:A5) and tells it the *range* in which to add, ie all numbers in the cells from A1 through to A5.

Press **ENTER** to transfer this formula to the spreadsheet and cell A6 should show the answer. If it doesn't you have made a mistake and should refer back to the earlier section on correcting errors.

Averages

The AVERAGE statement will find the average of the numbers in your list. The format is similar to that in the SUM statement in that it needs the statement title and range to be specified. Move the cursor to cell A7 and type:

AVERAGE(A1.A5)

Press **ENTER** and the average of the list of figures should appear in cell A7. *This formula can also be entered as AVG(a1.a5).*

Count

In some large spreadsheets it may be important to know just how many sets of numbers are involved in a particular range, and this can be found by using the COUNT statement. Once again the range needs to be specified:

COUNT(A1.A5)

Press **ENTER** and the answer (5) should appear in cell A8. This figure can be checked by counting how many cells there are between A1 and A5.

Maximum

In larger spreadsheets it may also be important to know which cell contains the largest number. Type in:

MAX(A1.A5)

Press **ENTER** and cell A9 should then show 80 as this is the largest number in the range.

Minimum

To find the cell which contains the smallest number you use the MIN statement. Type in:

MIN(A1.A5)

Cell A10 should show the answer as 12 as this is the smallest number in the range.

```
     |  A  ||  B  ||  C  ||  D  ||  E  ||  F  ||  G  ||  H  |
 1        22
 2        37
 3        12
 4        45
 5        80
 6       196
 7      39.2
 8         5
 9        80
10        12
11
12
13
14
15
16
17
18
19
20
  TEMP1!A11
Width:  9  Memory:  188  Last Col/Row:A10
  1>
READY F1:Help  F3:Names  Ctrl-Backspace:Undo  Ctrl-Break:Cancel
```

Fig 1.10

Other formulae

There are a number of other formulae that can be used for simpler arithmetical calculations.

Firstly, move the cursor to cell B1 using the **GoTo** command (remember it is either the = sign or **F5**). The next series of formulae can be entered in column B – this will show that formulae do not have to be entered in sequence but can be entered anywhere on the spreadsheet.

Type in the following and then press **ENTER**:

A1+A2

The value shown in cell B1 should now be 59 (ie: 22 + 37).

Move the cursor down to cell B2 if it isn't there already.

Now type: **A2–A3**

Press **ENTER** and this should subtract whatever value is in cell A3 from whatever value is in cell A2 (ie:37 – 12).

Now type in cell B3: **A6/A1**

Press **ENTER** and this will divide the value in cell A6 by whatever value is in cell A1 (ie: 196/22). (NB: Most computer keyboards do not have a proper division symbol so the / key is used instead.)

Now type in cell B4: **A4*A5**

Press **ENTER** and this will multiply whatever value is in cell A4 by the value in A5. (NB: The asterisk symbol is always used in computing as the multiplication key.)

Now type in cell B5: **10%A1**

Press **ENTER** and this will calculate 10% of whatever value is in A1 (ie: 10% of 22). *This formula could also have been entered as **A1*10/100** or **A1*.1**.*

It will often be necessary to increase a number by a set percentage.

Type in cell B6: **10%A1**

Press **ENTER** and a number which is 10% greater than that in A1 will appear in cell B6. *This formula could also have been entered as A1*110/100 or A1*1.1. All three versions will produce the same answer.*

Now type in cell B7: **A1+(A2/10)**

Press **ENTER** and this will divide the figure in A2 by 10 (ie: 37/10) and add it to the value in A1.

SuperCalc can also perform **IF THEN** statements which are useful where two alternatives are required. Your cursor should be in cell B8.

Type in: **IF(A1>10,2)**

This statement first asks if the value in A1 is greater than 10 and, if it is, then the value entered in the current cell (B8) will be 2.

Now type in cell B9: **IF(A1>10,A2+10)**

The statement now asks if A1 is greater than 10. If it is then the value in the current cell (B9) will be A2+10. If the value in A1 is less than 10 the answer in the current cell will be 0.

The IF THEN statement can include two options so that if the IF part is not true an alternative calculation can take place.

The statement below is used to ascertain whether the value in A1 is greater than 30; if it is greater than 30 then the value in B10 will be A2+10; but if the value in A1 is less than 30 then the value in B10 will be A3–3. Type the statement in cell B10 and see if you can work out what the answer should be:

IF(A1>30,A2+10,A3-3)

The SUM statement can be used again to show the total of all figures on the spreadsheet.

Type in cell B11: **SUM(A1:B10)**

```
      |  A  ||  B  ||  C  ||  D  ||  E  ||  F  ||  G  ||  H  |
 1          22       59
 2          37       25
 3          12 8.909091
 4          45     3600
 5          80      2.2
 6         196     24.2
 7        39.2     25.7
 8           5        2
 9          80       47
10          12        9
11             4331.209
12
13
14
15
16
17
18
19
20
  TEMP1!B12
Width:  9  Memory:  188  Last Col/Row:B11
  1>
READY F1:Help  F3:Names  Ctrl-Backspace:Undo  Ctrl-Break:Cancel
```

Fig 1.11

The screen should now show the same figures as those shown above. This formula has added all figures included in the range A1 (top left hand corner) to B10 (bottom right hand corner).

There are also less commonly used formulae that may be useful on some occasions or in certain areas. Some of these formulae will be familiar to most people, even if it is some time since they were last used! The first of these is the square root formula. This formula can be used to find the square root of the value in cell B11.

Type in cell B12: **SQRT(B11)**

This will give the answer to a suitable number of decimal places. If, however, you want to show the answer as a whole number only you can do this by using the **INTEGER** formula (remember that an integer is a whole number).

The cursor should already be in cell B13 so type in: **INT(B12)**

This should remove all decimal places from the answer in cell B12. (NB: INT does not round up but merely 'truncates' the value.)

On other occasions it may be appropriate to show an answer to a desired number of decimal places, and SuperCalc allows you to alter the display in two ways. The most efficient way will be demonstrated in later lessons, but the simplest way is to use the **ROUND** formula. This will allow you to round off a value to any number of decimal places required. You can now use this formula to round off the answer in cell B12 to two decimal places.

Type in: **ROUND(B12,2)**

Unlike the INT formula, this formula does actually round up when necessary. All of these formulae could have been used without reference to a cell number, for example,

type in: **ROUND(123.456,1)**

This considers the value in the first part of the cell and then displays it to one decimal place.

*If you do not have sufficient time available to complete this exercise then you can save the work done so far by using the **Save** command. Refer to the instructions at the end of this lesson.*

These formulae are in fact only a small sample of the many varied formulae available in SuperCalc. Most of the other formulae will be dealt with in later lessons.

1.7 Formula display

The screen now shows all of the answers to your formulae. Unfortunately you have almost certainly forgotten which value relates to which formula, and this could present a problem if you wanted to amend any of the formulae.

The cursor should be in cell B16. If you move it back up to cell B15 (using the arrow keys) then the screen should show the following display:

```
    |   A    ||   B    ||   C    ||   D    ||   E    ||   F    ||   G    ||   H    |
1          22       59
2          37       25
3          12 8.909091
4          45     3600
5          80      2.2
6         196     24.2
7        39.2     25.7
8           5        2
9          80       47
10         12        9
11           4331.209
12           65.81192
13                 65
14              65.81
15              123.5
16
17
18
19
20
 TEMP1!B15                   Form=ROUND(123.456,1)
Width:  9  Memory:  188  Last Col/Row:B15
 1>
READY F1:Help  F3:Names  Ctrl-Backspace:Undo  Ctrl-Break:Cancel
```

Fig 1.12

If your screen cursor is shown as < > then it will partly obscure the value in cell B15 – do not worry, this is not altering your figure, just temporarily covering it.

If you look at the *status line* it should display **Form=ROUND (123.456,1)**. The *status line* enables you to check the entry in any cell by displaying the **contents**. The spreadsheet is displaying the answers to the formulae, but the computer has stored the formulae used and these can be examined by moving the cursor to the desired cell and viewing the formula on the *status line*. All formulae can be examined in turn by moving the cursor. Now try this for yourself.

On some occasions you will want to check all the formulae at the same time. This can be done by using another of SuperCalc's / commands. Firstly, press the / key – the screen should change so that the *prompt line* shows the commands available The same thing happened when you used the **Zap** command, but this time the command you require is the **Global** command. To call up the **Global** command simply press the letter G or move the cursor onto the word **Global** and then press **ENTER**.

The **Global** command is one of the more powerful commands available in SuperCalc and the screen shows some of the options available when using the **Global** command. Most of the SuperCalc commands have a range of options to choose from (you have already seen the options available with the **Zap** command, but **Global** is a much more powerful command and consequently has many more options). What you are trying to do is to show all the **formulae** on the screen instead of the answers to the formulae. The option you require is **Formula**. Press the **F** key, or select it with the cursor, and the screen should change again to show the following display.

```
       |   A    ||   B    ||   C    ||   D    ||   E    ||   F    ||   G    ||   H    |
   1    22        A1+A2
   2    37        A2-A3
   3    12        A6/A1
   4    45        A4*A5
   5    80        10%A1
   6    SUM(A1:A  110%A1
   7    AVERAGE(  A1+(A2/10)
   8    COUNT(A1  IF(A1>10,2)
   9    MAX(A1:A  IF(A1>10,A2+10)
  10    MIN(A1:A  IF(A1>30,A2+10,A3-3)
  11              SUM(A1:B10)
  12              SQRT(B11)
  13              INT(B12)
  14              ROUND(B12,2)
  15              ROUND(123.456,1)
  16
  17
  18
  19
  20
 TEMP1!B15                          Form=ROUND(123.456,1)
Width:  9  Memory:  188  Last Col/Row:B15
  1>
READY F1:Help  F3:Names  Ctrl-Backspace:Undo  Ctrl-Break:Cancel
```

Fig 1.13

This now shows the formulae used instead of the values. The end of some of the formulae in column A have been cut off. This is because each column on the spreadsheet is only nine characters wide, and therefore only the first nine characters can be displayed – the remainder is cut off by the entries in column B. Column C has nothing in it so the computer can display the full formulae for column B.

This display is important as it shows what each cell actually contains, as opposed to what the result of what it contains. For example, cell B1 contains the formula **A1+A2** and not the **56** which was shown before.

The importance of this is that if the contents of either A1 or A2 are altered, then the contents of cell B1 will automatically alter as well. You can try this next.

To revert to normal display the process is simply repeated. Press:

/	to call up the commands
G	to select the **Global** command
F	to select the **Formula** display option

Alternatively, you can move the cursor onto the desired option by using the cursor movement keys.

Move the cursor to cell A1 (pressing the **HOME** key is quickest way). Type in 45 and press **ENTER**. The value shown in cell B1 should alter, and all other cells in column B that used cell A1 in their formula will change as well. Now change the entries in cell A2 to 50 and A4 to 75.

The effect of these changes is that the screen will now alter to that shown below. Note how many of the cells have been altered.

```
      |    A    ||    B    ||    C    ||    D    ||    E    ||    F    ||    G    ||    H    |
  1          45         95
  2          50         38
  3          12  5.822222
  4          75       6000
  5          80        4.5
  6         262       49.5
  7        52.4         50
  8           5          2
  9          80         60
 10          12         60
 11              7038.222
 12              83.89411
 13                     83
 14                  83.89
 15                  123.5
 16
 17
 18
 19
 20
  TEMP1!A5                         Form=80
Width:  9  Memory:  187  Last Col/Row:B15
  1>
READY F1:Help  F3:Names  Ctrl-Backspace:Undo  Ctrl-Break:Cancel
```

Fig 1.14

This is what is known as the WHAT IF effect of spreadsheets. Once the formulae are entered then the figures can be amended as often as desired and the revised answers will be re-calculated automatically.

1.8 Saving work

If you have not completed the lesson but do not have time to finish and would like to save the work done until your next session then you must first use the **Save** command. Press the / key and the commands should be shown on the *prompt line*. The letter for Save is **S**, so select this . The *prompt line* will then request a name for your file, but you will also have to designate which disk drive it will be saved to (see 'Introduction'). A suitable file name will be LESSON1, so if you are using a twin drive machine place your data disk in drive B, then enter the file name as B:LESSON1. If you are using a hard disk machine then place your data disk in the disk drive and enter the file name as A:LESSON1.

Press **ENTER** and you will then be asked if you want to **Save All, Values, Part, Duplicate, Level, Mode** or **Single**. A brief description of each option is given at the bottom of the screen and you can examine these by moving the cursor over each item in turn. A more detailed description can be found by pressing **F1**. This is also another way of examining the HELP menu as you can go straight to the topic which you require help on. Now press **F1**.

A simpler explanation of each option is:

All	saves everything
Values	saves answers only (not formulae)
Part	saves a specified range only (eg A1.A5)
Duplicate	saves file under another name
Level	saves files so that they can then be used by SuperCalc 3 or SuperCalc 4
Mode	specifies which sort of cells can be saved
Single	used with very large spreadsheets for saving just one section

Press **ESC** to return to the spreadsheet, then press **A** for **All**, and then you can follow the instructions to Quit.

When you want to recommence this lesson you need to load SuperCalc and then reload your file. To do this you use the **Load** command by pressing the / key and then selecting **Load**. The file name will be either A:LESSON1 or B:LESSON1, depending upon whether you are using a twin drive or hard disk machine.

1.9 Quitting SuperCalc

You can leave this lesson now if you wish, although you are advised to attempt the further exercises to reinforce the work covered.

If you have finished the lesson and intend to attempt the further exercises then you should now **zap** the screen as shown in the section on correcting errors. This will delete all of the work done so far and leave you with a fresh spreadsheet to start work on.

If you have completed the lesson but do not intend to attempt the further exercises yet then you should exit SuperCalc in the correct manner. It is never advisable to simply switch off the computer and all programs should be exited properly. To do this in SuperCalc requires the use of the **Quit** command. Press the / key and the *prompt line* should alter to show the various commands. Select the option for **Quit** and the *prompt line* will now show the options available with the **Quit** command.

These options are:

No	use this if you select quit by mistake
Yes	use this to finish the current session
To	use this to start another program
Save	use this to finish but save work first
DOS	use this to go to DOS temporarily

The option that you require should be **Yes**, so press **Y** or select this option with the cursor.

Further exercises

Start with a blank spreadsheet and enter the following figures **down** column A: 100, 234, 410, 120, 65, 89.

Move the cursor to column B and then enter the formulae going **down** column B to calculate the following:

Cell:	Formula:
B1	Add up all numbers in column A
B2	Find the Average of the numbers in column A
B3	Count the number of numbers in column A
B4	Find the largest number in column A
B5	Find the smallest number in column A
B6	Add the number in cell A1 to the number in cell A5
B7	Multiply the number in cell A2 by that in cell A6
B8	Divide A3 by A5
B9	Find 25% of the number in A2
B10	Add 10% to the number in cell A1
B11	If A1 is greater than 200, then enter A3 in this cell, if A1 is less than 200, then enter A4 in this cell

Now amend the numbers as follows: change A1 to 230, change A4 to 75, change A5 to 190.

Display formulae on screen.

When you have completed these exercises you can follow the instructions given previously to quit SuperCalc.

Lesson 2 *Common SuperCalc commands*

This lesson will examine some more of the more frequently used commands available in SuperCalc, and demonstrate how to use text and improve the layout of work.

At the end of this lesson you should be able to:

a) enter headings and text
b) underline headings and totals
c) round off figures (using the **Format** command)
d) copy formulae (using the **Copy** command)
e) insert additional rows/columns (using the **Insert** command)
f) delete excess rows/columns (using the **Delete** command)
g) widen columns (using the **Format** command)
h) allocate *names* to blocks (using the **Name** command)
i) Printout simple spreadsheets (using the **Output** command)

In this lesson you will learn how spreadsheets can be used to set up simple tables. The example we will use is an analysis of sales by product and area.

2.1 Copying formulae

Load SuperCalc as instructed. Type in the figures as shown in the following display:

```
     |   A    ||   B    ||   C    ||   D    ||   E    ||   F    ||   G    ||   H    |
  1        40
  2        55
  3        70
  4        85
  5        25
  6
  7
  8
  9
 10
 11
 12
 13
 14
 15
 16
 17
 18
 19
 20
TEMP1!A6
Width:  9  Memory:  189  Last Col/Row:A5
  1>
READY F1:Help  F3:Names  Ctrl-Backspace:Undo  Ctrl-Break:Cancel
```

Fig 2.1

These figures represent the sales of our product in the different regions of the country at the normal selling price. The titles of the different regions have deliberately been left out to show you that it is possible to set up your figures in a spreadsheet first and then make it tidier afterwards.

The figures shown represent the expected sales at a selling price of £10 per unit. If the selling price is increased by 10% then sales will reduce by 5%. A second column can be added to show the expected sales at the increased prices. The price does not need to be entered yet, just the reduction in sales. Move the cursor to cell B1 (using the cursor arrow keys or the **GoTo** command).

Instead of working out every answer separately, you can let SuperCalc do it for you by using the formulae you learned in lesson 1. The correct formula could be: **A1*95/100** or **A1*.95** or **95%A1**, all of which will produce the same answer. Type one of these formulae into cell B1 now.

The value in cell B1 should now be 38. The same formula needs to be repeated for every cell from B1 to B5, except that in B2 it will need to be A2*.95; in B3 it will need to be A3*.95 and so on. Make sure that you understand this logic before proceeding.

However, it will not be necessary to enter all of these formulae as SuperCalc can do it for you using the **Copy** command. **Copy** is the command used to *echo* a cells contents across any range desired.

To call up the **Copy** command you need to press the / key. When you have done this press C for Copy or select this option with the cursor keys. SuperCalc will then ask you to specify the range you want to copy from and the range you want to copy to.

What you want to do is to copy the formula in cell B1 to all of the cells in the range B2 to B5. To do this you will need to show that B1 is the cell to copy from, so your answer to the prompt **From:** is B1. You can either type this in or move the cursor back onto cell B1 by using the cursor keys. When the *status line* shows **/Copy,B1** press **ENTER** to accept this as the start cell.

The next prompt will ask where you want to copy **To:**. You can type in B2.B5 (note that ranges for all commands are specified as *start cell.end cell*, the **.** effectively means **to**), however, it is often more accurate (and easier to follow) if the area is highlighted on the screen. The *status line* should show **C1** as this is the current cell. As you want the new block to start from B2 move the cursor into this cell with the arrow keys and then, when the *status line* shows **/Copy,B1,B2**, press **ENTER** to show that this is the *starting cell* for the block and then move the cursor down to cell B5. As you do this the area to be copied to will be highlighted on the screen so that you can be sure that you know which range you are including. When you have reached cell B5 the status line should show **/Copy,B1,B2:B5** as this is the range required press **ENTER** to accept it and the screen should now show a list of values in cells B1 to B5. These should correspond with the values shown on the screen display shown in Fig 2.2.

This method of copying often takes some getting used to so remember that you can simply call up the **Copy** command and type in the cell ranges. However, experienced users usually prefer to designate ranges with the help of the cursor movement keys as the highlighting of ranges reduces the risk of error.

```
      |  A  ||  B  ||  C  ||  D  ||  E  ||  F  ||  G  ||  H  |
   1       40      38
   2       55   52.25
   3       70    66.5
   4       85   80.75
   5       25   23.75
   6
   7
   8
   9
  10
  11
  12
  13
  14
  15
  16
  17
  18
  19
  20
TEMP1!C1
Width:  9  Memory:  188  Last Col/Row:B5
  1>
READY F1:Help  F3:Names  Ctrl-Backspace:Undo  Ctrl-Break:Cancel
```

Fig 2.2

If you check these figures you will find that the entry in column B is 5% less than the adjacent entry in column A. This is because SuperCalc has automatically adjusted your original formula and updated for the new cells. If you use the Global, Formula command as described in Lesson 1 you should get the following display:

```
      |  A  ||  B  ||  C  ||  D  ||  E  ||  F  ||  G  ||  H  |
   1  40      95%A1
   2  55      95%A2
   3  70      95%A3
   4  85      95%A4
   5  25      95%A5
   6
   7
   8
   9
  10
  11
  12
  13
  14
  15
  16
  17
  18
  19
  20
TEMP1!C1
Width:  9  Memory:  188  Last Col/Row:B5
  1>
READY F1:Help  F3:Names  Ctrl-Backspace:Undo  Ctrl-Break:Cancel
```

Fig 2.3

This shows how SuperCalc has decided that the formula should be adjusted as it is entered in each new cell.

The **Copy** command can copy more than one column at a time. Let us assume that the number of sales will reduce by 5% every time there is a 10% increase in selling price. This will mean that column C will be used for a further 10% price increase and column D for yet another 10% increase.

This means that the values in column C will be 5% less than those in column B, and the values in column D will be 5% less than those in column C. You can enter these figures simply by using the **Copy** command.

All of the formulae in column B can be copied to columns C and D. Press the / key and select **Copy**. The range **F(rom)** will be all of the cells used in column B (ie: B1:B5), so type this in or select the block with the cursor keys and then press **ENTER**.

The range **T(o)** will be C1 to D1 (ie C1:D1). This often causes confusion as users expect the range *T(o)* to be C1:D5. What you need to understand is that **Copy** is copying a *block* of five values:

B1 |..|
B2 |..|
B3 |..|
B4 |..|
B5 |..|

If this block was copied to cell C1 only it would still fill the cells C1 to C5:

B1 |..| C1 |..|
B2 |..| C2 |..|
B3 |..| C3 |..|
B4 |..| C4 |..|
B5 |..| C5 |..|

If you have entered the range as C1:D1 you can press **ENTER.** This is one of the instances where the cursor keys make it much easier to see if the block is being copied to the correct cells than it would be if the cell range were typed in. All of the formulae should now be copied to the appropriate cells and the formulae updated at the same time.

The screen should now show the same values as those in Fig 2.4.

This still shows the formulae. Before changing back to show the values there is one other formula that can be entered. It would be useful to know what the total sales are for all of the regions, and this can be shown as the last entry in each column.

```
   |  A   ||   B    ||   C    ||   D    ||   E    ||   F    ||   G    ||   H    |
 1   40      95%A1     95%B1     95%C1
 2   55      95%A2     95%B2     95%C2
 3   70      95%A3     95%B3     95%C3
 4   85      95%A4     95%B4     95%C4
 5   25      95%A5     95%B5     95%C5
 6
 7
 8
 9
10
11
12
13
14
15
16
17
18
19
20
 TEMP1!C1                          Form=95%B1
Width:  9  Memory:  188  Last Col/Row:D5
  1>
READY F1:Help  F3:Names  Ctrl-Backspace:Undo  Ctrl-Break:Cancel
```

Fig 2.4

These totals can easily be found by finding the SUM of each column. This formula was covered in lesson 1 so you should know how to add up each column, and as you now know how to use the **Copy** command you should be able to copy the formula from cell A6 to the appropriate cells in the other columns. See if you can work out yourself how to enter the formula for SUM and how to copy it. The correct method is shown below but try and attempt it yourself first.

The formula for the SUM statement will need to be entered in cell A6, so you must move the cursor to that cell first. The formula is **SUM(A1:A5).** When you have entered this you can **copy** it to cells B5 to D5 by selecting the appropriate blocks with the cursor keys, or pressing the following keys:

/ C A6 (ENTER) B6:D6 (ENTER)

The screen should now show the same results as Fig 2.5.

```
   |  A  ||  B  ||  C  ||  D  ||  E  ||  F  ||  G  ||  H  |
1   40       95%A1    95%B1    95%C1
2   55       95%A2    95%B2    95%C2
3   70       95%A3    95%B3    95%C3
4   85       95%A4    95%B4    95%C4
5   25       95%A5    95%B5    95%C5
6   SUM(A1:A SUM(B1:B SUM(C1:C SUM(D1:D5)
7
8
9
10
11
12
13
14
15
16
17
18
19
20
TEMP1!A6                     Form=SUM(A1:A5)
Width:  9  Memory:  188  Last Col/Row:D6
  1>
READY F1:Help  F3:Names  Ctrl-Backspace:Undo  Ctrl-Break:Cancel
```

Fig 2.5

The screen cannot show all formulae as the columns are not wide enough. If you move the cursor onto a particular cell then the full formula will be displayed on the *status line*. Section 2.5 will explain how columns can be widened.

It is probably now worth reversing the screen display to show the values instead of the formulae. The method for this is to use the **Global, Form** command again. The keys to press are:

/ G F

The screen should now show:

```
        |  A  ||   B  ||    C   ||   D   ||  E  ||  F  ||  G  ||  H  |
 1         40       38     36.1   34.295
 2         55    52.25  49.6375 47.15563
 3         70     66.5   63.175 60.01625
 4         85    80.75  76.7125 72.87688
 5         25    23.75  22.5625 21.43438
 6        275   261.25 248.1875 235.7781
 7
 8
 9
10
11
12
13
14
15
16
17
18
19
20
TEMP1!A6                      Form=SUM(A1:A5)
Width:  9  Memory:  188  Last Col/Row:D6
  1>
READY F1:Help  F3:Names  Ctrl-Backspace:Undo  Ctrl-Break:Cancel
```

Fig 2.6

Whilst this screen shows the figures that are required it is not very clear what they relate to. What is needed are some headings and text to describe the different entries.

2.2 Inserting columns and rows

Unfortunately, there is no room at present to show headings either at the top or the side of the figures. SuperCalc will allow you to insert extra rows and columns by using the **Insert** command.

Firstly, you could do with an extra column so that you can enter the names of the different regions. Move the cursor into column **A** and then select the **Insert** command by pressing the / key. Then pressing **I** for Insert or select this option with the cursor keys.

You will then be asked to specify **Row, Column, Block** or **Page,** press **C** for **Column.**

The next prompt will ask you to specify the column letters – the default value provided will be the column that the cursor is currently in. If you want a different column you can simply type in the appropriate column letter. As you do require a new column inserted at column A just press **ENTER**, a new column A will be inserted, with the existing columns being moved over one column as shown below:

```
     |  A  ||  B  ||  C  ||  D  ||  E  ||  F  ||  G  ||  H  |
1               40       38      36.1    34.295
2               55    52.25   49.6375  47.15563
3               70     66.5    63.175  60.01625
4               85    80.75   76.7125  72.87688
5               25    23.75   22.5625  21.43438
6              275   261.25  248.1875  235.7781
7
8
9
10
11
12
13
14
15
16
17
18
19
20
TEMP1!A6
Width:  9  Memory:  188  Last Col/Row:E6
  1>
READY F1:Help  F3:Names  Ctrl-Backspace:Undo  Ctrl-Break:Cancel
```

Fig 2.7

This will now enable you to enter the names of the different regions in column A. However, before you do this you might like to insert some extra rows so that you can enter some headings for each of the columns. You will need five rows in total for the headings, so you want to insert some new rows at rows 1 to 5.

The sequence in which to do this is:

/	for commands
I	for **Insert**
R	for **Rows**
1:5	for rows 1 to 5
ENTER	

Key in the above in the sequence shown and the spreadsheet should then show:

```
   |    A    ||    B    ||    C    ||    D    ||    E    ||    F    ||    G    ||    H    |
 1
 2
 3
 4
 5
 6                      40         38      36.1    34.295
 7                      55      52.25   49.6375  47.15563
 8                      70       66.5    63.175  60.01625
 9                      85      80.75   76.7125  72.87688
10                      25      23.75   22.5625  21.43438
11                     275     261.25  248.1875  235.7781
12
13
14
15
16
17
18
19
20
TEMP1!A6
Width:  9  Memory:  188  Last Col/Row:E11
   1>
READY F1:Help  F3:Names  Ctrl-Backspace:Undo  Ctrl-Break:Cancel
```

Fig 2.8

2.3 Deleting columns and rows

Occasionally it will also be necessary to remove some unwanted columns or rows and the command for deleting rows or columns is, not surprisingly, **Delete**. Note that this command is not intended for use in deleting incorrect formula or text but more correctly for removing surplus columns or rows in order to improve spread-sheet layout.

In the last section five extra rows were **inserted** where, in fact, four would have been sufficient. The extra row can now be deleted. The sequence in which to do this is:

- **/** to call up commands
- **D** to select **Delete**
- **R** to select **Row**
- **5** to delete row 5
- **ENTER**

This should remove the existing row 5 and all other rows will be moved up to replace it. The **Delete** command can delete columns in a similar way and can also be used to delete surplus files.

2.4 Entering text

You should now be in a position to start entering the headings. It is worth remembering that earlier versions of SuperCalc required you to enter " before any text, but the more recent versions will add the " prefix automatically when the text is entered. This is useful to know as, if you attempt to enter a formula but make a mistake, SuperCalc will interpret it as text and insert the " prefix automatically. Consequently, if you try to **edit** the formula you will also have to delete the " at the beginning of the statement.

Move the cursor to cell A1 (press the **HOME** key). This cell will be used for the heading of your spreadsheet. The heading is:

Sales of Product: Alpha

Type this in on the entry line, note what the number is at the beginning of the *entry line*, then press **ENTER**. the heading should now be transferred to the spreadsheet.

As this is the main heading it would look better if underlined. Move the cursor to cell A2. The best key to use for underlining is the - key. The reason that it was suggested that you check the number that was shown at the beginning of the *entry line*, was so that you would know how many -s to enter. The number should have been 24. Type in - 24 times and then press **ENTER**.

You should now have the following displayed on your screen:

```
     |  A  ||  B  ||  C  ||  D  ||  E  ||  F  ||  G  ||  H  |
  1  Sales of Product: Alpha
  2  ------------------------
  3
  4
  5                  40      38     36.1   34.295
  6                  55   52.25  49.6375 47.15563
  7                  70    66.5   63.175 60.01625
  8                  85   80.75  76.7125 72.87688
  9                  25   23.75  22.5625 21.43438
 10                 275  261.25 248.1875 235.7781
 11
 12
 13
 14
 15
 16
 17
 18
 19
 20
  TEMP1!A3                                                  TEXT
 Width:  9  Memory:  188  Last Col/Row:E10
  1>
 READY F1:Help  F3:Names  Ctrl-Backspace:Undo  Ctrl-Break:Cancel
```

Fig 2.9

Row 3 will be used to show the changes in selling price. Move the cursor to cell A3 and type in:

Price: and press **ENTER**

The selling prices can be entered by using the **Copy** command again. Move the cursor to cell B3 and type in 10 – this represents the normal selling price of £10 per unit.

It would be possible to enter the selling price as £10, but this would make the figure *text* and formulae cannot be used with *text* entries.

Move the cursor to cell C3 and enter the following:

110%B3

This formula should add 10% onto the figure in B3. The **Copy** command can now be used to copy this formula to all of the other cells in row 3. You should know how to do this by now but just in case you need reminding, the method is:

/	for commands
C	for **Copy**
C3	for **From**
ENTER	
D3:E3	for **To**
ENTER	

When entering D3.E3, try to use the cursor keys and the full stop *anchor* to highlight the areas required, instead of merely typing it in, as you will find this method much easier once you get used to it.

```
    |  A  ||  B  ||  C  ||  D  ||  E  ||  F  ||  G  ||  H  |
 1  Sales of Product: Alpha
 2  ------------------------
 3  PRICE:          10       11     12.1     13.31
 4
 5                  40       38     36.1    34.295
 6                  55    52.25  49.6375  47.15563
 7                  70     66.5   63.175  60.01625
 8                  85    80.75  76.7125  72.87688
 9                  25    23.75  22.5625  21.43438
10                 275   261.25 248.1875  235.7781
11
12
13
14
15
16
17
18
19
20
 TEMP1!D3                        Form=110%C3
Width:  9  Memory:  187  Last Col/Row:E10
 1>
READY F1:Help  F3:Names  Ctrl-Backspace:Undo  Ctrl-Break:Cancel  CAPS
```

Fig 2.10

If you do not have sufficient time to complete this lesson then you can save the work done by following the instructions given at the end of Lesson 1. The filename for this work should be LESSON2.

These headings can be underlined as well, but this time you want the underline to continue right across the screen. This can be done quite easily be using the **Repeating Text** command.

Pressing the ' key before entering any text will have the effect of copying that text right across the row to the end of the available spreadsheet, or until it comes up against a cell that is being used.

To underline all headings in row 3, move the cursor to cell A4 then type:

'- ENTER

The - will be repeated in every cell across the screen as shown:

```
       |  A  ||  B  ||  C  ||  D  ||  E  ||  F  ||  G  ||  H  |
 1   Sales of Product: Alpha
 2   -----------------------
 3   PRICE:          10       11      12.1    13.31
 4   ------------------------------------------------------------------------
 5                   40       38      36.1   34.295
 6                   55    52.25 49.6375 47.15563
 7                   70     66.5  63.175 60.01625
 8                   85    80.75 76.7125 72.87688
 9                   25    23.75 22.5625 21.43438
10                  275   261.25 248.1875 235.7781
11
12
13
14
15
16
17
18
19
20
  TEMP1!A5
Width:  9  Memory:  187  Last Col/Row:E10
  1>
READY F1:Help  F3:Names  Ctrl-Backspace:Undo  Ctrl-Break:Cancel  CAPS
```

Fig 2.11

If you use the **GoTo** command to look at row 4 in the parts of the spreadsheet not shown on the screen, you should find that the underlining continues to the end of the spreadsheet.

2.5 Widening columns

The only other text to be entered is the names of the different regions. Move the cursor to cell A5, and type in **MIDLANDS** as the name of the first region.

Now move the cursor to cell A6 and type in **NORTH EAST** as the name of the second region.

You will now see that the spreadsheet does not show all of this text. The reason for this is that all columns are currently only 9 characters wide (see *Width: 9* on the *prompt line*). When you entered the main heading this was accepted, even though it was more than 9 characters, because there was no entry in the next cell (ie: B1).

But the spreadsheet will not allow this text to overlap the next column because there is an entry in cell A6.

The solution is to widen column A. The command used to widen columns is the **Format** command. This is a particularly useful command and will be looked at in greater detail in future lessons. At the moment you only need it to widen column A.

Call up the **Format** command by pressing **/ F**. You will then be presented with the following options:

Global	(ie: the entire spreadsheet)
Column	(ie: specified columns only)
Row	(ie: specified rows only)
Entry	(ie: part rows or columns)
User-Define	(ie: to define specific formats)
Hide-column	(to suppress the display of specified columns)

These options (with the exception of User-Define) are used to establish the range to be *formatted*. You want to **format** column A to make it wider so select Column. The column range will be A only, so press **A** (if this letter is not already shown) and then **ENTER**.

You will then be presented with an even more formidable list of options:

Accept	used when all options have been selected
Integer	all figures shown as whole numbers
General	all figures shown with the most suitable number of decimal places
Exponential	all numbers shown to the power of ten
$	all numbers shown to two decimal places
Right	all numbers shown as right-justified
Left	all numbers shown as left-justified
Centre	all numbers centred in each column
Text	alters justification of text
*****	simple graphic display
User-defined	apply a User-defined format already set up
Hide	hide confidential values
Default	returns all values to original settings
Width	alter width of columns

These options may seem totally confusing at present, but their applications should become clearer as you progress through this manual.

At present all you want to do is to widen column A. This column will need to be 15 characters wide. To widen it all you need to do is to select **Width,** and then type in the desired width (ie: 15) or press the right arrow key until the width shown is 15.

The display should then show that column A has been widened to 15 spaces.

You can now enter the other regions as shown in figure 2.12.

```
   |      A        ||  B  ||  C  ||  D  ||  E  ||  F  ||  G  |
1   Sales of Product: Alpha
2   ----------------------
3   PRICE:              10       11     12.1    13.31
4   -----------------------------------------------------------
5   MIDLANDS            40       38     36.1   34.295
6   NORTH EAST          55    52.25  49.6375 47.15563
7   NORTH WEST          70     66.5   63.175 60.01625
8   SOUTH EAST          85    80.75  76.7125 72.87688
9   SOUTH WEST          25    23.75  22.5625 21.43438
10                     275   261.25 248.1875 235.7781
11
12
13
14
15
16
17
18
19
20
  TEMP1!A10                                                      TEXT
Width: 15  Memory:  187  Last Col/Row:E10
  1>
READY F1:Help  F3:Names  Ctrl-Backspace:Undo  Ctrl-Break:Cancel  CAPS
```

Fig 2.12

2.6 Integer values

The one remaining problem with your spreadsheet is that it shows the units that you will sell as decimals (eg: D5 has the number of units as 36.1 units). It is not possible to sell fractions of units, only whole numbers.

The display needs to show integer values only. The formula **INT** was used in the previous chapter, but it is not much use here as you want to display a whole spreadsheet as integers. Fortunately there is another option for showing integer values.

If you glance back at the list of options in the **Format** command you should be able to see that one of the options is to display numbers as integers.

The **Format** command can be used to alter the screen display. To do this you must follow this sequence:

/	to call up the commands
F	to select **Format**
E	to define the range required
B5:E10	to specify the entry range

(this range can also be selected by using the cursor keys)

ENTER	
I	to select **Integer**
ENTER	

The screen will then show:

```
   |      A        ||   B   ||   C   ||   D   ||   E   ||   F   ||   G   |
 1  Sales of Product: Alpha
 2  ----------------------
 3  PRICE:                  10        11      12.1     13.31
 4  -------------------------------------------------------------------
 5  MIDLANDS                40        38        36        34
 6  NORTH EAST              55        52        50        47
 7  NORTH WEST              70        67        63        60
 8  SOUTH EAST              85        81        77        73
 9  SOUTH WEST              25        24        23        21
10                         275       261       248       236
11
12
13
14
15
16
17
18
19
20
 TEMP1!A10
Width: 15  Memory:  187  Last Col/Row:E10
  1>
READY F1:Help  F3:Names  Ctrl-Backspace:Undo  Ctrl-Break:Cancel  CAPS
```

Fig 2.13

2.7 Naming blocks

One of the new commands introduced in version 4 is the ability to *name* blocks to make it easier for the user to re-call blocks of figures. Blocks can be given names that refer to their content and this is easier to remember than a range of cells.

In the next lesson you will use the data that you have entered in this lesson, but you will probably understand it better if the *ranges* used are given names rather than cell ranges. For example, the contents of cells B5 to E5 refer to the sales of our product at the varying prices in the Midland region only. It will be much simpler if these figures can be called into subsequent calculations by referring to them as **Midlands** rather than as a range **B5.E5**.

In order to name a block of cells you will need to use the **Name** command. To designate the block B5.E5 as MIDLANDS enter the following commands:

/	to call up commands
N	to select the **Name** command
C	to select **Create**
MIDLANDS	to specify the range name

ENTER

The next entry is for the range required which will be B5.E5, but you do not have to type this in as, once you have entered the commands shown above, the *entry line* will show the cell reference that the cursor is currently in. If you use the arrow keys to move the screen cursor to cell B5 the entry line should change to show the new cursor position.

As you want the range to be B5.E5 you should now press either **.** or **:**, then use the cursor movement keys to move the cursor to cell E5. The entry line will now show the range as B5.E5 and the block will be highlighted on the screen so that you can check that the range is correct. If it is you can press **ENTER**.

New users of SuperCalc often find this method of designating blocks confusing to begin with, but you will understand it in time and discover how much more efficient it is.

```
    |      A      ||  B  ||  C  ||  D  ||  E  ||  F  ||  G  |
 1  Sales of Product: Alpha
 2  ----------------------
 3  PRICE:                 10      11    12.1   13.31
 4  ------------------------------------------------------------
 5  MIDLANDS               40      38     36     34
 6  NORTH EAST             55      52     50     47
 7  NORTH WEST             70      67     63     60
 8  SOUTH EAST             85      81     77     73
 9  SOUTH WEST             25      24     23     21
10                        275     261    248    236
11
12
13
14
15
16
17
18
19
20
 TEMP1!E5              I      Form=95%D5
Enter range
 28>/Name,Create,MIDLANDS,B5:E5
POINT F1:Help F2:Edit F3:Names Home:1st End-Arrow:last Ctrl-Break:Cancel
```

Fig 2.14

Now that you have designated **MIDLANDS** for the Midlands region you should be able to *create* names for the other four regions as well. Use the same procedure as for **MIDLANDS** and create names for the other regions to designate the block ranges as follows:

NORTH EAST B6.E6
NORTH WEST B7.E7
SOUTH EAST B8.E8
SOUTH WEST B9.E9

When you have finished naming the ranges you can check that they have all been stored by pressing **F3**, which is shown on the bottom of the screen to remind you how to obtain a list of names.

This facility is needed because you may forget which blocks have been designated or what names you have used. If you press **F3** now the screen should show the following.

```
NAMED RANGE DIRECTORY
MIDLANDS          NORTH EAST          NORTH WEST          SOUTH EAST          SOUTH WEST










Current selection: MIDLANDS  (B5:E5)
  1>
NAME  F1:Help  F4:Select range  Return:Select name  Ctrl-Break:Cancel
```

Fig 2.15

To return to the main screen press **Ctrl** and **Break** together.

This section has demonstrated how blocks can be defined using the names command, and the next lesson will show how this command can make data entry quicker by calling up blocks stored as names.

2.8 Printing spreadsheets

You have now devised a simple spreadsheet which will be used as the basis for lessons 3 and 4, so you will need to **save** it shortly. However, before you do that there is one other command that is very useful: printing out a spreadsheet.

The spreadsheet devised in this lesson is very basic and only covers a small part of the spreadsheet area available. Any simple spreadsheets that can be displayed entirely on one screen can be printed off very easily. However, most spreadsheets will be considerably larger than the example used here, and therefore a more sophisticated technique is needed to obtain a suitable printout. This will be explained in Lesson 5.

At present the procedure is very straightforward: firstly you will need to call up the command used for **printing**. This is not **/ P** as you might expect – if you press / now you will see that **P** is for the **Protect** command (explained in Lesson 7). The command for obtaining a printout is in fact **Output.**

To obtain a printout follow this sequence:

/ to call up commands
O to select **Output**
P to select **Printer**
R to select **Range**

This procedure will ensure that the data is sent to the **printer** rather than any other form of output such as a disk. The **range** enables the user to specify which parts of the spreadsheet should be included in the printout. The current spreadsheet covers the **range A1 to E10.** This could be entered as the range, but it is not really necessary as you want **all** of the spreadsheet included in the printout, so you can just type **all** as the range, followed by **ENTER** (NB: do not use all on large spreadsheets but type in the range instead).

```
   |      A      ||  B  ||  C  ||  D  ||  E  ||  F  ||  G  |
 1  Sales of Product: Alpha
 2  -----------------------
 3  PRICE:             10      11    12.1   13.31
 4  ---------------------------------------------------------
 5  MIDLANDS           40      38     36      34
 6  NORTH EAST         55      52     50      47
 7  NORTH WEST         70      67     63      60
 8  SOUTH EAST         85      81     77      73
 9  SOUTH WEST         25      24     23      21
10                    275     261    248     236
11
12
13
14
15
16
17
18
19
20
 TEMP1!A10
Enter range , "-" to clear
 26>/Output,Printer,Range,ALL
EDIT  F1:Help  F3:Names  Ctrl-Backspace:Undo  Ctrl-Break:Cancel  CAPS
```

Fig 2.16

Note: the hyphens in row 4 (which extend to cell IV4) are ignored outside the range A1—E10 since they are created by cell A4.

The spreadsheet should now be ready to print but will not start immediately as the program will give you the chance to ensure that you are connected to a printer and that the printer is **On-Line** before it starts to print. If you have checked the printer then select **Go** to start printing.

This should produce a printout similar to that shown in Fig 2.17. If your printout is different it is because the printout options have been set differently on your computer. A more detailed explanation of the **Output** command is given in lesson 5 and this will include an explanation of how to alter the printer options.

This is the end of lesson 2, but the work done in the lesson will be used in the next lesson so it is essential that you **save** your spreadsheet. Follow the instructions at the end of lesson 1 to save your spreadsheet (make sure that you know whether you are saving to disk A: or B:) and call the file **LESSON2.**

Once you have saved your work you can **quit**, but it is recommended that you attempt the further exercises.

```
Sales of Product: Alpha
-----------------------
PRICE:                10        11      12.1     13.31
--------------------------------------------------------
MIDLANDS              40        38        36        34
NORTH EAST            55        52        50        47
NORTH WEST            70        67        63        60
SOUTH EAST            85        81        77        73
SOUTH WEST            25        24        23        21
                     275       261       248       236
```

Fig 2.17

Further exercises

Save the work that you have done so far, as detailed above. You can continue to use the existing work as the basis for the further exercises. These will involve producing a further spreadsheet from the information already obtained.

Firstly, you want to enter a new heading; move the cursor to cell A15 and enter the new heading as:

Sales per quarter:

You can underline this heading and then move the cursor to cell A17 and enter the column headings for the columns A to E as follows:

QUARTER: 1 2 3 4

Underline these headings with the repeating text key.

The row headings will be the same regions as used in the previous part of the spreadsheet so you can copy these to the appropriate cells, starting at cell A19, using the **Copy** command.

This spreadsheet will be used to record the sales for the different regions in each of the different quarters.

The sales for the first quarter are as follows:

Midlands	9
North East	12
North West	16
South East	19
South West	5

All sales are expected to increase by 10% for the second quarter, increase by 20% for the third quarter and then reduce by 10% in the last quarter. You will have to enter the formula for the first region but should then be able to use **COPY** to copy it to all of the other regions.

If you can do this successfully, then save this file as you can use it for the further exercises at the end of the next lesson. Save the spreadsheet to the same filename (LESSON2). This time SuperCalc will inform you that *the file already exists*, so you should press **O** for **Overwrite** and then proceed as normal.

Lesson 3 *Sales graphs*

All versions of SuperCalc since *SuperCalc3 release 1* have had some advanced graph features. Earlier versions did possess a very basic bar graph function, but this was never very presentable.

SuperCalc can produce seven different types of graph, of which four are particularly useful for accounting and business functions. The remainder are more commonly associated with mathematics and will not be considered in this manual.

The number of graphs that can be produced from one spreadsheet is limited only by the memory of your computer.

SuperCalc produces graphs from an existing spreadsheet, therefore the data for the graph must first be entered onto the spreadsheet in the normal way. This is, in fact, an advantage as it means that a spreadsheet can be prepared using the standard formulae and then, if required, a graph can be produced from the existing work. This will be demonstrated to you in this lesson by using the spreadsheet from the last lesson as the basis for producing graphs.

You can assume that the work done in Lesson 2 was devised so that the firm would have some idea of its forecast sales. Now that the spreadsheet has been devised the data can be presented in a better style by producing graphs from the various figures.

At the end of this lesson, and the subsequent lesson you should be able to produce:

a) simple bar graphs
b) bar graphs with complete headings
c) line graphs
d) stacked bar charts
e) pie charts
f) exploded pie charts
g) printouts of various types of graphs

3.1 The Graphics command

The first step is to reload the spreadsheet from Lesson 2 (you were told to save this – if you haven't then you will need to key in the figures again). The sequence to **load** spreadsheets is as follows:

/	to select the commands
L	to select the **Load** command
B:LESSON2	if you are using a twin drive machine
or	
A:LESSON2	if you are using a hard disk machine
R	to clear the current file and load LESSON2

You can now proceed to devise some graphs to illustrate this data. The logical choice of command would be G for graph, but G has already been used for the **Global** command. The command for graphs is accessed from SuperCalc's second *string* of

commands which is called up by pressing / twice. Press this now (//) and you should get the display shown in Fig 3.1.

```
  |      A      || B  ||  C  ||  D  ||  E  ||  F  ||  G  |
1  Sales of Product: Alpha
2  ---------------------
3  PRICE:            10     11    12.1   13.31
4  -----------------------------------------------------------
5  MIDLANDS          40     38     36     34
6  NORTH EAST        55     52     50     47
7  NORTH WEST        70     67     63     60
8  SOUTH EAST        85     81     77     73
9  SOUTH WEST        25     24     23     21
10                  275    261    248    236
11
12
13
14
15
16
17
18
19
20
Add-in  Data  Export  File  Graphics  Import  Macro  Network  Restrict
Spreadsheets  Test
  3>//
MENU  Attach, detach, invoke Add-in programs
```

Fig 3.1

This is the list of additional commands available in SuperCalc 5. The command for setting up graphs is Graphics, so select this now by either positioning the cursor or by pressing G.

The display will now show the various options used in the **Graphics** command (Fig 3.2). These options are used for the following purposes:

- **View** displays the finished graph
- **Type** selects the type of graph required (bar chart, line graph, pie chart, etc)
- **Data** specifies the data to be used for the graph variables
- **Labels** selects headings and titles for inclusion in the graph
- **Axis** specifies scales required on each axis
- **Options** selects various alternatives to normal graph displays (eg: exploded or 3D pie charts)
- **Global** selects various alternative output devices and/or various types of monitor
- **Name** stores graphs under a designated name for later retrieval
- **Plot** prints out the current graph

Zap erases the graph currently in use
Quit quits the Graphics command

```
   |    A     ||   B   ||   C   ||   D   ||   E   ||   F   ||   G   |
1  Sales of Product: Alpha
2  -----------------------
3  PRICE:               10      11     12.1    13.31
4  ---------------------------------------------------------------------
5  MIDLANDS             40      38      36      34
6  NORTH EAST           55      52      50      47
7  NORTH WEST           70      67      63      60
8  SOUTH EAST           85      81      77      73
9  SOUTH WEST           25      24      23      21
10                     275     261     248     236
11
12
13
14
15
16
17
18
19
20
 LESSON2!A10
View  Type  Data  Labels  Axis  Options  Global  Name  Plot  Zap  Quit
 12>//Graphics,
MENU  View the current chart
```

Fig 3.2

In this lesson you will learn how to use most of these options.

3.2 Designating data

The first step in setting up a graph is to decide what data to include. It has been decided that your graph will show the expected sales at the different prices and, therefore, the data used will be the figures for sales for each region at the different prices. This means that your graph will show the one line or bar for sales in the Midlands region at each of the different prices, one line or bar for the North East and so on.

To specify the data you have to select the **Data** option, to do this just press **D**.

The display will change to that shown in Fig 3.3. The columns on this screen are used to enter details of the data for each variable required (eg: for each separate bar on a bar chart). You are going to plot the data for each of the regions – there are five different regions so you will need to enter five sets of variables.

```
CHART DATA APPEARANCE AND OPTIONS MENU      TYPE: BAR

                          1     |      2      |      3      |      4      |      5
SERIES RANGE                    |             |             |             |
                                |             |             |             |
SERIES OPTIONS                  |             |             |             |
 Color          9LtBlue         | 10LtGreen   | 11LtCyan    | 12LtRed     | 13LtMagent
 Hide           No              | No          | No          | No          | No
 Fill Pattern   MediumSlan      | MediumHori  | MediumVert  | MediumHatc  | MediumCros
 Outline Color  Black           | Black       | Black       | Black       | Black
 Outline Style  Solid           | Solid       | Solid       | Solid       | Solid
 Outline Width  Auto            | Auto        | Auto        | Auto        | Auto
 Y-axis         Left            | Left        | Left        | Left        | Left
 Pie Explosion  No              | No          | No          | No          | No


 17>//Graphics,Data,
MENU  F4:Point  F5:Row/Col  F6:Copy  Ctrl / More series
```

Fig 3.3

The cursor should be in column 1 next to SERIES RANGE . This is requesting details of the cell range for the first variable which will be the data for the Midlands region. Unfortunately you cannot tell which cells are involved as the spreadsheet has been replaced by the Data screen. However, if you examine the HELP line you will notice F4:Point, if you select this the display will revert to the spreadsheet to enable you to select the required range. Press F4 now.

SuperCalc will now ask you to enter the variable range for variable 1. This needs to be the sales figures for the Midlands and these are in cells B5 to E5 on the spreadsheet. The prompt line will show that the range is currently blank. Cell B5 is the first cell in the range required, so select this by moving the cursor to cell B5. The last cell should be E5. In order to enter this press, the full stop key and then right arrow key. Continue pressing it until the area highlighted covers the range B5 to E5, then press **ENTER**.

The screen should change back to the CHART DATA APPEARANCE AND OPTIONS MENU and the **SERIES RANGE** for variable 1 should show **B5:E55**.

CHART DATA APPEARANCE AND OPTIONS MENU TYPE: BAR

	1	2	3	4	5
SERIES RANGE	B5:E5				
SERIES OPTIONS					
Color	9LtBlue	10LtGreen	11LtCyan	12LtRed	13LtMagent
Hide	No	No	No	No	No
Fill Pattern	MediumSlan	MediumHori	MediumVert	MediumHatc	MediumCros
Outline Color	Black	Black	Black	Black	Black
Outline Style	Solid	Solid	Solid	Solid	Solid
Outline Width	Auto	Auto	Auto	Auto	Auto
Y-axis	Left	Left	Left	Left	Left
Pie Explosion	No	No	No	No	No

```
B5:E5
 17>//Graphics,Data,
MENU  F4:Point  F5:Row/Col  F6:Copy  Ctrl / More series
```

Fig 3.4

3.2.1 Designating data with names

Move the cursor into the second column and repeat this procedure to enter the range for variable 2 as **B6:E6**. This is the simplest way to enter the ranges for variables but an easier way is to use the **Name** command to enter variable data for use in both graphs and spreadsheets.

All of the regions were used to create names in Lesson 2. You can now use the names to designate variable data for the graph instead of typing in the ranges.

Move the cursor into column 3 and, instead of highlighting the cell range for the variable **North West**, you can simply type in the name. Type **N** and the cursor will jump to the bottom left hand corner of the screen – this is the position that data is entered if it is keyed in instead of being highlighted. Type in the remainder of the name **North West**, then press **ENTER**. The variable range for variable 3 will be shown on the menu as **B7:E7** as this is the range specified by the name North West.

Repeat the process to enter the names for the other two regions (**South East** and **South West**) in columns 4 and 5. The menu should now show the following:

CHART DATA APPEARANCE AND OPTIONS MENU   TYPE: BAR

	1	2	3	4	5
SERIES RANGE	B5:E5	B6:E6	B7:E7	B8:E8	B9:E9
SERIES OPTIONS					
Color	9LtBlue	10LtGreen	11LtCyan	12LtRed	13LtMagent
Hide	No	No	No	No	No
Fill Pattern	MediumSlan	MediumHori	MediumVert	MediumHatc	MediumCros
Outline Color	Black	Black	Black	Black	Black
Outline Style	Solid	Solid	Solid	Solid	Solid
Outline Width	Auto	Auto	Auto	Auto	Auto
Y-axis	Left	Left	Left	Left	Left
Pie Explosion	No	No	No	No	No

```
B9:E9
 17>//Graphics,Data,
MENU  F4:Point  F5:Row/Col  F6:Copy  Ctrl / More series
```

Fig 3.5

It is possible to include up to ten variables in a graph. If you press the **right arrow** the menu will scroll to the right and show an additional five columns for variables 6 to 10.

The other items on this menu relate to the appearance of data when it is graphed. These items are not essential and will be explained in the next chapter. Return to the **Graphics** command line by pressing **Esc.**

3.3 Headings on graphs

All graphs should have a heading to explain what their contents refer to, and the next stage will be to place headings on the graph. SuperCalc will allow you to enter headings as titles, sub-headings, and footnotes. You can also include headings on each axis and labels for the variables used for data.

3.3.1 Axis labels

The option for entering headings is **Labels**, so select this either from the menu or by pressing **L**. The *prompt line* will then show the various categories of labels available. In order to demonstrate how these work you can work through each option in turn. Select **Axis-labels** first and the following screen should appear:

```
                    AXIS LABELS OPTIONS MENU             TYPE: BAR

                             Y1-AXIS    |   Y2-AXIS    |   X-AXIS
X-AXIS LABEL RANGE         ------------ | ------------ |
                                        |              |
AXIS LABEL OPTIONS                      |              |
  Color                      Black      |   Black      |   Black
  Font                       Auto       |   Auto       |   Script
  Size                       Auto       |   Auto       |   Auto
  Justify                    Auto       |   Auto       |   Auto
  Format                     General    |   General    |   General
  Date Format                D1         |   D1         |   D1

CHART BOX
  Fill Color                 Grey
  Outline Color              White

AXIS BOX
  Fill Color                 White
  Outline Color              Black
  Outline Width              Auto


  31>//Graphics,Labels,Axis-labels,
 MENU  F4:Point
```

Fig 3.6

This option will designate the labels that will be included as the ranges on both the X axis (horizontal) and Y axis (vertical). The first option asks for the range for the X axis. This range will usually be the *time* range as the X axis is normally divided into *time* periods, however in your example the periods will be the different prices.

The range can be entered in the same way as the variable data was entered in the previous section – if you know what the range is you can simply type it in or alternatively you can select it using the **Point** facility of **F4**. As you probably cannot remember the range you will have to select it using **F4**. Press this now.

The screen should now revert to the spreadsheet display. The range required is that containing the different prices (ie: B3 to E3). Highlight this range as before and then press **ENTER**.

The Y axis will show the different numbers of units sold at each price level. You do not have to specify a range for this axis as SuperCalc will determine the most suitable bands.

The other options on this menu determine changes in the layout and style of graphs. These will be examined in the next chapter.

The axis labels are now complete so you can press **Esc** to quit this menu.

The graph is far from complete but you can examine what you have included so far. If you press **F10** at any time whilst using the **Graphics** command the graph currently defined will appear on screen. Press **F10** to view the graph designed so far.

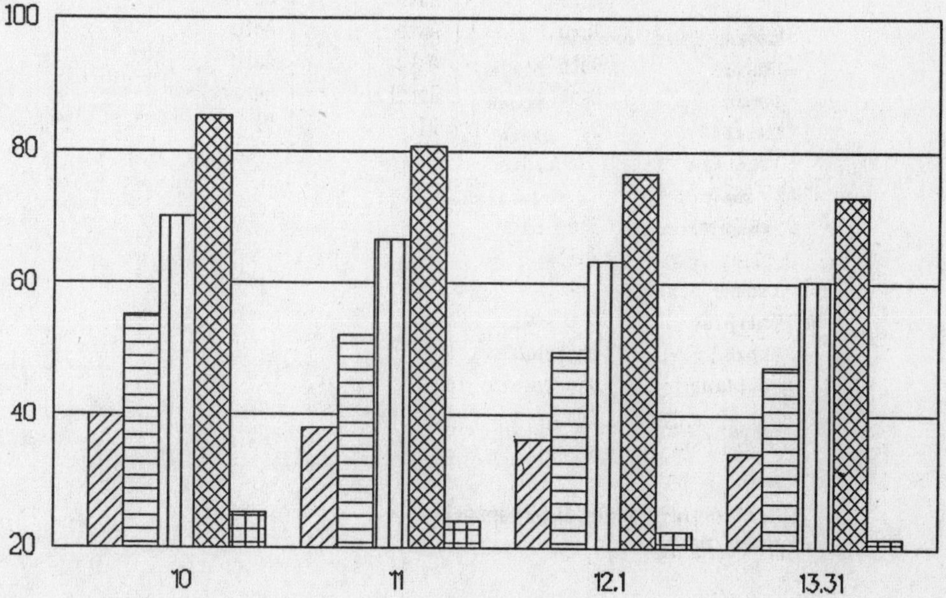

Fig 3.7

If the screen does not show a chart then you will need to use the ***Global, Optimum*** *command to configure your computer to accept graphs (see Appendix 1).*

Note that the graph shows five bars (one for each region) and that the labels on the X axis are the price ranges in cells B3 to E3. SuperCalc has calculated what is considered to be the most appropriate labels/divisions on the Y axis.

The next step is to add more headings – to return to the normal spreadsheet just press any key.

3.3.2 Legend labels

The *prompt line* should still show the **Graphics, Labels** options as you are always returned to the last position you were at. The next option is to include **Legend-labels**. If you select this option the screen will appear as in Fig 3.8.

```
                    LEGEND LABEL DEFINITION AND OPTIONS MENU      TYPE: BAR

LEGEND LABEL RANGE

LEGEND LOCATION
 Position             UpperRight
 Placement            Outside

LEGEND LABEL OPTIONS
 Color                Black
 Font                 Roman
 Size                 Auto
 Justify              Auto
 Format               General
 Date Format          D1

LEGEND BOX
 Display              Yes
 Color                White
 Outline              Black


Auto
 33>//Graphics,Labels,Legend-labels,
MENU  F4:Point                                                    NUM
```

Fig 3.8

Legend labels are the **keys** to the graph and will be used to show on the graph what each bar or line refers to. You have included five variables on the graph and the graph should show what each bar (variable) refers to.

Legend labels are entered in the same way as variables and the X axis. Press **F4** to revert to the spreadsheet display. The legend labels should be the different regions, which are shown in cells **A5.A9.** Highlight these now by moving the cursor, then press **ENTER.**

The screen will now show the LEGEND LABEL DEFINITION AND OPTIONS MENU again. Press **F10** and the graph display should now include a **key** which is **the legend label.**

If you press any key the screen will revert to the LEGEND LABEL DEFINITION AND OPTIONS MENU . This menu is broken down into four sections: the first section allows you to specify the range for the legend labels, and the other three sections enable the user to alter the presentation of these labels.

The second section is headed **LEGEND LOCATION** and the options in this section allow you to select where you want the labels to appear on the graph. All of the options on this menu have default values but you can alter any item. Move the cursor down to the word **UpperRight** alongside **Position**. If you want to alter the position just press **ENTER** and the options will appear in a sub-menu. Do this now and you should get the following screen:

```
                    LEGEND LABEL DEFINITION AND OPTIONS MENU      TYPE: BAR

LEGEND LABEL RANGE    A5:A9

LEGEND LOCATION
 Position             UpperRight ╔==Position==╗
 Placement            Outside    ║ Top        ║
                                 ║ Bottom     ║
LEGEND LABEL OPTIONS             ║ Right      ║
 Color                Black      ║ Left       ║
 Font                 Roman      ║ UpperRight ║
 Size                 Auto       ║ LowerRight ║
 Justify              Auto       ║ UpperLeft  ║
 Format               General    ║ LowerLeft  ║
 Date Format          D1         ╚============╝

LEGEND BOX
 Display              Yes
 Color                White
 Outline              Black


UpperRight
 33>//Graphics,Labels,Legend-labels,
MENU  F4:Point
```

Fig 3.9

This menu shows the various positions where the labels can be displayed. Move the cursor to **Right** and press **ENTER** to select this position.

Now move the cursor down to the entry alongside **Placement** and press **ENTER** again. This sub-menu only has two options – the labels can be displayed inside or outside the graph. The default is **Outside**, but you can select **Inside**, just to see what it will look like.

The remaining options on this menu will be explained in the next lesson. You can view the current graph now by pressing **F10** again – the label should appear on the right of the graph and inside the graph.

There are still some other items that should be included in the graph, so you can press Esc twice to return to the **//Graphics, Labels** *entry line.*

3.3.3 Data labels

The next item on offer is **Data-labels**. Select this item now and you will then get the DATA LABELS OPTIONS MENU as shown. This menu allows you to include the values for each item as part of the graph. The first item is the **DATA LABEL RANGE** and should include the cell ranges that include the values shown on the graph. Normally this will be the same ranges used in the **Data** section of the **Graphics** command. They can be selected by pressing the **F4** key or typing them in if you remember what they are. The ranges to be used are shown on the following screen. Type these in as shown:

```
                              DATA LABELS OPTIONS MENU                TYPE: BAR

                         1  |      2  |      3  |      4  |      5
DATA LABEL RANGE B5:E5      | B6:E6   | B7:E7   | B8:E8   | B9:E9
                            |         |         |         |

DATA LABEL OPTIONS
 Location       Point
 Placement      Outside
 Source         Range
 Color          Black
 Font           Auto
 Size           Auto
 Format         General
 Date Format    D1




B9:E9
 31>//Graphics,Labels,Data-labels,
MENU  F4:Point  F5:Row/Col  F6:Copy  Ctrl / More series
```

Fig 3.10

Once you have entered these ranges use F10 to view the current graph, which should show that the Data-label function takes the value from each cell and includes it as part of the bar or line on the graph.

Unfortunately, your graph should show the decimal places in each cell. This did originally appear on the spreadsheet but you used the **Format, Integer** command to round off the answers. This option is also available on graphic displays and any values can be displayed as Integers or to a specified number of decimal places. Move the cursor into the section **DATA LABEL OPTIONS** and select the item alongside **Format**. If you press **ENTER** you should obtain a sub-menu which enables you to specify the number of decimal places required, or whether you just want the integer values shown. Select **Integer** by highlighting this item and then pressing **ENTER**.

In the previous display the value was shown inside the bar. If you move the cursor up to the item for **Placement** you can now alter this to position the data outside the bar.

Press **F10** again and the display should now show:

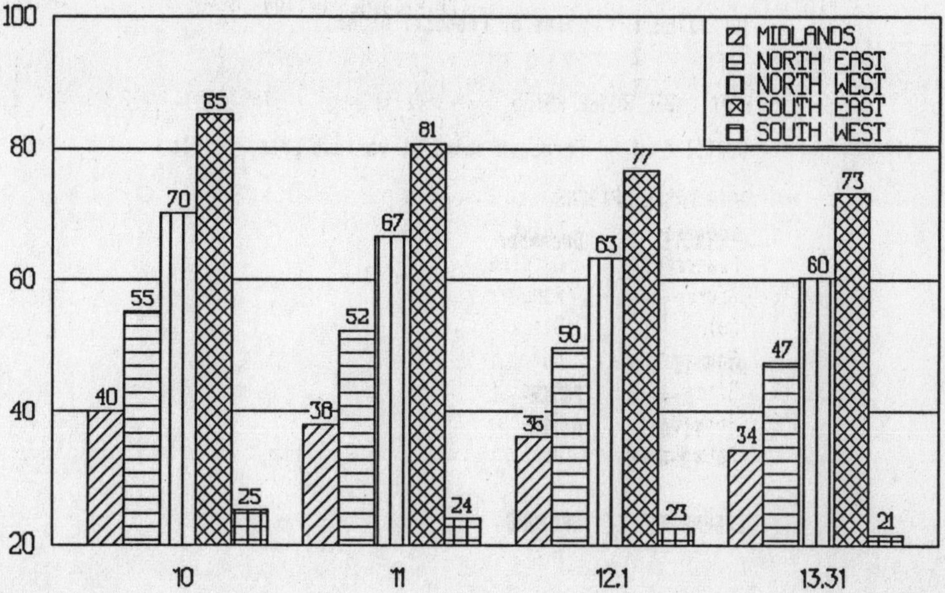

Fig 3.11

Press any key to revert to the DATA LABELS OPTIONS MENU and then press Esc to go back to the other Graphics, Labels options.

3.3.4 Titles

The only other label option is **Titles**. Select this now.

The screen should then show the TITLES ENTRY MENU. This allows you to enter three lines for a main (**TOP**) **TITLE**, two lines for a **SUBTITLE**, three lines as a **FOOTNOTE** and titles or headings for both the **X** and **Y** axes, and also for the **key**.

The headings to be included on the graph can either be typed in now or selected from the spreadsheet. For example the **main** heading should be **Sales of Product: Alpha** – there is no need to type this in as it already appears on the spreadsheet in cell A1 and, therefore it can be selected by the **Point** option or just by typing in A1 alongside **TOP TITLE 1**.

The other items that can be selected from the spreadsheet are the **Axis** titles. Move the cursor down to this section and select cell A3 (**PRICE**) for the X axis. There is no suitable title on the existing spreadsheet for the Y axis, but as this shows the number of units you can simply type in **Units** alongside this item.

You can also include some titles for the other items by moving the cursor to the appropriate point and typing in the required title.

Enter the other headings as shown below:

```
                    TITLES ENTRY MENU                TYPE: BAR

TOP TITLE 1   Sales of Product: Alpha
          2
          3

SUBTITLE 1    Forecast sales at various price levels
         2

FOOTNOTE 1    December
         2
         3

AXIS TITLES
     X-Axis   PRICE
    Y1-Axis   Units
    Y2-Axis

LEGEND TITLE  REGIONS


December
 26>//Graphics,Labels,Titles,
MENU  F4:Point  F5:Row/Col  PgDn:Options
```

Fig 3.12

Once you have entered these items you can press **F10** to view the graph again. Unfortunately the display will now show that the legend labels are partly obscuring the bars for a price of £13.31. See if you can get back to the legend labels menu and change the placement of the legend label box so that it is back outside the graph.

3.4 Printing graphs

Most dot matrix printers will produce a printout of your graph. Obtaining a printout should be very straightforward: all that you need to do is press either **Alt** and **F10** or select **Plot** from the **Graphics** command list (first check that you are *On-Line*).

The printout will be produced *sideways* and is much slower to print than normal printouts because it is printing in *graphics mode*.

If you have any difficulty in obtaining a printout it is probably because SuperCalc has not been configured for your printer. SuperCalc can be adapted to most printers by using the **Global** command. If you cannot get a printout of your graph then select the **Global, Graphics, Device** command. This will provide a list of printers that will be accepted by SuperCalc and allow the user to specify the printer required.

Graphs can be printed on a Plotter if you have one. In order to do this you need to select the corresponding plotter configuration file from the Global, Graphics menu.

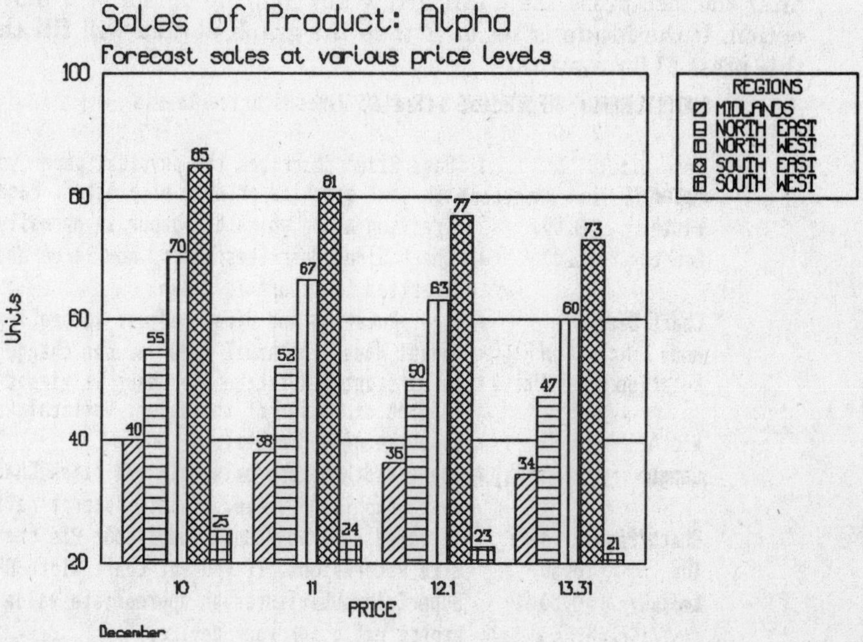

Printout 3.1

3.5 Altering graph size

The default for plotting graphs is to print vertically (ie: sideways). SuperCalc will produce a graph that will fill a normal size of printer paper.

It is possible to alter the direction and size of printing by using the **Global, Graphics**, command. This is especially useful if you want to reduce the graph size so that it can be pasted into a word-processed report.

To alter the size of your graph you must first quit the **Graphics** command (**Ctrl** and **Break**), then select the following:

/	to call up commands
G	to select **Global**
G	to select **Graphics**
L	to select **Layout**

You should then get the same screen as shown in Fig 3.13.

This screen contains the options available for altering graph size and a brief explanation of each item. The **Page Size** section allows you to alter the paper size – this will not be necessary in most cases.

The **Graph Size** determines the direction of printing and graph dimensions. To alter the size press the down arrow key and the cursor will move onto **the Mode** option. If the **Mode** is set at **F** then the graph plotted will **fill** the paper. To alter this press **M** for **manual**.

```
LAYOUT MENU: SELECTIONS FOR PLOTTING

Page Size:           • "Page Size" describes the physical paper you are using
Paper         1        with your graphics printer or plotter. Page Width is the
Width      8.50        direction along which the paper is normally read.
Length    11.00      • "Chart Size" describes where, how large and in which
                       direction the chart is drawn.
Chart Size:          • Size, Rotation and Offset adjust automatically EXCEPT in
Mode          M        Manual Mode. In Manual Mode you can change chart settings.
Rotation      V      • In Horizontal Rotation the chart is viewed in the normal
                       reading direction of the paper. Vertical Rotation is the
Width      9.75        opposite of Horizontal.
Length     7.25      • Chart Width is approximately 1.3 times Chart Length for
                       most graphics devices. If this "aspect ratio" is changed
Chart/Page Offset:     (allowed only in Manual Mode) your Pie charts will look
Top        0.50        like watermelons. If you set Chart Width OR Length to 0.00
Left       0.50        SuperCalc substitutes an appropriate value using the
                       aspect ratio for your device.
                     • "Chart/Page Offset" tells SuperCalc where on the page
                       (measured from the Top and Left) to start the chart.


H(orizontal) or V(ertical)?
 24>/Global,Graphics,Layout
MENU  Specify graph layout - Keepable defaults
```

Fig 3.13

The cursor will then move into the **Rotation** option, which will currently be **V for vertical**. Press **H** to change this to **horizontal**. This will change the direction of printing so that the graph will now be printed in the normal direction.

The next two items to adjust are the **Width** and **Length**. If you read the instructions on the screen you will notice that it recommends that the **Width** is set at approximately 1.3 times the **Length**. Fortunately you do not have to calculate this yourself as, if one of the options is set at zero, then SuperCalc will automatically adjust the other item.

Therefore you can set **Width** to 5.00 and **Length** to zero. The cursor will then move to **Graph/Page offset**. This is used to set margins and the amounts are in inches. These do not require altering at the moment so you can now leave this screen by pressing **Esc**.

The screen will still show the **Global, Graphics** *entry line,* but you can obtain a printout of the new graph without loading the **Graphics** command by simply selecting **Alt** and **F10**.

The dimensions given above for the width of the graph are an example only and you can change these figures at any time to select the graph size that you require.

3.6 Saving and retrieving graphs

It is possible to create more than one graph per spreadsheet by using the **Graphics, Name** option. This will allow you to save and retrieve graphs by allocating a name to each graph.

Select this option now by pressing:

//	to select the second band of commands
G	to select **Graphics**
N	to select **Name**

This will show that there are four options with this command:

Retrieve	is used to load graphs previously saved
Store	is used to save the current graph
Delete	is used to delete obsolete graphs
Zap	deletes all graphs except the current graph

This graph will be required for the next lesson so you can save it now as follows: select **Store** or press **S**; the next prompt will ask you to **Enter the chart name:.** Type in **alpha1** as the name and then press **ENTER**.

You should remember that this command only saves the graph as part of the spreadsheet and if you intend to use the graph again in a future work session then you must also ***save*** *the spreadsheet.*

To **Retrieve** (load) graphs, select the **Graphics, Name, Retrieve** command again, and the prompt will ask for the chart name. There will be occasions when you have forgotten the name, but if you press **F3** the screen will provide a display of all graphs available. The required graph can be selected by moving the cursor onto the name and then pressing **ENTER**. You do not need to do this now as you already have the graph in memory, so press **Esc** to quit this option.

```
CHART LIST

Name
ALPHA1




















  26>//Graphics,Name,Retrieve,
FILE  F1:Help   ↵:Select file/directory Ctrl-Break:Cancel
```

Fig 3.14

3.7 Starting new graphs

The **Graphics, Name** command allows you to save and retrieve graphs from previous sessions, but you may also want to devise more than one graph during the same session. In order to do this you should first **store** the first graph when completed. The graph will still be in the memory of your computer and must be **zapped** by using the **Graphics, Zap** command.

You should still have the Graphics command line on screen, so **Zap** is selected by moving the cursor onto this item and pressing **ENTER**, or by pressing **Z.** Note that SuperCalc does not ask you *if you are sure* so make certain that you have stored the graph, or do not need it again, before using **Zap**.

Save your file as it will be needed for Lesson 4.

Further exercises

If you attempted the *Further exercises* at the end of the last lesson you will have some additional work saved on your spreadsheet. Use this data to create a new graph using the items covered in this lesson, enter headings and labels where appropriate.

Practice using the **Global, Graphics, Layout** command to produce a printout of a reasonable size.

When complete use the **Graphics, Name** command to **Store** your new graph as **alpha2**.

Lesson 4 *Improving sales graphs*

This lesson is a continuation of the previous lesson and demonstrates some further possibilities with graphs. It is necessary to break this topic into two sections as the range of options available for devising graphs in SuperCalc is now very extensive.

In this lesson you will use the graph you created in Lesson 3, so you need to Load the file LESSON2 as shown at the beginning of Lesson 3, and use the Graphics, Name command to Retrieve your graph alpha1. This was explained in section 3.6.

Once you have loaded the graph press F10 to make sure that all items have been saved correctly. The screen display should show the following:

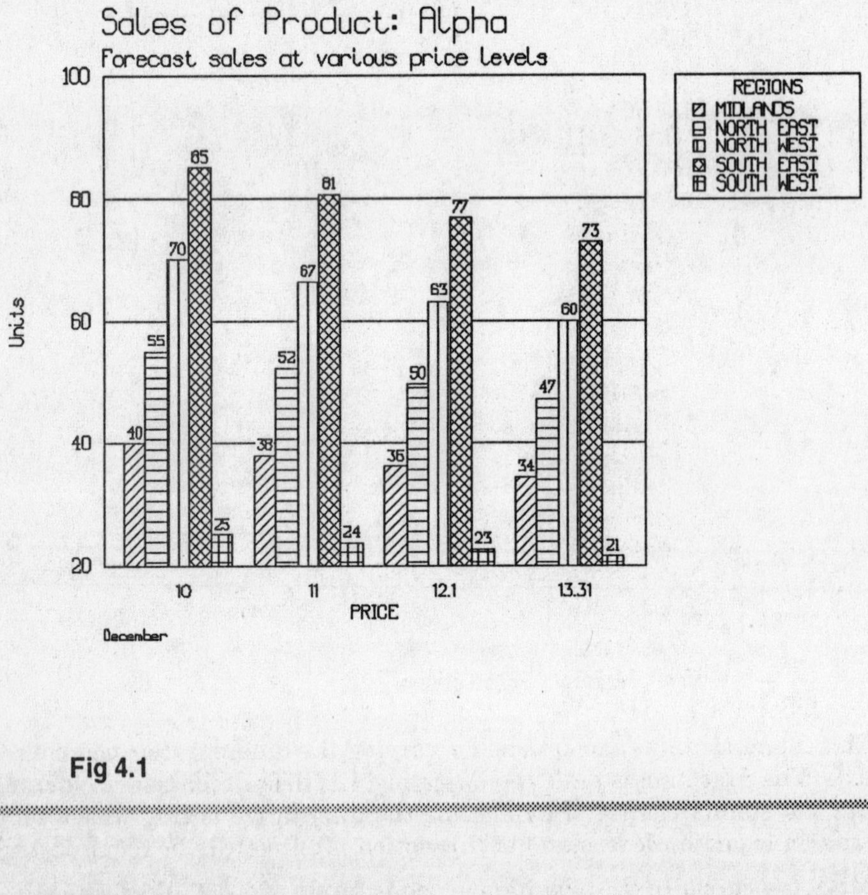

Fig 4.1

4.1 Setting the scale and axis options

If you examine the graph carefully you will notice that the Y axis starts at 20. SuperCalc will automatically calculate what is considered to be the most appropriate scale for this axis and will set the **minimum** and **maximum** levels accordingly. In most cases the scales selected will be acceptable, but there will be occasions when a specific scale is required. For example, your graph would probably have more impact if the scale started at zero and went to a

You can set the scale manually if required by pressing:

/	to call up commands
/	to select the second line of commands
G	to select **Graphics**
A	to select **Axis**

This will call up the AXIS SCALING OPTIONS MENU as shown below:

AXIS SCALING OPTIONS MENU TYPE: BAR

	Y1-AXIS	Y2-AXIS	X-AXIS
TYPE	Normal	----------------	Normal
MODE	Auto	Auto	Auto
LOW VALUE	0	0	0
HIGH VALUE	0	0	0
MANUAL LABEL RANGE			
TICKS:			
NORMAL MAJOR			
Divisions	5	5	5
Increment			
NORMAL MINOR			
Divisions	0	0	0
Increment			
LOG MAJOR			
Divisions/Decade	1	1	1
Decades/Division			
LOG MINOR			
Divisions/Decade	9	9	9
Decades/Division			

Normal
17>//Graphics,Axis,
MENU F4:Point PgDn:Options

Fig 4.2

This menu contains the options for varying the different items on both the **X** and **Y** axis. The first item is for **Type** of scaling, the default for this is **Normal** which will use the standard style of numbering the alternative is **Log** which will display the scale in logarithmic format, but this option is unlikely to be required very often.

Move the cursor to the next item which is **Mode**, the default of which is **Auto** which means that SuperCalc selects the most suitable scale. If you press **ENTER** the other options will appear.

The other two options allow you to designate the scale that you require (**Manual**) or will start the scale from **Zero**. Select **Zero** and press **ENTER**.

If you press **F10** now to check what the altered graph looks like the scale will start from zero but will still go up to 100.

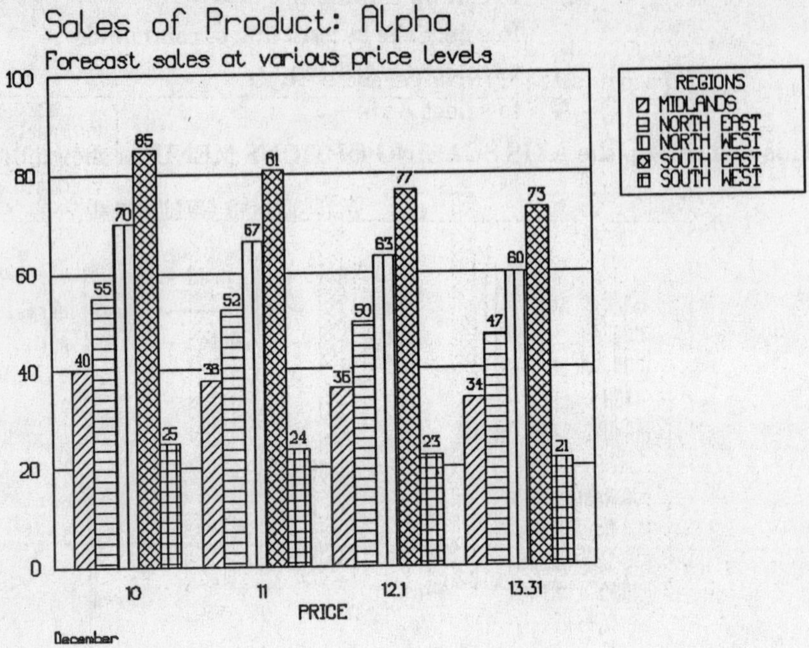

Fig 4.3

Unfortunately, the **Zero** option only enables you to start the graph from zero and all other values are still selected automatically. In order to use the other options you will have to set the **Mode** to **Manual.**

In some instances you will want to enter an exact scale. To do this you would select **Manual**, and then enter the lowest point and highest point next to **LOW VALUE** and **HIGH VALUE.** The **low value** we require is **0** and the **high value is 100.** Enter these now.

The next section headed **TICKS** refers to the divisions on the axis. The current setting is 5 which means that your Y axis will show the scale as 0 - 20 - 40 - 60 - 80 - 100. Change this value to **4**, and this will change the scale so that the divisions are set a 0 - 25 - 50 - 75 - 100.

The other option under this item is **Increment.** This is used as an alternative to **Divisions** and can be used where you are unsure how many divisions you require but do know what *gap* you want between them. It is not possible to use both **Increment** and **Divisions** at the same time as they both perform the same task.

The **NORMAL MINOR** options will include some additional, smaller ticks in between the **MAJOR** divisions. If you enter **5** as the number here it will include another five smaller ticks in the gap between each larger division – this will provide ticks for every five units.

Press **F10** and the graph should include both of these changes.

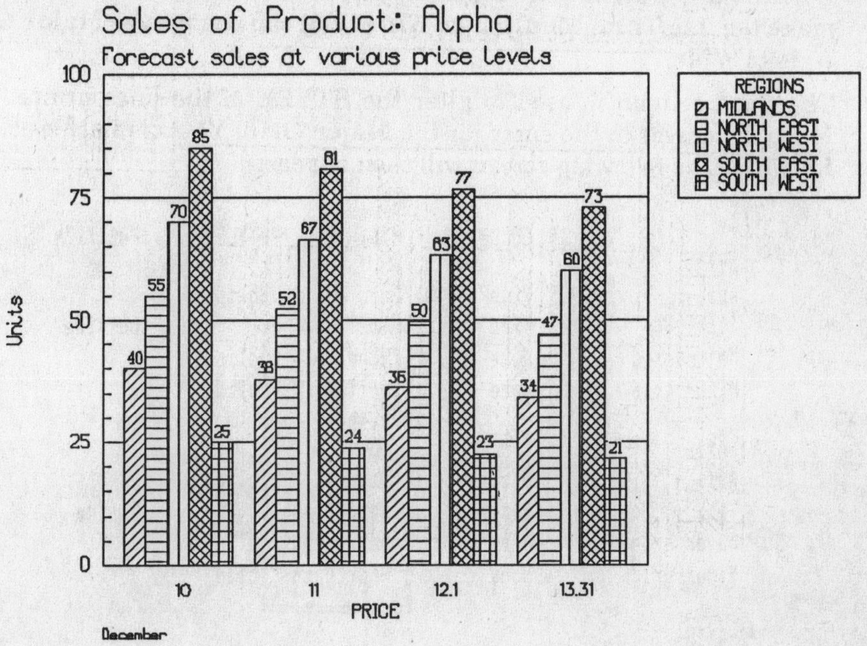

Fig 4.4

4.1.1 Altering axis appearance

If you return to the AXIS SCALING OPTIONS MENU then you will notice that the **Help** line shows additional options that can be obtained by pressing **PgDn**. If you press this key you will be presented with the AXIS APPEARANCE OPTIONS MENU.

These options may look complicated but in fact most of them are repetitions for the different axes. The first column is **COLOR** and enables you to change the colour of each axis or the ticks on each axis. This is only relevant if you have a colour monitor. However, to demonstrate the possibilities you can press **ENTER** to select a new colour for the X axis. The display should show a sub-menu detailing the different colours that can be used. This list is more extensive than it appears and if you continue to press the down arrow key you will see that there are over 70 colours on offer. Select a new colour if you wish or just press **Esc**.

The same list is available for all of the other items including the ticks and major/minor grids on each axis. if you do have a colour monitor or printer you should be a little cautious about spending a lot of time changing these colours as this option only changes the colour of the lines. As the lines are fairly small and narrow you are unlikely to notice much difference.

The second column will allow you to alter the **WIDTH** of the axis line. The default setting is **Auto** but if you move the cursor onto any of these items and press **ENTER** a sub-menu will appear which shows that you can alter the **WIDTH** to make the line **Thin, Medium** or **Wide**. You can change the **Major Grid** on the **Y1-Axis** to **Wide**.

The third column is used to alter the **STYLE** of the lines printed on the graph. Move the cursor to the entry for the **Major Grid, Y1-Axis** in this column and press **ENTER**. The following screen will then appear:

```
                      COLOR        WIDTH        STYLE        POSITION
X-AXIS
  Axis                BluePurple   Auto         Solid
  Tick                4Red        ╔═══STYLE════╗             Outside
  Major grid          None        ║ None       ║olid
  Minor grid          None        ║ Solid      ║olid
                                  ║ Dash       ║
Y1-AXIS                           ║ Dot        ║
  Axis                Black       ║ DashDot    ║olid
  Tick                Black       ║ MediumDash ║             Inside
  Major grid          Grey        ║ DashDotDot ║olid
  Minor grid          None        ║ ShortDash  ║olid
                                  ╚════════════╝
Y2-AXIS
  Axis                Black        Auto         Solid
  Tick                Black        Auto                      Inside
  Major grid          Grey         Auto         Solid
  Minor grid          None         Auto         Solid


Solid
 17>//Graphics,Axis,
MENU F4:Point  F6:Copy  PgUp:Axis Menu
```

Fig 4.5

This shows the alternative styles of drawing for the lines. The default is to draw a solid line, but various alternatives can be used. Select **Dash** and this will then draw the **Major Grid** as a series of dashes instead of a continuous line.

The last option on this menu is the **POSITION.** This determines the position in which the ticks are shown. There are only two alternatives: **Inside** the graph box or **Outside** the graph box. As you have not selected any ticks on the **X-Axis** the only axis you can use in this option will be the **Y1-Axis.** Move the cursor to this option and press **ENTER** – when the menu appears change the position to **Outside.**

If you press **F10** you can now view all of the changes made to your graph. Notice that the **Y1-Axis** now has the ticks which are printed on the outside of the box and that the grid line is wide and printed as a series of dashes.

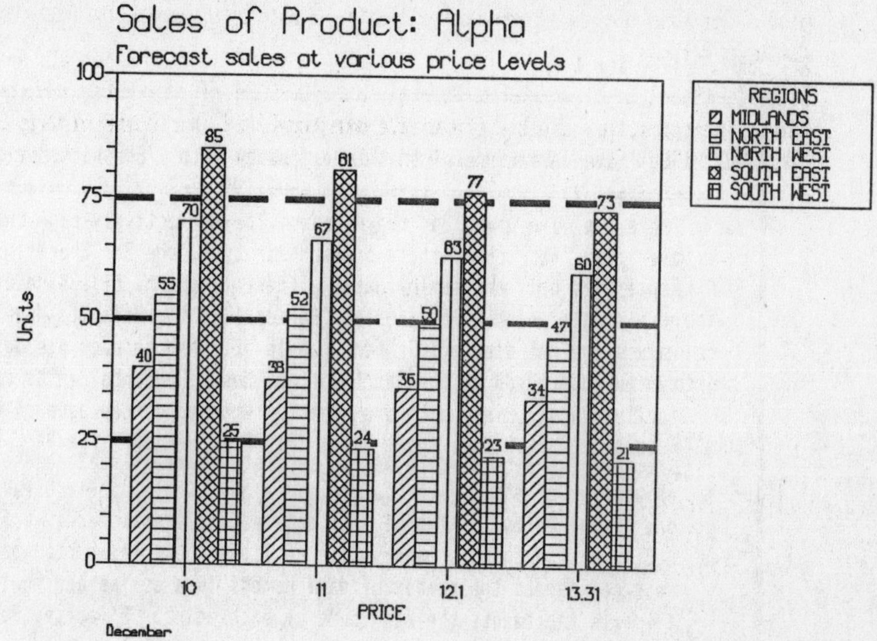

Fig 4.6

4.2 Graph types

SuperCalc will normally show graphs as bar charts as the default graph type. However, bar charts will not be appropriate for all data and graphs so alternative graph types are available.

The alternative types of graph can be obtained very simply and quickly by using the **Graphics, Type** option.

To examine the other types of graph available select the following:

Press any key to revert to the spreadsheet display
Press **Esc** to quit the **Axis options menu**
Press **T** to select **Graph type**

The different types of graph available include *bar, pie, dual, line, Hi-Lo, X-Y, radar* and *word.* The function of each of these graphs varies substantially.

Press **F1** and the first HELP menu on graph types will appear.

If you read the contents of this screen and the subsequent screen (page 2) you should have a better idea of the types of graph that can be used and where each type is appropriate. It is especially important that you realise that **pie charts** are normally only suitable where there is only one set of data – your current example uses 5 sets of data so a **pie chart** would not be suitable.

```
Chart Types Page 1                                        SuperCalc AnswerScreen

 //Graphics,Type selects the main chart type. All chart types (except Pie and
 and Hi-Lo) have variations of that type (change with //Graphics,Options).

 Bar   There are five basic Bar chart types. They effectively show changes
       over time. For more details on each Bar type, see Bar Charts.
 Pie   Represents only one set of data, either all points of a single series,
       or a single point of all series. Series 1 is the default. Negative
       values are not plotted. Segment labels attached to each pie segment
       can be suppressed at the Chart Options Menu. Segments can be exploded
       (pulled away). Pie charts are best for showing percentages of a whole.
 Dual  Each of the four dual chart types (Pie-Pie, Bar-Bar, Pie-Bar, Bar-Pie)
       presents two sets of data as two separate charts.  Dual charts are
       effective for showing the larger parts of a whole, and a breakdown of
       one of the parts, or two sets of data as different charts.
 Line  A Simple-Line chart presents data as lines where the horizontal (X)
       axis represents the number of data points in a series and the vertical
       (Y) axis represents the magnitude of each point.  Effective for showing
       trends for several series over many time intervals.
       A Stacked-Line chart accumulates all series for each period in a single
       line. Effective for showing accumulating trends.  See next page.

RELATED TOPICS:   Page 2          Bar Charts          Graphics Topics
ESC=Return to SuperCalc    F2 = How to use Help    F3 = Help Index
```

Fig 4.7

4.2.1 Line charts

A **line chart**, however, would be suitable. Press **Esc** to quit the HELP menu and then select **Line**. The *entry line* will revert to the main **Graphics** commands.

If you press **F10** the graph will now appear in line chart format as shown in Fig 4.8.

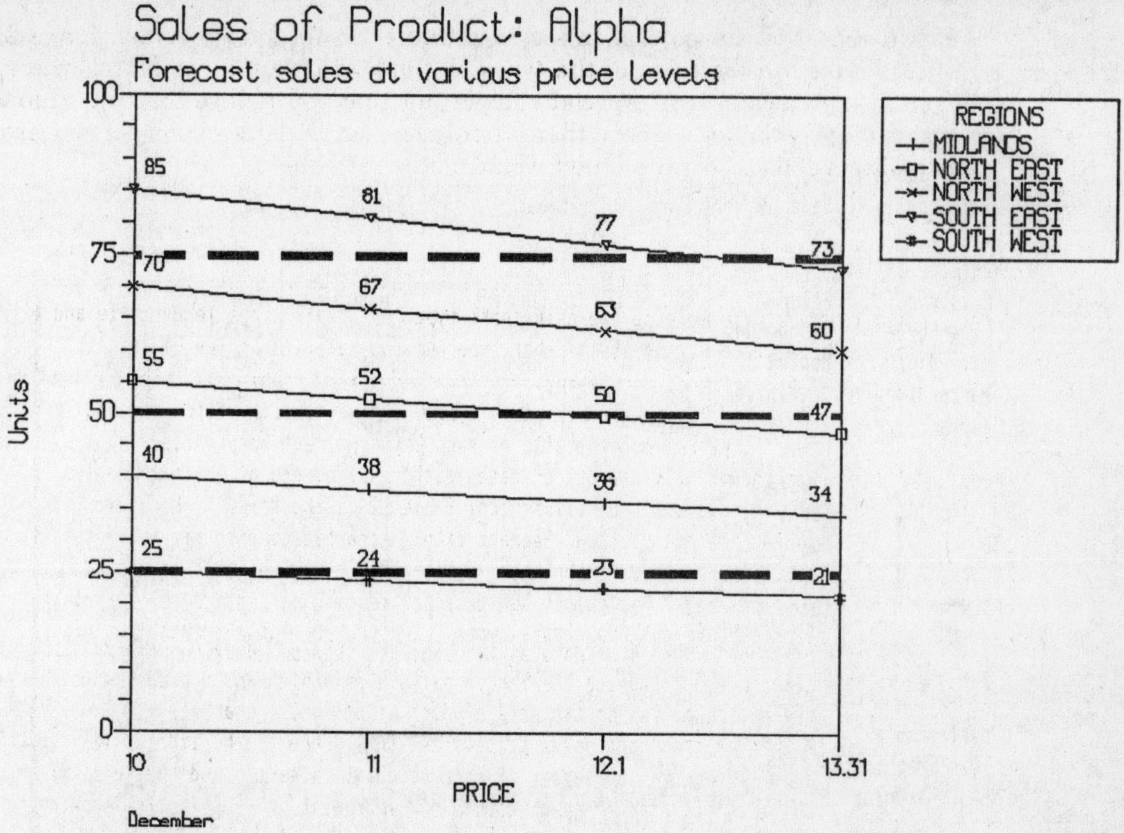

Fig 4.8

The most frequently used types of graph will be bar, line and pie charts as the other types are more commonly used in mathematical displays, but it is possible to improve on the style of the standard graphs.

4.3 Improving graph types

Clear the screen and use the **Graphics, Type** command to turn the graph type back to **Bar**.

It is possible to improve on the style of the display, particularly if the display is in **bar** or **line** type. The *entry line* should be showing the main **Graphics** commands. Move the cursor to the item **Options** or press **O** to select this item.

The screen will then show the BAR CHART OPTIONS MENU (this menu will also be relevant for line graphs). The first part of this menu relates to **BAR OPTIONS** and will determine the sequence in which data appears on the graph (*Group / Stack*) and whether it should be displayed as a **bar** or **line**. Move the cursor to the word **Bar** in column **1** and press **ENTER**. When the sub-menu appears select **Line.** This will mean that your graph will mix bars with lines.

The next block of options, **BAR/LINE OPTIONS** is similar to that demonstrated for **AXIS OPTIONS** and is used to alter the appearance of the lines that make up each variable. Alter the settings to those shown in Fig 4.9.

```
                         BAR CHART OPTIONS MENU                TYPE: BAR

                       1     |     2     |     3     |     4      |     5
BAR OPTIONS                  |
 Group/Stack £  1            | 1         | 1         | 2          | 4
 Bar/Line       Line         | Bar       | Bar       | Bar        | Bar
                             |           |           |            |
BAR/LINE OPTIONS             |           |           |            |
 Fit Type       Stepped      | Connect   | Connect   | Connect    | Connect
 Line Style     DashDotDot   | Solid     | Solid     | Solid      | Solid
 Line Width     Medium       | Auto      | Auto      | Auto       | Auto
 Marker Type    DownTriang   | Box       | X         | DownTriang | Pound
 Marker Size    2            | Auto      | Auto      | Auto       | Auto

TYPE            Simple
HORIZONTAL      No
3D              No
%OVERLAP        0
FILL            Auto


DownTriangle
 20>//Graphics,Options,
MENU  F4:Point  F5:Row/Col  F6:Copy  Ctrl / More series
```

Fig 4.9

The different items perform the following functions:

Fit type	determines which method is used to link lines
Line Style	alters the way the lines around the data are shown
Line Width	alters the thickness of surrounding lines
Marker Type	used in line graphs as the symbol for marking points
Marker Size	used in line graphs to alter size of symbol

Most of these options will make more difference on a **line** graph but are included on this menu as it covers both **bar** and **line** charts. As you have only got one set of data (*Group 1*) in the form of a **line** this is the only set of data that would be affected by these options.

The last few items on this menu will alter the variables for all groups of data and consequently only need to appear once.

4.3.1 Stacked bar charts

The **Type** option or the BAR CHART OPTIONS MENU will allow you to alter the appearance of bar charts. **Stacked** is possibly the most useful option as it will show the total sales at each price, but the bar will be subdivided into the different regions. Before you select this type of graph you will have to adjust the scaling because the maximum scale has been set manually at 100 units and the **stacked**

bar graph will show the total sales at each price – the total for sales at £10 is 275 so this would disappear off the top of the graph. The scales can be reset so that SuperCalc will automatically adjust the scale.

Type in the following:

//	to call up commands
G	to select **Graphics**
A	to select **Axis**

When the AXIS SCALING OPTIONS MENU appears change the **Mode** for the **Y1-AXIS** back to **Auto**. The major grid previously selected from this menu is not really very impressive so you might as well adjust that whilst you are amending the axis options. Press **PgDn** to obtain the screen showing the remaining options and alter the **WIDTH** of the **Y1-AXIS Major Grid** to **Thin**.

Now press **F10**, your graph should now show:

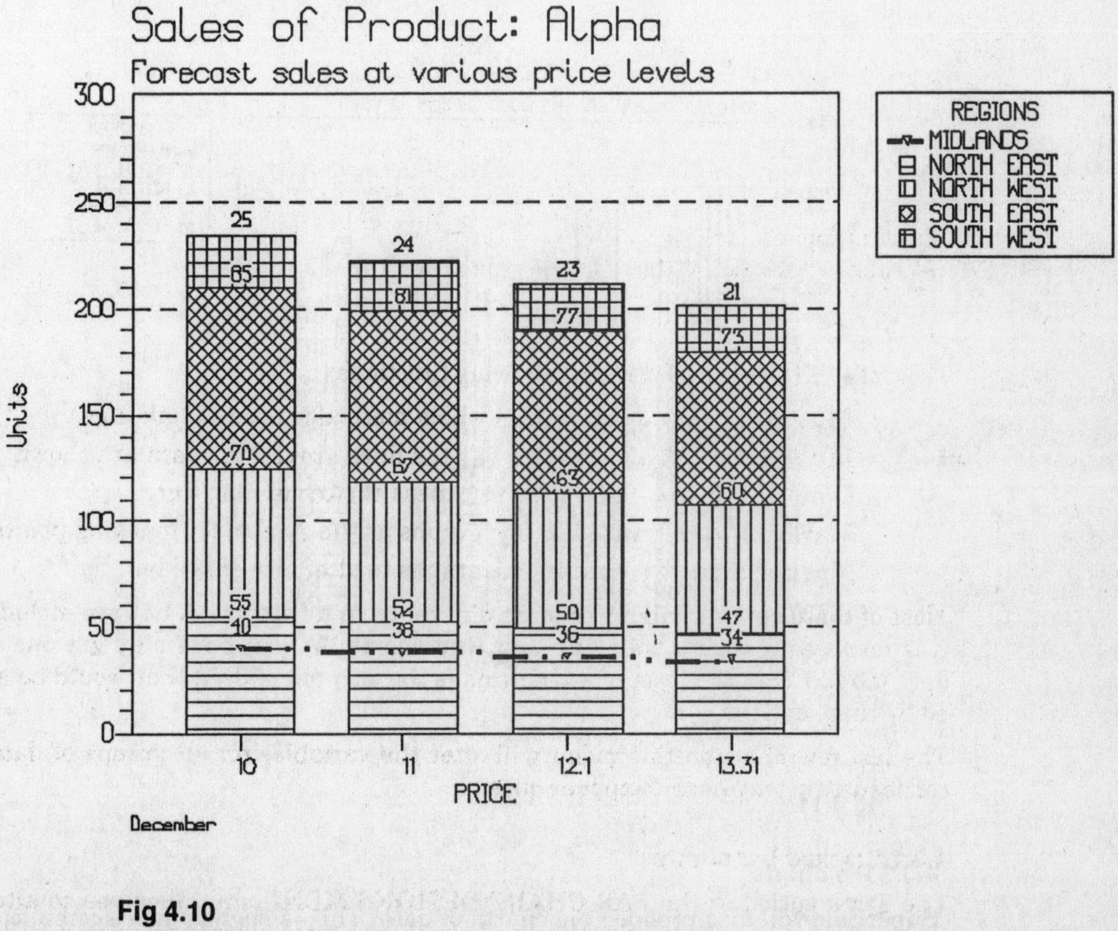

Fig 4.10

This graph shows the data stacked one on top of the other, with the exception of the **Midlands** region which is still shown as a line.

4.3.2 Grouped bar charts

The BAR CHART OPTIONS MENU will also enable you to group data. You can now use this option to have two stacked bars, one showing data for the two Northern regions and one showing data for the two Southern regions.

First clear the screen, then select **Options** again. The first step is to change the **Type** from **Stacked** to **Grouped**. You will then need to designate your different groups.

The top line on this menu shows **Group/Stack #**, this is where you enter the numbers for the groups . The group for Northern regions will be group 1 and the Southern regions group 2. The Northern regions are columns 2 and 3, so you can amend the figure for **Group/Stack #** in column 3 to show number 1.

Then alter columns 4 and 5 to show the group as number 2. Once you have done this press **F10** or select **View** and the graph displayed should show the following:

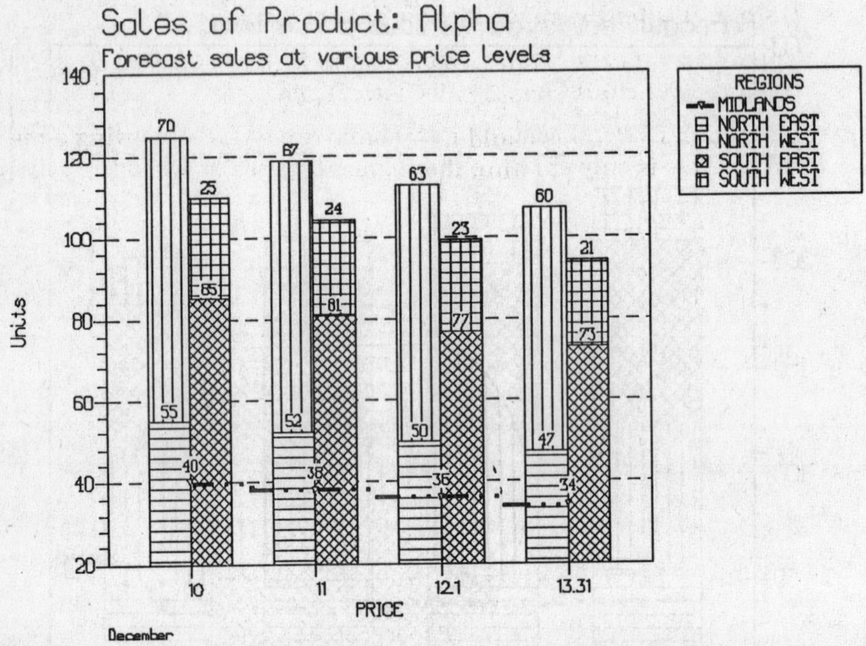

Fig 4.11

4.3.3 Pie charts

SuperCalc will also produce pie charts of data. This is slightly more complicated as a pie chart may look more impressive than a bar chart or line graph, but they can only show *one variable* at a time. Your current graph shows five variables: Midlands, South East, South West, etc, all sub-divided into four groups (ie: the prices).

To devise a pie chart select the following (assuming that you are still in **Graphics** mode):

T to select **Type**
P to select **pie**

Press **F10** or select **View** and you will find that SuperCalc produces a pie chart which shows the different prices. This is not really what is required, but it is not possible to show all data on a pie chart. It should be possible to produce a pie chart which shows the percentages of sales in each region.

However, it will first be necessary to adjust the data so that the pie chart shows the percentages of sales in each region for *one price only.*

The best way of creating a pie chart in this example is to start a brand new graph. The existing graph has already been **Stored** once using **Name** but you have made some alterations so you can **Store** it as **alpha1** again. To do this follow the procedure in section 3.6 to store and zap graphs.

Your new pie chart will show the sales in each region when the price is £10. Select **Data** and enter the range for this data as **B5.B9**.

Then return to the main **Graphics** command and select **Type** as Pie charts again (the previous chart should have been zapped).

If you press **F10** you should now obtain a pie Chart showing a pie chart like the one below. This is only showing the segments for sales when the price is £10.

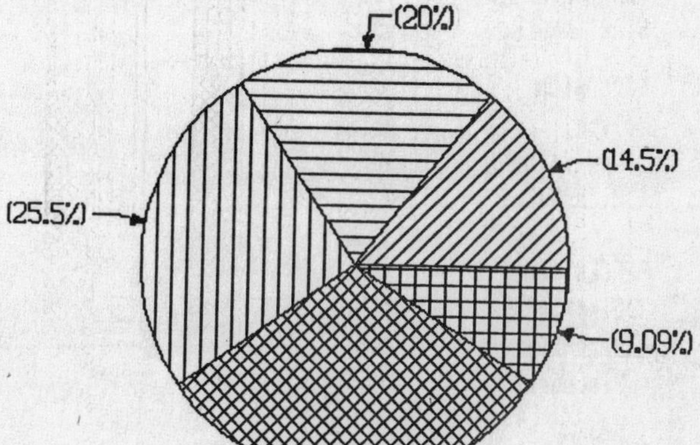

Fig 4.12

Unfortunately the use of pie charts is limited to graphs which have only one variable.

If you select **Options** again the screen will change to display the PIE CHART OPTIONS MENU. These options will allow you to alter the following:

3D	selects three-dimensional display
FILL	fills segments with a pattern or a colour
SORT	sorts segments into order of value
ANGLE	specifies angle from which the chart is drawn
EXPLOSION	separates segments from the rest of the pie
LABELS	determines position and display of labels

Alter the options as shown in Fig 4.13.

This will produce a pie chart in three-dimensional display, with segments sorted into order of size and segments filled with patterns. The graph will be drawn from an angle of 45° and all segments with a value (not a %) below 60 will be *exploded* . The labels will show the values in parentheses (brackets) and will appear inside the segment (if there is sufficient room).

```
                         PIE CHART OPTIONS MENU           TYPE: PIE

DATA SOURCE
  Pie mode           Series
  Series/Point £     1

3D                   Yes
FILL                 Auto
SORT SEGMENTS        Yes
START ANGLE          45

EXPLOSION
  Type               Below
  Low Value          60
  High Value         0

PERCENT LABELS
  Display            Both
  Parentheses        Yes
  Placement          Inside



Inside
 20>//Graphics,Options,
MENU  F4:Point
```

Fig 4.13

If you press **F10** once more the screen will show the pie chart with the above contents. Note that the chart does not yet contain any headings or data labels. pie charts will always show the percentages involved in each segment as the default value, however, it is possible to show the actual amounts by using the **Data-label** option.

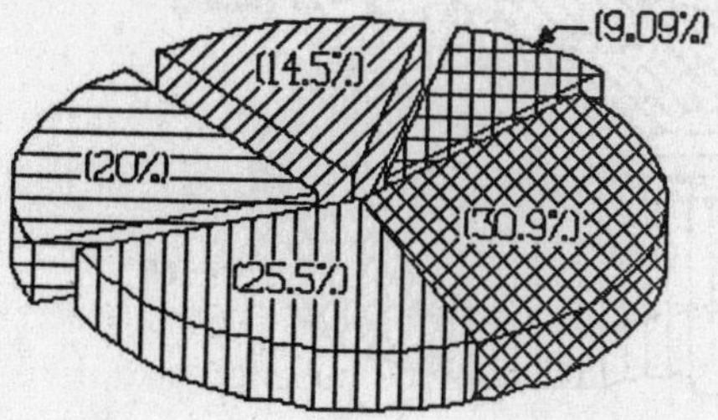

Fig 4.14

4.3.4 Changing fonts

To include the actual values for each segment you will have to designate some **data labels**. Select **Labels** from the **Graphics** menu and then choose **Data-labels**.

The **DATA LABEL RANGE** Should be the same as the range for the data, ie: **B5.B9**, either type this in direct or use **F4** to **point** out the data. A quicker way of entering this data is to use the **Source** option. This is currently displaying **Range** but the alternative is **Data**. If you select this the data label range will automatically use the data from the **Graphics, Data** command.

Whilst you are in the DATA LABEL OPTIONS MENU you can make use of some of the other options not yet examined. The options for **Placement** and **Format** were used in section 3.3.3.

Move the cursor down to **FONT** and press **ENTER**. The screen will now show the different fonts offered by SuperCalc (NB: these fonts can all be displayed on the screen but can only be printed if your printer is capable of accepting them). These will alter the appearance of the data labels in the graph. Select **Script** from this menu and then move to **Size**.

If you press **ENTER** on this item another sub-menu will appear which contains a list of numbers. These refer to the different sizes in which the label can be printed. The usual default is **Auto**, but you can select your own size if required. 1 is used for very small text and 20 for very large. Select **3** for this example. Press **F10** and the display should now look like that in Fig 4.15.

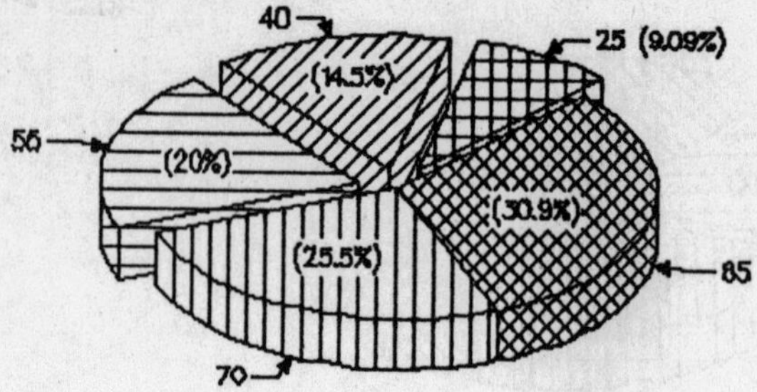

Fig 4.15

Your chart could also do with some headings. Exit the data label menu and select **Legend-labels**. Enter the details as shown in Fig 4.16.

The range selects the names of the different regions but all of the other items affect the position and style of the legend labels. The items for **Font** and **Size** contain the same choices as the data label menu, but different items have been chosen so that you can see the sort of effect that can created by changing options.

```
                      LEGEND LABEL DEFINITION AND OPTIONS MENU      TYPE: PIE

LEGEND LABEL RANGE    A5:A9

LEGEND LOCATION
 Position             Left
 Placement            Outside

LEGEND LABEL OPTIONS
 Color                Brown
 Font                 Italic
 Size                 5
 Justify              Auto
 Format               General
 Date Format          D1

LEGEND BOX
 Display              Yes
 Color                Beige
 Outline              Blue


Blue
 33>//Graphics,Labels,Legend-labels,
MENU  F4:Point
```

Fig 4.16

Press **F10** and the pie chart will now look like the following:

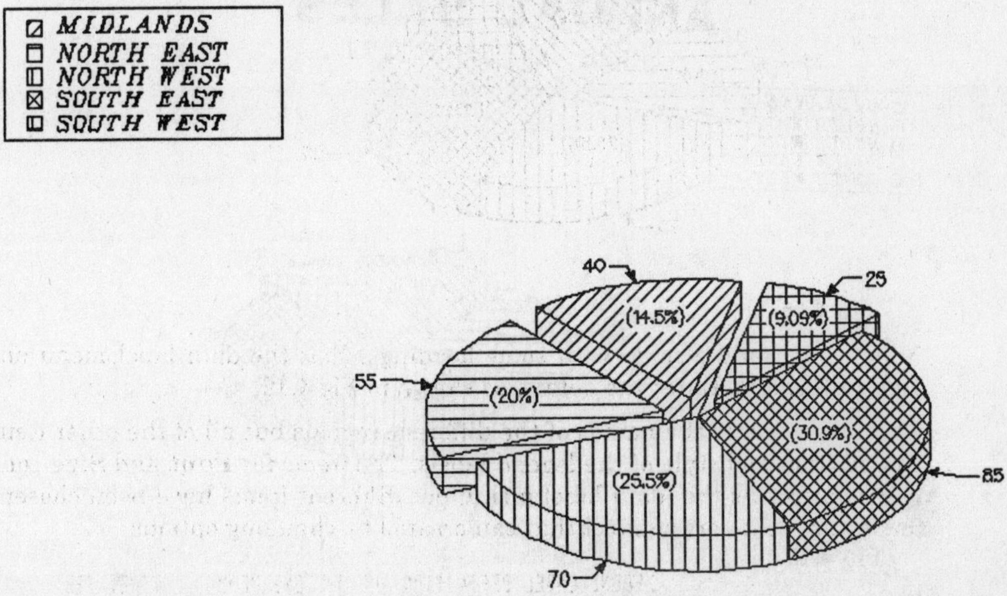

Fig 4.17

Axis labels are not relevant on pie charts but you can include some headings. Select **Titles** and enter the **TOP TITLE** as **Annual Sales**. Then enter a **SUBTITLE** as **Sales for price £10.**

The HELP line shows that there are some further options which can be accessed by pressing **PgDn**. Press this now.

These options should now be more familiar to you. The choice of options can be used (in most cases) for all titles, including those on the axes.

Change the **TOP TITLE** so that the **FONT** is **HelvBold** and the **SIZE** is **14**. Change the **SUBTITLE FONT** to **Block** and the **Size** to **12**. Note that this menu will also allow you to change the fonts on axis titles and the legend title. The position of the axis titles can be repositioned as **Horizontal** or **Vertical** by using this option menu. However, as you do not have any axes on a pie chart these options are not relevant in this example.

Press **F10** again and the pie chart will now show the percentages of sales for each region, including all of the titles and fonts selected during this session.

Fig 4.18

4.3.5 Three-dimensional and horizontal graphs

The work that you have just completed demonstrates how pie charts can be drawn in three-dimensional style. This option is also possible with bar charts, which explains why the bar charts options all refer to the **Y1-Axis** and the **Y2-Axis**. This section demonstrates how easy it is to produce a 3D bar chart.

First, you must clear the existing graph by selecting **Zap** from the command line. Then select the **Name** option and **Retrieve** the graph called **alpha1**.

Use the **View** option to check that this graph is in **grouped bar chart** format. If it is displayed as a pie chart you will have to select **Type** then **Bar** to revert to the bar chart display.

To change to **3D** mode select **Options**. When the BAR CHART OPTIONS MENU appears move the cursor to the bottom of column **1** to the position adjacent to **3D** and press **ENTER** – a sub-menu will appear offering the choice of **No** or **Yes**. Select **Yes** and press **ENTER**.

Press **F10** and the graph should now appear in three-dimensional style, this graph now has two Y axes which are the **Y1-Axis** and **Y2-Axis** referred to above. The **Axis** options can be used to alter the scaling and grids on either of these axes and the axis option on the **Labels** menu can be used to alter the colour, size, font and justification of these axes.

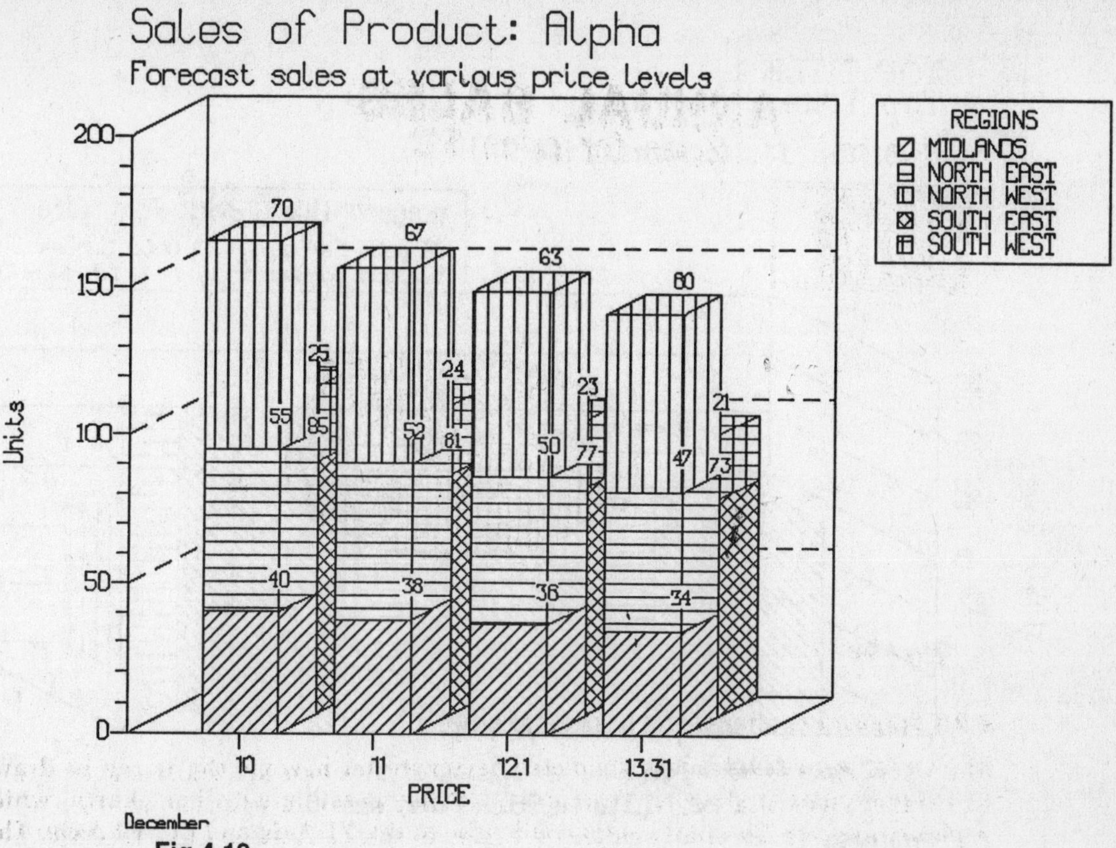

Fig 4.19

4.4 Graphics options

There is a large choice of options and variations possible with the **Graphics** command, but it is difficult to remember what all of these relate to if you are not using **Graphics** continuously. The following section is designed to illustrate what each of the main options refer to so that you can quickly refer back to this in the future.

One major cause of confusion is what each item on the **Graphics** menu refers to. The following graph illustrates what these items will look like on a bar chart and where they will appear.

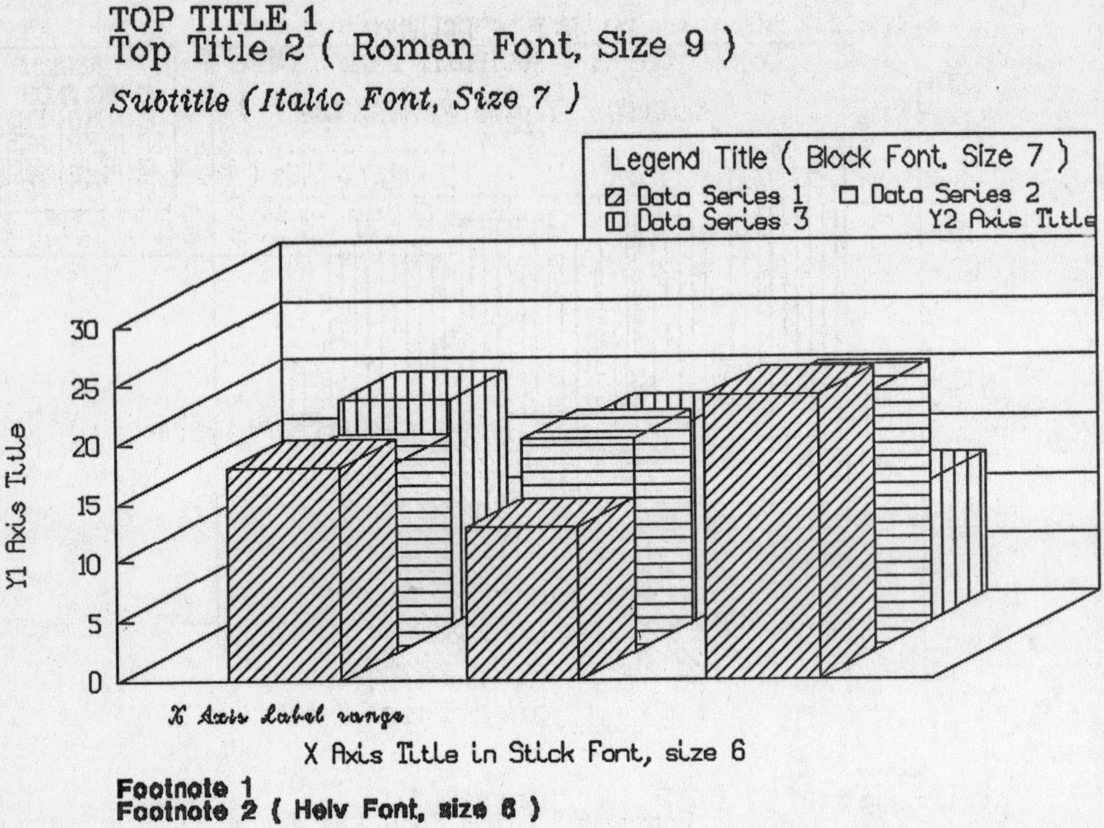

Fig 4.20

The next graph shows more or less the same information but this time using a pie chart as the example – remember when using pie charts that you can only effectively use one variable.

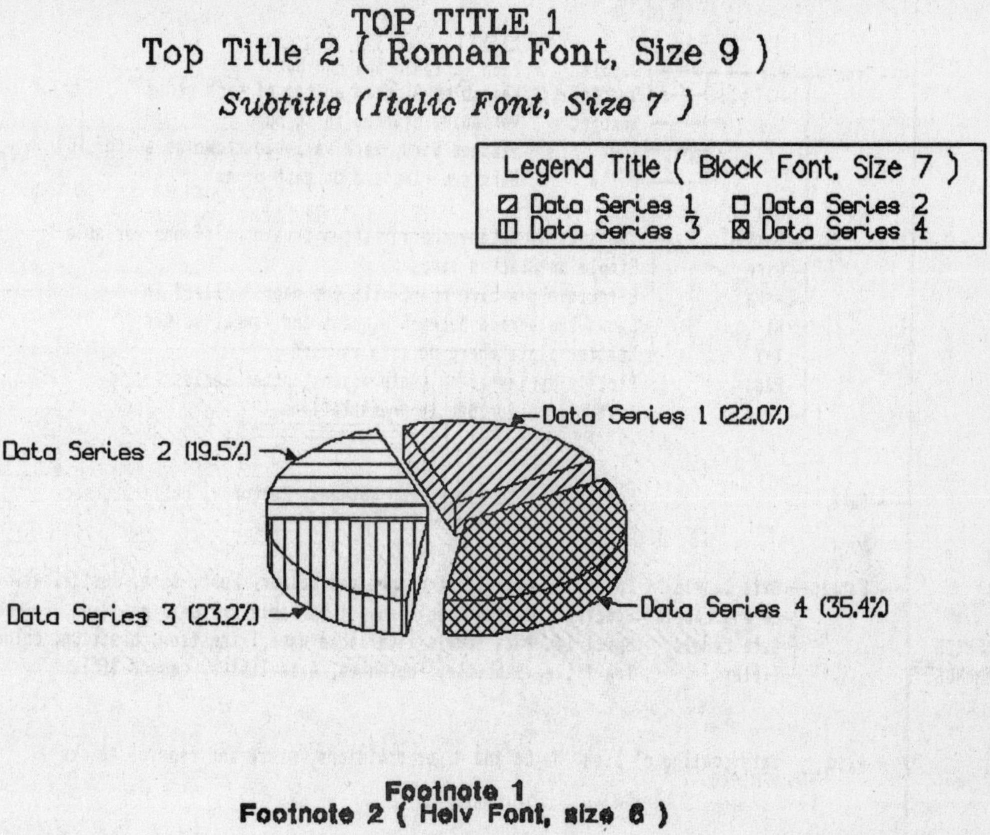

Fig 4.21

The other problem with the **Graphics** command is that there are so many options. A full list of commands is provided in the appendix to this manual but the chart shown below shows the different options available in **Graphics,** and where they appear within the structure of the **Graphics** command.

GRAPHICS COMMANDS

Command	Option	Sub-option	Description
View			Displays graph onscreen (F10)
Type	Bar	Simple	Each variable has own Bar
		Stacked	Variables stacked on top of each other
		Grouped	Variables stacked in "groups"
		100%	Stacked bars, each variable shown as a % of 100
		Delta	Bars superimposed on each other
	Pie		
	Dual		Two sets of data (one set shows breakdown of one variable)
	Line		Simple or Stacked lines
	Area		Effectively a Line chart with the gaps "filled" in
	Hi-Lo		Shows the spread between highest and lowest values
	X-Y		Scatter plots where no axis is used
	Radar		Plots a series as an angle against other series
	Word		Text blocks for use in presentations
Data			Specifies data ranges and Colours, Patterns, Outlines, etc
Labels	Axis Labels		Specifies axis label ranges and Colour, Font, size, Justification, Format, etc
	Legend Labels		Specifies Legend label range (Variable titles) position, Colour, Font, size, etc
	Data Labels		Specifies Data labels (variable name) location, position, colour, font, size, etc
	Titles		Top Title, Subtitle, Footnotes, Axis Titles, Legend Titles
Axis			Sets scaling of axes, Major and Minor divisions, width and type of "ticks"
Options	Bar charts		Selects groups for "Stacking", Marker type, bar or line, % overlap, 3D, Horizontal
	Pie charts		Selects 3D, Fill type, start angle, segments for "Explosion", label display options
	Dual charts		Selects options for both charts; 3D, fill type, Explosion, segment labels
	Line charts		Selects type, width, marker type, horizontal, 3D, etc
			Similar option menus for other Types of graphs
Global	Drivers		Selects settings for output to a device other than a printer (Normal, PIC Files, C
	Options		Selects option settings for printers and monitors (printer and monitor resolution)
Name	Retrieve		Re-loads graphs previously STORED and SAVED
	Store		Saves graphs for future use (use with SAVE command)
	Delete		Delete NAMED graphs
	Zap		Delete all NAMED graphs
Plot			Plots (prints) current graph (Alt F10)
Zap			Deletes all current graphs
Quit			Exits Graphics command

Fig 4.22

Further exercises

Those of you who attempted the further exercises at the end of the last lesson will have some additional work saved on your spreadsheet. Use this data to create the various types of graphs covered in this lesson, enter headings and labels where appropriate. Also produce a pie chart to show total sales for each region.

You can also practice changing the fonts to see which you like best and which will work on your printer.

Lesson 5 *Budgets*

One of the main uses of spreadsheets in business is the preparation and amendment of budgets. Some of the more advanced spreadsheets are often referred to as *Financial Planning Packages*, because the commands used are specifically designed for use with budgets and other financial uses. In this lesson you will be shown how SuperCalc can be used in budgeting.

At the end of this lesson you should be able to:

a) copy data with the **Copy** command
b) lock **titles** on the screen
c) split the screen into **windows**
d) print out spreadsheets

The lesson will involve a budget for sales and purchases which will be merged to form the Cash Budget.

5.1 Entering headings

All of the budgets will record the income and payments made by the firm in each month. Therefore, the headings required will be the months of the year. Type **JAN** in A1, **FEB** in B1, **MAR** in C1 and so on, up to DEC. Now move the cursor back to A1 (use the **HOME** key).

```
  |    A    ||    B    ||    C    ||    D    ||    E    ||    F    ||    G    ||    H    |
 1 JAN       FEB        MAR        APR        MAY        JUN        JUL        AUG
 2
 3
 4
 5
 6
 7
 8
 9
10
11
12
13
14
15
16
17
18
19
20
 TEMP1!A1                    Text="JAN
Width:  9  Memory:  188  Last Col/Row:L1
 1>
READY F1:Help  F3:Names  Ctrl-Backspace:Undo  Ctrl-Break:Cancel  CAPS
```

Fig 5.1

Unfortunately this has not left any room for headings alongside the months. You will need to enter descriptions in column A, and will therefore have to use the **Insert** command to enter a new column A (demonstrated in Lesson 2). In case you cannot remember it, the sequence is:

/	to call up the commands
I	to call up the **Insert** command
C	to select column
A	to select a new column A
ENTER	

You will also need a new row at the top of the spreadsheet to enter the name of the budget. Insert a new row now as shown:

```
    |  A  ||  B  ||  C  ||  D  ||  E  ||  F  ||  G  ||  H  |
 1
 2           JAN     FEB     MAR     APR     MAY     JUN     JUL
 3
 4
 5
 6
 7
 8
 9
10
11
12
13
14
15
16
17
18
19
20
 TEMP1!A1
Width:  9  Memory:  188  Last Col/Row:M2
  1>
READY F1:Help  F3:Names  Ctrl-Backspace:Undo  Ctrl-Break:Cancel  CAPS
```

Fig 5.2

The first budget is the Sales Budget. This will show the anticipated level of sales of the firms product. Enter the heading as SALES BUDGET in cell A1.

Next, move the cursor to cell B3 and underline the months – the **Repeating Text** key ' will repeat the entry across the entire spreadsheet.

Enter **Units** in cell A4 as the description for row 4. Now move the cursor into B4 and enter the following as the number of units sold, in the appropriate cell:

	Jan	Feb	Mar	Apr	May	Jun	Jul	Aug	Sep	Oct	Nov	Dec
Units	200	220	240	260	260	250	300	370	400	380	360	220

This only shows the number of units sold and not the cash received from sales. Each of the units is going to be sold for £10, but all sales are on a credit basis, with debtors being offered one months credit. This means that the sales in January will not be paid for until February, the sales in February will not be paid for until March, and so on. Consequently you now require a Debtors Budget to show the receipts from sales.

5.2 Copying data

Move the cursor to A6 (use **GoTo**) and type **DEBTORS BUDGET** as the next heading.

Your budget will be easier to follow if you enter the months again, but you don't need to re-type them. Use the **Copy** command to copy the headings from row 2.

First press the / key to call up the commands, and select **Copy** command by pressing the letter **C**. The next prompt will ask you the range to **copy from**; the range you require is all cells between B2 and M2. Try and enter this range by using the cursor keys to designate the start and finish cells rather than typing in the range.

Once you have entered the range to copy from you can press **ENTER**. You will now be asked to enter the **Cell to copy to**, which is cell B7, so type this in, or select it with the cursor keys, and then press **ENTER**.

The sequence that you should have followed is:

/	to select commands
C	to select **Copy**
B2.M3	to specify the range to copy from
ENTER	
B7	to specify the range to copy to
ENTER	

The screen should now look like the one shown below:

```
    |   A    ||   B    ||   C    ||   D    ||   E    ||   F    ||   G    ||   H    |
 6   DEBTORS BUDGET
 7            JAN       FEB       MAR       APR       MAY       JUN       JUL
 8            ----------------------------------------------------------------------
 9
10
11
12
13
14
15
16
17
18
19
20
21
22
23
24
25
 TEMP1!B9
 Width:  9  Memory:  187  Last Col/Row:M8
   1>
 READY F1:Help  F3:Names  Ctrl-Backspace:Undo  Ctrl-Break:Cancel  CAPS
```

Fig 5.3

Move the cursor to cell A9 and enter **RECEIPTS** as the heading, and then move the cursor into cell B9.

As cash from sales is not received until a month after the units have been sold, the receipts in January will be in respect of sales made in December. You can assume that the sales last December were 190 units. This can be entered in cell B9 as a formula to show the actual cash receipts. This formula will be:

Units sold x Selling price

ie: **190*10**

Enter this formula into cell B9 now.

The formula for the other cells will be much easier to enter as the **Copy** command can do most of the work for you. All that you have to do is enter the formula in cell C9.

The receipts in February will be in respect of January's sales (cell B4) and multiplied by the selling price (£10). Can you work out a suitable formula?

The best formula will be:

B4*10

This should be entered in cell C9. This is the best formula as it can be Copied to all of the other cells in row 9. The sequence for this is:

/ to call up the commands

C to select **Copy**

The screen will now change to show the command line for the **Copy** command. In previous examples of the **Copy** command you have been given the option of using the cursor keys or typing in the ranges required, however you should by now be able to use the **Point** facility to select the ranges required. You will notice that Super-Calc is showing cell C9 as the default value. For this example you want to copy cell C9 to cells D9 across to M9, therefore cell C9 is the cell **To copy from,** so press **ENTER** and this value will be stored as the **copy from** cell.

The *prompt line* will now ask for the cell to **copy to**, and will show C9 as the default for that range as well. This is not the cell required, but you can mark out the range on the screen by using the cursor keys. The first cell to copy to is cell D9 so press the right-movement cursor key and the cursor and prompt will move to D9.

Now press **.** (the full stop key) to mark that cell as the start point, and then move the cursor across the screen to cell M9. This range will now be highlighted on the screen so that you can see exactly which cells you have selected. If the cells marked are correct (ie: D9.M9) then you can press **ENTER**.

This method is not necessarily quicker for specifying cell ranges but is usually more accurate as you can actually see which cell ranges you are selecting and can be used in a wide range of commands (including **Graphics**).

The screen should now show:

```
   |  A  ||  B  ||  C  ||  D  ||  E  ||  F  ||  G  ||  H  |
 6  DEBTORS BUDGET
 7           JAN       FEB       MAR      APR      MAY       JUN       JUL
 8           ------------------------------------------------------------
 9  RECEIPTS      1900      2000      2200      2400      2600      2600      2500
10
11
12
13
14
15
16
17
18
19
20
21
22
23
24
25
 TEMP1!D9                          Form=C4*10
Width:  9  Memory:  187  Last Col/Row:M9
  1>
READY F1:Help  F3:Names  Ctrl-Backspace:Undo  Ctrl-Break:Cancel  CAPS
```

Fig 5.4

If necessary a whole group of subsidiary budgets could be prepared in this way. It is also possible to subdivide each of the budgets between different products; however, the work already done should be sufficient to demonstrate the procedure for doing this.

The next stage is to combine the budgets and draw up the Cash Budget. The Cash Budget will show details of all receipts and payments of cash. It is then possible to see how much Cash the firm has at the end of each month.

The first step is to enter the heading **CASH BUDGET**; enter this in cell A11.

The budget will be clearer if the months are shown in each column. Use the **Copy** command to copy the months into cells B12 to M12 – try using the **Point** facility instead of keying in the ranges (refer back to previous work if you cannot remember the method).

The entries required in the Cash Budget are shown in Fig 5.5. Enter these into your spreadsheet now.

```
        | A     || B     || C     || D     || E     || F     || G     || H   |
 9  RECEIPTS        1900     2000     2200     2400     2600     2600     2500
10
11  CASH BUDGET
12           JAN      FEB      MAR      APR      MAY      JUN      JUL
13           ----------------------------------------------------------------
14  RECEIPTS
15
16  PURCHASES
17  WAGES
18  LIGHT/HEAT
19  INSURANCE
20  OFFICE EXPENSES
21
22
23
24  SURPLUS
25  OPENING BAL
26
27  CLOSING BAL
28
 TEMP1!A28                                                                TEXT
Width:  9  Memory:  186  Last Col/Row:M27
  1>
READY F1:Help  F3:Names  Ctrl-Backspace:Undo  Ctrl-Break:Cancel  CAPS
```

Fig 5.5

5.3 Copying values

Before you start entering the formulae and figures for the items shown on the screen you will have to widen column A. If you check with the screen display you will see that the entries for **LIGHT/HEAT**, **OFFICE EXPENSES**, **OPENING BAL** and **CLOSING BAL** all over-run into column B. This is not a problem at the moment but will be when data is entered in column B.

Therefore column A will need to be widened to accommodate the text entries. This involves the **Format** command and was demonstrated in Lesson 2. The longest entry in column A is **office expenses**, which means that column A will need to be at least 17 characters wide to make it fit. See if you can remember how to widen the column (make it 18 characters wide). The correct procedure is given below:

/ to call up the commands

F to select **Format**

C to select **Column**

A to select column range

ENTER

W to select **Width**

18 to select width required

ENTER

The next step is to enter figures into the spreadsheet. The first figures will be those for **RECEIPTS**. These are the figures shown in the **DEBTORS BUDGET** and the **Copy** command can be used instead of having to re-type them all.

Press **HOME** so that the top of the spreadsheet is displayed on the screen. The range to **Copy** from is B9 to M9, and the cell to **Copy** to is B14. Use the **Copy** command to copy this now.

```
   |      A      ||    B  ||    C  ||    D  ||    E  ||    F  ||    G  |
1   SALES BUDGET
2                   JAN      FEB      MAR      APR      MAY      JUN
3                   ---------------------------------------------------
4   Units              200      220      240      260      260      250
5
6   DEBTORS BUDGET
7                   JAN      FEB      MAR      APR      MAY      JUN
8                   ---------------------------------------------------
9   RECEIPTS          1900     2000     2200     2400     2600     2600
10
11  CASH BUDGET
12                  JAN      FEB      MAR      APR      MAY      JUN
13                  ---------------------------------------------------
14  RECEIPTS          1900    19000    20000    22000    24000    26000
15
16  PURCHASES
17  WAGES
18  LIGHT/HEAT
19  INSURANCE
20  OFFICE EXPENSES
 TEMP1!B14                    Form=190*10
Width:  9  Memory:  186  Last Col/Row:M27
 1>
READY F1:Help  F3:Names  Ctrl-Backspace:Undo  Ctrl-Break:Cancel  CAPS
```

Fig 5.6

If you have done this correctly your screen should look like the one in Fig 5.6. If you look closely you will notice that they are incorrect, except for B14. SuperCalc has decided that as you were using the **Copy** command you wanted the formula to be updated for the new cells. when you copied the formula from cell C9 (to calculate receipts), the formula was automatically updated for the new cells – use the **Global** command to display **Formula** on screen if you cannot follow this reasoning. The sequence is:

/	to call up commands
G	to select **Global**
F	to select **Form**

The display should now become:

```
      |      A         ||   B   ||   C   ||   D   ||   E   ||   F   ||   G   |
  1    SALES BUDGET
  2                      JAN      FEB      MAR      APR      MAY      JUN
  3                      ------------------------------------------------------
  4    Units             200      220      240      260      260      250
  5
  6    DEBTORS BUDGET
  7                      JAN      FEB      MAR      APR      MAY      JUN
  8                      ------------------------------------------------------
  9    RECEIPTS          190*10   B4*10    C4*10    D4*10    E4*10    F4*10
 10
 11    CASH BUDGET
 12                      JAN      FEB      MAR      APR      MAY      JUN
 13                      ------------------------------------------------------
 14    RECEIPTS          190*10   B9*10    C9*10    D9*10    E9*10    F9*10
 15
 16    PURCHASES
 17    WAGES
 18    LIGHT/HEAT
 19    INSURANCE
 20    OFFICE EXPENSES
  TEMP1!B14                    Form=190*10
 Width:  9  Memory:  186  Last Col/Row:M27
   1>
 READY F1:Help  F3:Names  Ctrl-Backspace:Undo  Ctrl-Break:Cancel  CAPS
```

Fig 5.7

As you can see the formula in cells C14 to M14 have been altered and therefore have produced different answers to those in cells C9 to M9. In order to stop **Copy** from automatically updating formulae you have to use some of the options available with this command.

Select **Copy** again, but this time follow this sequence:

/	to call up commands
C	to select **Copy**
B9.M9	to specify the range to copy from
ENTER	
B14	to specify range to copy to
,	to call up **Options** (as shown on screen)
N	to select **No Adjustment**

This will then **Copy** the formula exactly as it is in cells B9 to M9. The Option for **Values** would have copied the answers and not the formula and so would have achieved the same result. The other options will be examined in a later lesson. Revert the display by selecting **Global, Form** again.

The cost of **Purchases** will be £3 per unit, paid in the same month as units are sold. The easiest way of entering this is to use a formula that multiplies units sold (row 4) by the purchase price (£3). Move the cursor to cell B16, and the appropriate formula and then copy it to all other cells in row 16. Try and do this on your own; the correct answers are shown on the following display. If you cannot do this on your own then the formula is shown below (however, it might be worthwhile for you to repeat the previous lessons).

```
      |        A        ||   B   ||   C   ||   D   ||   E   ||   F   ||   G   |
   1   SALES BUDGET
   2                       JAN      FEB      MAR      APR      MAY      JUN
   3                     ------------------------------------------------------
   4   Units                  200      220      240      260      260      250
   5
   6   DEBTORS BUDGET
   7                       JAN      FEB      MAR      APR      MAY      JUN
   8                     ------------------------------------------------------
   9   RECEIPTS              1900     2000     2200     2400     2600     2600
  10
  11   CASH BUDGET
  12                       JAN      FEB      MAR      APR      MAY      JUN
  13                     ------------------------------------------------------
  14   RECEIPTS              1900     2000     2200     2400     2600     2600
  15
  16   PURCHASES              600      660      720      780      780      750
  17   WAGES
  18   LIGHT/HEAT
  19   INSURANCE
  20   OFFICE EXPENSES
   TEMP1!B16                   Form=B4*3
  Width:  9  Memory:  185  Last Col/Row:M27
   1>
  READY F1:Help  F3:Names  Ctrl-Backspace:Undo  Ctrl-Break:Cancel  CAPS
```

Fig 5.8

The correct formula is:

B4*3

The sequence to **Copy** the formula is:

/
Copy
B16
ENTER
C16.M16
ENTER

Wages paid work out at £2 per unit. Enter the formula for this and then **Copy** to all cells in row 17 – no help this time!

Light and Heat are what is known as a Semi-Variable cost. The total cost is divided into Fixed Costs (which are the same amount each month), and variable costs (which vary in accordance with output). The fixed amount is £100 per month, and the variable proportion £0.50 per unit sold. The formula for January will be:

(B4*.5)+100

The first part of the formula calculates the variable part of the cost and as it is a separate part of the calculation needs to be in brackets. It is worth noting that using a spreadsheet does not necessarily mean that all figures will be correct – most errors on spreadsheets are the result of incorrect formulae, so always take great care in devising formulae and use brackets whenever in doubt. Enter this formula and then **Copy** it as before.

Insurance costs £1,000 per year, paid in two equal instalments in January and July. This cost will have to be entered manually. Enter **500** in cell B19 and then move the cursor to cell H19 and enter **500** again.

Column A will have disappeared as you scrolled across the screen. If you use the **GoTo** command to jump back to cell A20 then this cell will become the top left-hand cell on the screen. In order to keep all of your work on the screen it is better to press the **END** key (NB: this doesn't do anything on its own) and then press the **left arrow** key which will take you back to cell A19.

Office expenses are fixed costs and remain at £500 per month. Type **600** in cell B20 and then **Copy** to the remainder of row 20.

Move the cursor into cell B22. This cell will be used to calculate the total costs for each month (rows 16 to 20). You will have to use the SUM statement to calculate this total. Type in:

SUM(B16.B20)

This will need copying, but don't do it just yet. Move the cursor into cell B24. The Surplus is the receipts less the costs in each month. The formula to calculate this is quite simple and you should be able to work it out for yourself (try and enter it on your own).

These two formulae will need to be repeated right across the spreadsheet, so use the **Copy** command to copy the contents of cells B22 to B24 to all cells between C22 and M22.

```
     |        A        || B  || C  || D  || E  || F  || G  |
7                        JAN   FEB   MAR   APR   MAY   JUN
8                        ------------------------------------------
9    RECEIPTS            1900  2000  2200  2400  2600  2600
10
11   CASH BUDGET
12                       JAN   FEB   MAR   APR   MAY   JUN
13                       ------------------------------------------
14   RECEIPTS            1900  2000  2200  2400  2600  2600
15
16   PURCHASES            600   660   720   780   780   750
17   WAGES                400   440   480   520   520   500
18   LIGHT/HEAT           200   210   220   230   230   225
19   INSURANCE            500
20   OFFICE EXPENSES      600   600   600   600   600   600
21
22                       2300  1910  2020  2130  2130  2075
23
24   SURPLUS             -400    90   180   270   470   525
25   OPENING BAL
26
TEMP1!B24                Form=B14-B22
Width:  9  Memory:  183  Last Col/Row:M27
  1>
READY F1:Help  F3:Names  Ctrl-Backspace:Undo  Ctrl-Break:Cancel  CAPS
```

Fig 5.9

The **Opening Bal** represents the *cash in hand* at the beginning of each month. The balance at 1st January was £100. Type this into cell B25. The **Closing Bal** represents the *cash in hand* at the end of each month – this will be the surplus for the month plus the opening balance (ie: B24+B25). Enter this formula now.

The **closing balance** for January will be the **opening balance** for February. Therefore you will need to copy 300 into cell C25, but if you type in **-300** then you have two problems:

1) You cannot **copy** as the number -300 would be copied to all cells, and this balance will be only be correct for February.

2) If any alterations are made to any of the other figures in the spreadsheet then the figure in cell C25 would not be amended.

The solution is to enter this figure as a *formula*; if you type in **B27** as the entry for cell C25, it will show the value as **-300**. (Do this now to show that it works.) The advantage of doing this is that if any of the figures in January alter then this figure should alter as well.

The closing balance for February will be calculated in the same way as before (Ie: **C24+C25**). Type this in now and then **copy** the range C25:C27 to all other cells in that block for all of the other months – use the **Point** facility as shown previously.

The end result should be:

```
         |        A        ||   B   ||   C   ||   D   ||   E   ||   F   ||   G   |
 9  RECEIPTS                    1900     2000     2200     2400     2600     2600
10
11  CASH BUDGET
12                     JAN       FEB      MAR      APR      MAY      JUN
13                     ----------------------------------------------------------
14  RECEIPTS                    1900     2000     2200     2400     2600     2600
15
16  PURCHASES                    600      660      720      780      780      750
17  WAGES                        400      440      480      520      520      500
18  LIGHT/HEAT                   200      210      220      230      230      225
19  INSURANCE                    500
20  OFFICE EXPENSES              600      600      600      600      600      600
21
22                              2300     1910     2020     2130     2130     2075
23
24  SURPLUS                     -400       90      180      270      470      525
25  OPENING BAL                  100     -300     -210      -30      240      710
26
27  CLOSING BAL                 -300     -210      -30      240      710     1235
28
 TEMP1!C25                Form=B27
Width:  9  Memory:  182  Last Col/Row:M27
  1>
READY F1:Help  F3:Names  Ctrl-Backspace:Undo  Ctrl-Break:Cancel  CAPS
```

Fig 5.10

If you have problems with this it is probably because you are trying to **copy** C25:C27 to D25:M27. The correct range **to** is D25:M25.

5.4 Locking titles

If you scroll the spreadsheet to examine the entries for December you should be able to check that the final Closing balance is £5970.

The problem in doing this is that you will lose the titles and headings as they are contained in those cells that are now obscured. This can be a major problem in large spreadsheets as it is difficult to tell which heading each entry is being made under.

SuperCalc uses the **Title** and **Window** commands to *lock* headings onto the screen. Move the cursor back to column A (the row number is irrelevant).

It will be easier to examine the spreadsheet entries if the headings in column A are displayed at all times. To do this you need to select the **Title** command. The correct sequence is:

/	to call up the commands
T	to select the **Title** command
V	to select the Vertical headings

The *entry line* will then revert to normal and nothing appears to have happened. However if you scroll the screen to the *right*, then column A will remain on the screen at all times.

```
     |          A        ||  G  ||  H  ||  I  ||  J  ||  K  ||  L  |
 11  CASH BUDGET
 12                          JUN     JUL     AUG     SEP     OCT     NOV
 13                          ----------------------------------------------
 14  RECEIPTS                2600    2500    3000    3700    4000    3800
 15
 16  PURCHASES                750     900    1110    1200    1140    1080
 17  WAGES                    500     600     740     800     760     720
 18  LIGHT/HEAT               225     250     285     300     290     280
 19  INSURANCE                        500
 20  OFFICE EXPENSES          600     600     600     600     600     600
 21
 22                          2075    2850    2735    2900    2790    2680
 23
 24  SURPLUS                  525    -350     265     800    1210    1120
 25  OPENING BAL              710    1235     885    1150    1950    3160
 26
 27  CLOSING BAL             1235     885    1150    1950    3160    4280
 28
 29
 30
  TEMP1!L27                       Form=L24+L25
 Width:  9  Memory:  182  Last Col/Row:M27
   1>
 READY F1:Help  F3:Names  Ctrl-Backspace:Undo  Ctrl-Break:Cancel  CAPS
```

Fig 5.11

The **Title** command can be used to lock *vertical* or *horizontal* titles on the screen, or both at the same time. Move the cursor to cell A13 using the **GoTo** command, then press:

- **/** to call up commands
- **T** to select **Title**
- **B** to lock **both** vertical & horizontal headings

Now move the cursor down the screen – the screen should only scroll from row 13 down, leaving the months will on the screen at all times. If you scroll to the right then the months will move in line with the entries but the headings will remain on the screen.

The **Title** lock is removed/released by pressing:

- **/** to call up commands
- **T** to select **Title**
- **C** to **clear** title lock

Do this now and you can then examine the other method of retaining headings.

5.4.1. Locking windows

The alternative to **Title** is the **Window** command. **Window** is more powerful than **Title** and is designed for a slightly different purpose.

Title is intended to be used on large spreadsheets where the user wants to retain the headings on the screen at all times. **Window** is also used on large spreadsheets, but enables the user to make alterations in one part of the spreadsheet and, simultaneously, see what effect the changes will have on totals.

Move the cursor to A1 by pressing the **HOME** key, then move the cursor down to cell A10. Your spreadsheet should now show the top left hand portion of the spreadsheet. The window will be inserted at row 10 to split the screen between the minor budgets and the Cash Budget.

To select **Window** press / then **W**. the options now available are **Horizontal, Vertical, Clear, Synchronize, Unsynchronize.** These are similar to the options available when using **Title** (NB: SuperCalc will not allow you to use **Title** and **Window** together on the same level, although you can use one for a **vertical** hold and the other for a **horizontal** hold).

At present you require a **Horizontal Window**, so select **H**. The screen will now show a second border between rows 9 and 10.

Your spreadsheet is actually split into two parts by this border. If you now move the cursor across the screen, the top part of the **window** will remain fixed.

```
   |      A      ||   B   ||   C   ||   D   ||   E   ||   F   ||   G   |
 1  SALES BUDGET
 2                   JAN      FEB      MAR      APR      MAY      JUN
 3                   ---------------------------------------------------
 4  Units                200      220      240      260      260      250
 5
 6  DEBTORS BUDGET
 7                   JAN      FEB      MAR      APR      MAY      JUN
 8                   ---------------------------------------------------
 9  RECEIPTS            1900     2000     2200     2400     2600     2600
   |   F   ||   G   ||   H   ||   I   ||   J   ||   K   ||   L   ||   M   |
10
11
12 MAY      JUN      JUL      AUG      SEP      OCT      NOV      DEC
13 -----------------------------------------------------------------------
14     2600     2600     2500     3000     3700     4000     3800     3600
15
16      780      750      900     1110     1200     1140     1080      660
17      520      500      600      740      800      760      720      440
18      230      225      250      285      300      290      280      210
19                        500
  TEMP1!M10
Width:  9  Memory:  182  Last Col/Row:M27
  1>
READY F1:Help  F3:Names  Ctrl-Backspace:Undo  Ctrl-Break:Cancel  CAPS
```

Fig 5.12

To move the windows together you need to select the **Windows, synchronize** option; this is:

/	to call up the commands
W	to select **Window**
S	to select **Synchronize**

Now if you move the cursor both parts of the screen will move together. Try this now.

The major advantage of **Window** as compared to **Title** is that **Window** will allow you to *jump* between the two different parts of the window. Move the cursor to cell A24 using the **GoTo** command.

The bottom window now shows the balances on the Cash budget. If you press **F6** the cursor will *toggle* into the top window. Press **F6** again and the cursor will move back into the bottom window.

Each window can have its own commands and display. Move the cursor back into the top window and then select the option for displaying **formulae.** Just in case you have forgotten it, this is:

/
Global
Form

```
    |          A          ||   B   ||   C   ||   D   ||   E   ||   F   ||   G   |
 9  RECEIPTS                190*10   B4*10    C4*10    D4*10    E4*10    F4*10
10
11  CASH BUDGET
12                          JAN      FEB      MAR      APR      MAY      JUN
13                          ------------------------------------------------------
14  RECEIPTS                190*10   B4*10    C4*10    D4*10    E4*10    F4*10
15
16  PURCHASES               B4*3     C4*3     D4*3     E4*3     F4*3     G4*3
17  WAGES                   B4*2     C4*2     D4*2     E4*2     F4*2     G4*2
    |          A          ||   B   ||   C   ||   D   ||   E   ||   F   ||   G   |
24  SURPLUS                    -400       90      180      270      470      525
25  OPENING BAL                 100     -300     -210      -30      240      710
26
27  CLOSING BAL                -300     -210      -30      240      710     1235
28
29
30
31
32
33
 TEMP1!A9                          Text="RECEIPTS
Width: 18  Memory:  182  Last Col/Row:M27
  1>
READY F1:Help  F3:Names  Ctrl-Backspace:Undo  Ctrl-Break:Cancel  CAPS
```

Fig 5.13

It would be possible to show cells A1 to H9 in both windows and therefore if you alter the formula in any of the cells in the top window you can see the effect in the bottom window.

Revert to normal display by selecting **/ G F** again. Now move the cursor to the column for **Feb** and change the units to **230**. This should change the balances in the bottom window.

It is possible to **save** a spreadsheet with a **window**, but if you obtain a printout it will only show the normal display.

To clear the window select the following:

/	to call up commands
W	to select **Window**
C	to select **Clear**

The display should now revert to normal.

Remember that the **Window** and **Title** commands are available if you are producing a very large spreadsheet and want to retain headings.

5.5 Obtaining printouts

In the last lesson you should have obtained a printout of your graph, and in Lesson 2 you should have produced a simple printout. This spreadsheet is slightly more complicated, mainly because it is more than 80 characters wide (the standard printer width).

Hopefully you will have remembered that the procedure for obtaining a printout of a normal spreadsheet is to use the **Output** command, instead of the **Graphics** command which is only used for obtaining printouts of graphs.

The logical choice for a printout would be a **Print** command, but the letter P has been reserved for the **Protect** command (this will be examined in Lesson 7).

You do not have to **save** a spreadsheet before printing it – it can be printed at any time. However, it is recommended that you do **save** any work before you start printing just in case the computer should *crash*. Save your spreadsheet as LESSON5 before continuing.

To select **Output** press:

/	to call up commands
O	to select **Output**

You will then have the first choice of options:

Printer	to print the report
File	to send the report to a file on disk
Attributes	to alter fonts, shading, lines and boxes (usually only works with laser printers)
Grid	to turn the grid display on or off in the report (usually only works with laser printers)
Lines	to define horizontal or vertical lines in reports

New-Page	to insert a page-break (ie: start a new page)

Most of these options will be examined in later lessons, but this lesson will concentrate on the more commonly used **Output** commands. Select **Printer**.

The *prompt line* will now show the second string of options:

Range	to specify range required in the printout (as used in Lesson 2)
Go	to start the printer (as used in Lesson 2)
Console	to display the printout on the screen first (to enable the document to be checked)
Line-Advance	to advance the printer by one line before printing (to line up the paper)
Page-Advance	to advance the printer by one sheet before printing
Options	to set additional options for special reports
Zap	to remove all options and attributes (for starting a new printout)
Align	to reset line and page counters – for new documents (always select this for second printouts)
Width	to identify range widths for setting printer width (calculates width of printout)

The first step will be to specify the range required, ie the length and the width of the spreadsheet to be included in the printout. Select **Range** from the options shown.

The choice of **Range** enables you to select which parts of the spreadsheet you want printed out (eg: A1:M4 will just print out the Sales Budget). If, as is more usual, you want a printout of the entire spreadsheet then you could just type **all** and then press **ENTER** (see Lesson 2). However, there are certain problems that need to be considered first so do not type in **all** just yet.

The cursor will be flashing in the last cell used. Press **HOME** and the cursor will jump to cell A1. For the first printout you can specify the range as A1 to G27; this will printout the budget for the first six months only. The start point of the printout has been selected as the current cursor position (A1) , press the full stop to accept this as the start point. To specify the full range move the cursor to column G and then down to row 27 – the area included in the range will be highlighted on the screen. When the *entry line* shows the range as **A1:G27** you can press **ENTER**.

The display will revert to the **/Output, Printer** options. If you select **Console** the report that you have specified will appear on screen. Press **C** now.

This will only print out the first 20 lines of the report – to view remainder press **ENTER**. Notice that the report has removed the border (ie: the column and row numbers) – this is the default option on SuperCalc 5. Return to the command line by pressing any key as instructed.

OFFICE EXPENSES	600	600	600	600	600	600
	2300	1965	2020	2130	2130	2075
SURPLUS	-400	35	280	270	470	525
OPENING BAL	100	-300	-265	15	285	755
CLOSING BAL	-300	-265	15	285	755	1280

```
TEMP1!A2
End of Report...Press any key to continue
24>/Output,Printer,Console
MENU  Display the report on the console                        CAPS
```

Fig 5.14

If you feel that the report is satisfactory, then you can obtain a printout by selecting **Go** from the command line – make sure that you have set up the printer first as failure to do this can, and often does, result in the keyboard becoming locked and/or the computer crashing (hence the advice to **save** your spreadsheet before printing). It may also be advisable to press **Align** first, to ensure that the printout starts on a new sheet of paper.

You should now obtain the printout shown below.

SALES BUDGET

	JAN	FEB	MAR	APR	MAY	JUN
Units	200	230	240	260	260	250

DEBTORS BUDGET

	JAN	FEB	MAR	APR	MAY	JUN
RECEIPTS	1900	2000	2300	2400	2600	2600

CASH BUDGET

	JAN	FEB	MAR	APR	MAY	JUN
RECEIPTS	1900	2000	2300	2400	2600	2600
PURCHASES	600	690	720	780	780	750
WAGES	400	460	480	520	520	500
LIGHT/HEAT	200	215	220	230	230	225
INSURANCE	500					
OFFICE EXPENSES	600	600	600	600	600	600
	2300	1965	2020	2130	2130	2075
SURPLUS	-400	35	280	270	470	525
OPENING BAL	100	-300	-265	15	285	755
CLOSING BAL	-300	-265	15	285	755	1280

Fig 5.15

5.6 Altering printer width

Most printers have a standard width of 80 characters, which is exactly the same width as your computer screen. Your spreadsheet extends past the border of your screen and goes to column M; therefore, if you select the **Range** as **A1.M27** the result will be that your printer will reproduce the spreadsheet in two halves, cells A1 to G27 first and then the remainder afterwards on a separate sheet. This does not look very presentable so the **Options** allow you to alter the printer width from SuperCalc. Select range **A1.M27** now.

In this example the width of the spreadsheet obviously exceeds 80 characters and you will have to adjust the printer commands so that your printer will print out 132 characters per line. However, even this width may not be sufficiently wide, so you can check how wide your spreadsheet will be by using the **Width** option.

Select **Width** and the cursor will again be highlighted in the last position used. Move the cursor to column A and press either the full stop (.) or the colon (:), then move the cursor to the extreme right of the spreadsheet (column M). If you now press **ENTER** a prompt will appear in the bottom right-hand corner informing you of the width of the spreadsheet.

The width of your spreadsheet only needs to be 126 characters, so it can be printed across one sheet of paper if you reset the printer width to 132 characters. Select **Options** and you will be given the menu shown in Fig 5.16.

```
OUTPUT OPTIONS MENU: (*Indicates options saved with /Global,Keep)
*Report Format            *Layout                    *Paper
 Formatted    Draft        Page-length    66          Wait          Yes
 Contents        No        Width          80          Auto-page      No
 Spool           No        Left            4          Double         No
                           Top             2          Line-feed     Yes
 Titles       None         Bottom          2
 Horiz.       None         Orientation  Portrait     *Borders        No
 Vert.        None        *Copies          1          Character       |
 Headers
1:
2:
3:
4:
 Footers
1:
2:
3:
4:
*Setup String (default)             (Output range is currently A1:M27)

 TEMP1!A2
Quit  Report  Layout  Paper  Titles  Copies  Borders  Headers  Footers  Setup
 25>/Output,Printer,Options,
MENU  Done with output options; return to /Output,Printer or File menu
```

Fig 5.16

This screen contains the options available for altering the style and layout of printouts. You will usually use it to alter printer width, but it does have a number of other uses; the various options perform the following functions:

Report This determines whether the printout shows the *Values* in the cells or the *Formula*. The latter is useful for checking spreadsheets.

Layout This option will allow you to alter the page length and width, NB: it does not alter the printer width and if the printer width is not altered as well then the printout will be split between a number of different pages. This option can also be used to alter printing from *Portrait* orientation (down the page) to *Landscape* (sideways across the page) – this option will only usually work with laser printers.

Paper This option will allow you alter paper settings such as whether you want a line or sheet feed before printing, whether you are using single sheets or form feeds, etc.

Titles	This option will allow you to include headings on the printout. These can be entered *Manually* (by typing in the required headings) or by *Auto* (copying headings set with / **Titles**).
Copies	This sets the number of copies required, and may be useful if multiple copies are required.
Borders	This determines whether or not the printout should include the column and row characters/numbers. It can also be used to include additional characters if required.
Headers	This is similar to **Titles** and can be used to include up to four lines as a heading or footnote. Each line can include up to 255 characters.
Setup	This option allows you to include *Printer Control Characters* as messages to be sent to the printer. To make effective use of this option you will need to examine your printer manual to identify what characters your printer can produce. It will normally be used for altering the printer width.

First, select **Layout** and move the cursor to **Page width**; alter this figure to **132** – your printout will only be 126 characters wide, but it is always better to play safe. You will have to select **Quit** to return to the normal **Options** command line.

Now select **Setup**. The cursor should now move to the blank line beneath this item. This enables you to enter the printer codes applicable to your printer, which will condense the printer width or enable you to enter special characters.

The codes will vary depending upon which printer you are using and you may need to look up the codes in your printer manual. However, most modern dot matrix printers will be compatible with either IBM or Epson printers. The control code to condense print width will be either:

Ctrl O hold the **Ctrl** key down and press **O** (not zero)

or

\015 (note that this time it is zero not O)

Try **Ctrl O** first, and if that doesn't work try the other method.

Select one of these now and then press **ENTER**, then press **ENTER** again to return to the main **Output** command line.

If you try printing out more than once the computer program will *count* the number of lines that have been printed – if you use the printer controls to *feed* through more paper these commands will not be counted by the program, which means that the printout will never start at the top of the page. To avoid this press **Align** and the program counter will return to zero. You should try and get into the habit of pressing **Align** as this will save a lot of time and paper!

Check whether you are attached to a printer and ensure that the printer is **on-line**; if so select **Align** followed by **Go**. You should obtain the printout shown in Fig 5.17.

SALES BUDGET

	JAN	FEB	MAR	APR	MAY	JUN	JUL	AUG	SEP	OCT	NOV	DEC
Units	200	230	240	260	260	250	300	370	400	380	360	2

DEBTORS BUDGET

	JAN	FEB	MAR	APR	MAY	JUN	JUL	AUG	SEP	OCT	NOV	DEC
RECEIPTS	1900	2000	2300	2400	2600	2600	2500	3000	3700	4000	3800	36

CASH BUDGET

	JAN	FEB	MAR	APR	MAY	JUN	JUL	AUG	SEP	OCT	NOV	DEC
RECEIPTS	1900	2000	2300	2400	2600	2600	2500	3000	3700	4000	3800	36
PURCHASES	600	690	720	780	780	750	900	1110	1200	1140	1080	[illegible]
WAGES	400	460	480	520	520	500	600	740	800	760	720	[illegible]
LIGHT/HEAT	200	215	220	230	230	225	250	285	300	290	280	[illegible]
INSURANCE	500						500					
OFFICE EXPENSES	600	600	600	600	600	600	600	600	600	600	600	[illegible]
	2300	1965	2020	2130	2130	2075	2850	2735	2900	2790	2680	1
SURPLUS	-400	35	280	270	470	525	-350	265	800	1210	1120	1
OPENING BAL	100	-300	-265	15	285	755	1280	930	1195	1995	3205	4
CLOSING BAL	-300	-265	15	285	755	1280	930	1195	1995	3205	4325	6

Fig 5.17

5.7 Printing formulae

SuperCalc version 5 tends to refer to printouts as *reports* rather than simply printouts. One of the justifications for this more impressive title is that SuperCalc 5 can now produce printouts with a fairly high degree of sophistication. Unfortunately the ability to make use of the increased power of the **Output** command will depend how many different printer fonts (styles) your printer can support.

In order to ensure that you are making the most effective use of your printer you should use the **Global, Spreadsheet, Device** command to specify your printer from the list of printers supported by SuperCalc.

Your printer should already have been selected when SuperCalc was set up but if you examine the **Fonts** option in **Global, Spreadsheets** you will get some idea of what fonts can be used. It must be said that SuperCalc does not appear to provide as many fonts as the printer manufacturers claim their printers are capable of!

However, even if your printer does not allow you to make use of different fonts you can still improve your printout. Lesson 6 will demonstrate some ways of doing this, but we will finish this lesson by investigating another useful skill – obtaining a printout of formulae.

If you have devised a large spreadsheet it can be very irritating to have to continually refer back to previous rows/columns to check what formula has been used (even if you are using window). Also, if you are using SuperCalc for an assignment as part of a course, you might be asked to provide details of formulae used so that your tutor can check your work properly.

If you return to the **Options** menu in the **Output** command you will notice that under the option for **Report** there is an item called **Contents**. This is intended to be used as a means of printing out the exact contents of cells and includes details of formulae, and therefore would appear to be suitable for a printout of formulae. Unfortunately the **Report, Contents** option will print out the formulae in every single cell, allowing one line for each cell – even on this fairly simple spreadsheet that would amount to over 300 lines. In most cases the **Report, Contents** option is not needed as the formulae used in column B are virtually the same as those in columns C to M. Therefore a much simpler way of printing formulae is to change the display to **Global, Formula** and then just print out column A to show titles and headings and column B to show the formulae.

In order to do this you will first have to leave the **Output** command and select **Global, Form**. Unfortunately, the formulae in some of the rows in column B are too long to be seen. This can be remedied by widening column B to a new width of 14 spaces. The screen required is that shown in Fig 5.18.

```
   |      A       ||      B      ||  C  ||  D  ||  E  ||  F  |
 2                 JAN            FEB      MAR     APR     MAY
 3                 ---------------------------------------------
 4  Units          200            230      240     260     260
 5
 6  DEBTORS BUDGET
 7                 JAN            FEB      MAR     APR     MAY
 8                 ---------------------------------------------
 9  RECEIPTS       190*10         B4*10    C4*10   D4*10   E4*10
10
11  CASH BUDGET
12                 JAN            FEB      MAR     APR     MAY
13                 ---------------------------------------------
14  RECEIPTS       190*10         B4*10    C4*10   D4*10   E4*10
15
16  PURCHASES      B4*3           C4*3     D4*3    E4*3    F4*3
17  WAGES          B4*2           C4*2     D4*2    E4*2    F4*2
18  LIGHT/HEAT     (B4*.5)+100    (C4*.5)+ (D4*.5)+ (E4*.5)+ (F4*.5)+
19  INSURANCE      500
20  OFFICE EXPENSES 600           600      600     600     600
21
 TEMP1!B2                   Text="JAN
Width: 14  Memory:  182  Last Col/Row:M27
  1>
READY F1:Help  F3:Names  Ctrl-Backspace:Undo  Ctrl-Break:Cancel  CAPS
```

Fig 5.18

This can be achieved by using the following commands:

/	to call up commands
F	to select **Format**
C	to select **Column**
B	to select column B
ENTER	
W	to select **Width**
14	to specify new width as **14**
ENTER	

All of the required formulae can now be seen and all that remains to do is to obtain a printout. Select **Output, Printer** again and then set the **Range** as **A1.B27** – it will not be necessary to print the formulae in columns C to M as they should be virtually the same as column B.

As the total width of this printout will not exceed 80 characters you could alter the *Printer Control Codes* used in the **Options** under **Setup String** by selecting this option and then deleting the current entry, but this is not essential. The only other thing to do is to check that the printer is ready and then select **Align** (just to be on the safe side) followed by **Go**. This should produce the printout shown in Fig 5.19.

```
SALES BUDGET
                  JAN
                  --------------
Units              200

DEBTORS BUDGET
                  JAN
                  --------------
RECEIPTS           190*10

CASH BUDGET
                  JAN
                  --------------
RECEIPTS           190*10

PURCHASES          B4*3
WAGES              B4*2
LIGHT/HEAT         (B4*.5)+100
INSURANCE          500
OFFICE EXPENSES    600

                   SUM(B16:B20)

SURPLUS            B14-B22
OPENING BAL        100

CLOSING BAL        B24+B25
```

Fig 5.19

This lesson has demonstrated the most commonly used printout commands; most of the other items will be covered in future lessons.

This is the end of Lesson 5 and you can now **quit** or attempt the further exercises.

Further exercises

Use the **Zap** command to clear the existing spreadsheet. Now create a budget to record your Personal income and expenditure, on a monthly basis.

When you have finished use the **Graphics** command to devise a pie chart showing the different expenditure items. Remember that a pie chart can only have one dimension of variables and therefore will have to be for one month only or for annual totals.

Lesson 6 *Break even analysis*

In this lesson you will learn about another accounting application: break even analysis. This technique enables a firm to calculate how many of its products must be sold in order for it to break-even (ie: cover its costs). If the number of units sold is less than the break-even point then the firm will have made a loss; if the units sold are more than the break-even point then the firm will have made a profit. You will devise a break-even chart that will enable the firm to calculate how much profit (or loss) will be made at varying levels of sales.

The lesson will concentrate on the **Format** command and demonstrate how it can be used to tidy up presentation. At the end of this lesson you should be able to:

a) alter the position of text
b) alter the position of numbers
c) alter the presentation of numbers
d) alter the program settings (with **Global,Optimum**)
e) use the **Undo** key
f) devise blocks of dates and numbers (with **Data**)
g) improve printout quality to include headings (with **Output**)

6.1 Setting the Undo command

If you load SuperCalc and then glance at the HELP line at the bottom of the screen you should see that there is a command called **Undo** which is operated by the **Ctrl** and **BACKSPACE** keys. The **Undo** command is used to delete any entries or commands which are subsequently found to be incorrect. In most cases this command will not work at first as it needs to be set by the **Global** command.

The first task will be to see if **Undo** is enabled. You should have a blank Spreadsheet, so type in any number in cell A1. Then press **Ctrl** and the **BACKSPACE** keys together. The entry in cell A1 will either be deleted or a message will appear to state that **Undo is not enabled.**

If the **Undo** key did not work then you can now proceed to set it. Even if it did work it may be worthwhile following the next set of instructions so that you can see some of the other options available in the **Global** command.

The command required is the **Global, Optimum** command so you can select this now. This should give two options: **Present** and **Next**. This gives you the choice of setting options for the current session or for future sessions, but the **Next** option will be examined in a future lesson. For the time being you can select **Present**.

This should produce the screen shown in Fig 6.1 which displays all of the default options which can be set by this command.

These options perform the following functions:

```
OPTIMUM SPREADSHEET CONDITIONS MENU (Current sessions)
You can change these settings for the current OR for future work sessions:

Punctuation - Decimal,
  operand, thousands               1    ( . , , )
Before currency string             $
After currency string
Time                               12hr

Minimal recalculation              Auto
Interruptible recalculation        Yes
Undo enabled                       Yes
Extension Type Default             CAL

Regraph                            Manual
Flash suppression                  No

LICS characters translated         Yes


Punctuation  Before  After  Time  Minimal  Interruptible  Undo  Extension
Regraph  Flash  LICS  Quit
 25>/Global,Optimum,Present,
MENU  Set punctuation for foreign currency:  decimal/operand/thousands
```

Fig 6.1

Punctuation	will alter the position of the *decimal* place (not all foreign currencies are decimal)
Before	sets a standard character to appear before all figures (eg: a $ sign)
After	sets a standard character to appear after all figures
Time	determines whether the clock is 12 hour or 24 hour
Minimal	determines which cells should be recalculated on changes (useful to speed up large files)
Interruptible	stops calculations part way through
Undo	reverses previous entry (ie: deletes it)
Extensions	sets extensions for files so that they can be used on other programs (default is CAL)
Regraph	redraws graph automatically if secondary monitor is in use
Flash	changes colour set – used on colour monitors where borders *blink*
LICS	enables Lotus files to be read and saved
Quit	

The only option required at present is **Undo**, so select this item and then select **Yes** to enable the command. The screen will now show that **Undo** will be enabled **after the next // Spreadsheet Zap.**

The **Spreadsheet** command has not been used yet as it is mainly used where more than one Spreadsheet is open at a time. However, you can select this command and **Zap** all existing spreadsheets by pressing:

/	to call up commands
/	to call up the second row of commands
S	to select **Spreadsheets**
Z	to select **Zap**
Y	to **zap** all existing spreadsheets

The **Undo** command should now be operational. Do not try to use it now to delete the entry in cell A1 as it will only delete the last command or entry (ie: the **Spreadsheet, Zap** command). Instead you can use the normal **Zap** command to clear the Spreadsheet.

If you want to keep **Undo** on the system for use in future sessions then you will also have to store it using the **Global, Keep** command. Select this option by selecting **Global** then **Keep**. This will give you four alternatives.

At present, **Undo** will be available for the current work session only. If you are using this manual on your own machine it is probably worthwhile to retain the **Undo** function for future sessions, however, if you are using a machine at a College or University, then do not store the **Undo** function but accept **No** in answer to the **Global, Keep** prompts. To store the command under normal circumstances select **Yes.**

The other two alternatives are included in case your SuperCalc **Configuration** file is held in another directory. If you know what this means you will also know which directory to store **To** or load **From**. For those who don't already know, this is normally part of a technique that is used to load software programs automatically or through the use of a menu system.

6.2 Automatic data entry

In order to understand this lesson you need to first understand how to calculate a break-even point. It is calculated by the following formula:

$$\frac{\text{fixed costs}}{\text{selling price} - \text{variable costs}}$$

For this lesson you can use the following details: a firm sells its product for £5 per unit. The **fixed costs** (rent, rates, etc) are £20,000, and the **variable costs** are £3 per unit. The break-even point will be:

$$\frac{\text{£20,000}}{\text{£2}} = \text{10,000 units}$$

This shows the number of products that the firm needs to sell to break even, but does not show the profit or loss at the different levels of sales. You will now prepare a break-even chart to show the different figures for profit/loss.

The first step is to enter the headings. The main heading will be **Break Even Analysis**, so you can enter this in A1. Underline this heading by using the **Repeating Text** key (ie ') and then enter the headings shown below. Note that each item is to be entered in a separate cell (eg: **Units** is in cell A3 and **Produced** is in cell A4).

```
     |  A  ||  B  ||  C  ||  D  ||  E  ||  F  ||  G  ||  H  |
1    Break Even Analysis
2    ------------------------------------------------------------------------
3    Units    Fixed     Variable Total     Revenue  Profit/
4    Produced Costs     Costs    Costs              Loss
5    ------------------------------------------------------------------------
6
7
8
9
10
11
12
13
14
15
16
17
18
19
20
 TEMP1!A6
Width:  9  Memory:  184  Last Col/Row:F5
  1>
READY F1:Help  F3:Names  Ctrl-Backspace:Undo  Ctrl-Break:Cancel
```

Fig 6.2

Underline these headings as shown by using the **Repeating Text** key.

The first column (**Units Produced**) will show the quantities of units sold; these will be at intervals of 1,000 units, and could be entered by typing in zero in cell A6 and then using a formula (A6+1000) in cell A7 which could be **copied** to all other cells. But there is another way of entering figures that follow this sort of sequence, by using the **Data** command.

This command can be used to enter figures that follow a set sequence and increase or decrease in the same proportions or by the same factors. Note that if the increases involve a complex formula it is usually wiser to enter the values as formulae.

The **Data** command is mainly used for *database* analysis and will be covered in detail in Lesson 10; this lesson will simply demonstrate how to enter values onto the Spreadsheet. To select the **Data** command you will need to press / twice. Do this now and you should get the screen shown in Fig 6.3.

```
   |  A  ||  B  ||  C  ||  D  ||  E  ||  F  ||  G  ||  H  |
 1 Break Even Analysis
 2 -------------------------------------------------------------
 3 Units    Fixed    Variable Total    Revenue  Profit/
 4 Produced Costs    Costs    Costs             Loss
 5 -------------------------------------------------------------
 6
 7
 8
 9
10
11
12
13
14
15
16
17
18
19
20
Quit  Input  Criterion  Output  Find  Extract  Unique  Select  Remain  Delete
Analysis  Block  Matrix  Parse  Table
  8>//Data,
MENU  Leave //Data menu
```

Fig 6.3

The majority of these options are for use with the database facility but the one that you require is the **Block** option. Select this option and the following options will be displayed:

Number	this will generate numbers for inclusion on the Spreadsheet
Growth	this will also generate numbers but in a *geometric* progression
Dates	this will generate a series of dates in a progression
Order	this determines whether the values are entered in a column or row

All of these options, with the exception of **Order**, follow the same pattern in that they all require a **Start** value, a **Step** value and a **Stop** value.

In order to demonstrate the **Data** command and the **Undo** command the next few tasks are not related to the lesson but show how both these commands can be used. Your first attempt with the **Data** command will be to set a sequence of dates in column **A**.

To do this enter the following:

O	to select **Order** (always do this first in **Data**)
C	to select column order
A6.A26	to specify the **Range** (use the cursor keys if you prefer)
D	to select **Date**
M	to select **Month** (each new line will increase by one month)
DATE(1,1,90)	to enter the start date (this date is in American format – Month, Day, Year)
1	to increase each step by one month at a time
ENTER	to accept the default stop date of **DATE(2,28,2100)**

The screen should now show:

```
   |  A  ||  B  ||  C  ||  D  ||  E  ||  F  ||  G  ||  H  |
 1 Break Even Analysis
 2 ----------------------------------------------------------------
 3 Units    Fixed    Variable Total    Revenue  Profit/
 4 Produced Costs    Costs    Costs             Loss
 5 ----------------------------------------------------------------
 6   1/ 1/90
 7   2/ 1/90
 8   3/ 1/90
 9   4/ 1/90
10   5/ 1/90
11   6/ 1/90
12   7/ 1/90
13   8/ 1/90
14   9/ 1/90
15  10/ 1/90
16  11/ 1/90
17  12/ 1/90
18   1/ 1/91
19   2/ 1/91
20   3/ 1/91
 TEMP1!A6                     Form=DVAL(32814)
Width:  9  Memory:  183  Last Col/Row:F26
  1>
READY F1:Help  F3:Names  Ctrl-Backspace:Undo  Ctrl-Break:Cancel
```

Fig 6.4

The **Date** formula has not been used before but is designed to allow you to include dates in spreadsheets. If you enter a date as **12/1/90** this will be interpreted as 12 divided by 1 divided by 90. The default style for dates is the American layout of Month, Day then Year. This can be altered to European format and will be explained in Lesson 8.

The **stop** value in this example was 28th February 2100. This is the last date stored on SuperCalc and is far higher than we need, but this does not matter as the **range** only goes down to A26, and the command will always end at the last cell in the **range**.

This should have demonstrated how to enter a sequence of dates but has no application in this lesson, so you can now use the **Undo** command to reverse the last command. If you press **Ctrl** and **BACKSPACE** then all of the entries in cells A6 to A26 should be deleted.

What you require is a sequence of numbers in this range going from 0 to 20,000. You can now use the **Data** command to enter these numbers for you. Type in:

/	to call up commands
/	to call up the second row of commands
D	to select **Data**
O	to select **Order** (always do this first in **Data**)
C	to select Column order
A6.A26	to specify the **Range** (use the cursor keys if you prefer)
N	to select **Number**
0	to enter the **start** value
1000	to increase each **step** by 1,000
ENTER	to accept the default **stop** value of 99999999999

The values in column A should now start at 0 and increase by 1,000 in each row to a total of 20,000.

```
   |    A    ||    B    ||    C    ||    D    ||    E    ||    F    ||    G    ||    H    |
 1  Break Even Analysis
 2  ---------------------------------------------------------------------------------
 3  Units    Fixed      Variable  Total      Revenue   Profit/
 4  Produced Costs      Costs     Costs                Loss
 5  ---------------------------------------------------------------------------------
 6         0
 7      1000
 8      2000
 9      3000
10      4000
11      5000
12      6000
13      7000
14      8000
15      9000
16     10000
17     11000
18     12000
19     13000
20     14000
 TEMP1!A6                                Form=0
Width:  9  Memory:  183  Last Col/Row:F26
 1>
READY F1:Help  F3:Names  Ctrl-Backspace:Undo  Ctrl-Break:Cancel
```

Fig 6.5

6.3 Copying blocks

The next stage will be to enter the costs and income for each level of production. Move the cursor to cell B6. This should show the amount of **fixed costs**, which is £20,000, so type **20000** in cell B6. This will need to be **copied** to all other cells down to B26 but you needn't do it just yet. Instead move the cursor to cell C6 for **variable costs**.

The variable costs are £3 per unit; this figure can be calculated by using a formula, as the entry in column C will be the units produced multiplied by 3. Type the following formula in cell C6:

A6*3 ENTER

The answer should appear as 0. If you check this you will find that it is correct as the units sold in this row are zero. Once again, this will need to be **copied**, but don't do it yet. The next entry will be for **total costs** – this will be **fixed costs plus variable costs**, and can also be entered as a formula

B6+C6 ENTER

This should produce an answer of 20000. The entry for Revenue will be the number of units sold multiplied by the selling price per unit. Each unit is sold for £5 and this can be calculated by formula as well. This formula will be:

A6*5 ENTER

This will appear as zero because no units have been sold in this row.

The last entry will be for **profit/loss** and will be **revenue less total costs**; the formula is:

E6-D6 ENTER

Your screen should show the following:

```
     |  A  ||  B  ||  C  ||  D  ||  E  ||  F  ||  G  ||  H  |
1    Break Even Analysis
2    ---------------------------------------------------------------
3    Units    Fixed    Variable Total    Revenue  Profit/
4    Produced Costs    Costs    Costs             Loss
5    ---------------------------------------------------------------
6           0    20000        0    20000        0   -20000
7        1000
8        2000
9        3000
10       4000
11       5000
12       6000
13       7000
14       8000
15       9000
16      10000
17      11000
18      12000
19      13000
20      14000
 TEMP1!G6
Width:  9  Memory:  183  Last Col/Row:F26
  1>
READY F1:Help  F3:Names  Ctrl-Backspace:Undo  Ctrl-Break:Cancel
```

Fig 6.6

All of the formula in row 6 can now be **copied** in one go. Type in the following:

/	to call up commands
C	to select **Copy**
B6.F6	to select **range from**
ENTER	
B7.B26	to select **range to**
ENTER	

The screen should now show:

```
    |  A  ||  B  ||  C  ||  D  ||  E  ||  F  ||  G  ||  H  |
 1   Break Even Analysis
 2   ----------------------------------------------------------------
 3   Units    Fixed    Variable Total    Revenue  Profit/
 4   Produced Costs    Costs    Costs             Loss
 5   ----------------------------------------------------------------
 6          0    20000        0    20000        0   -20000
 7       1000    20000     3000    23000     5000   -18000
 8       2000    20000     6000    26000    10000   -16000
 9       3000    20000     9000    29000    15000   -14000
10       4000    20000    12000    32000    20000   -12000
11       5000    20000    15000    35000    25000   -10000
12       6000    20000    18000    38000    30000    -8000
13       7000    20000    21000    41000    35000    -6000
14       8000    20000    24000    44000    40000    -4000
15       9000    20000    27000    47000    45000    -2000
16      10000    20000    30000    50000    50000        0
17      11000    20000    33000    53000    55000     2000
18      12000    20000    36000    56000    60000     4000
19      13000    20000    39000    59000    65000     6000
20      14000    20000    42000    62000    70000     8000
 TEMP1!G6
Width:  9  Memory:  180  Last Col/Row:F26
  1>
READY F1:Help  F3:Names  Ctrl-Backspace:Undo  Ctrl-Break:Cancel
```

Fig 6.7

6.4 Adjusting text

It should be apparent that the headings in rows 3 and 4 do not *match up* with the entries beneath them. This is because SuperCalc will automatically assume that *text* should be left-justified – ie: start from the the left and work to the right (the way in which you write), and that *numbers* should be right-justified - ie: start from the right and work to the left (the way in which you add up).

Normally this is what you will require, but when you have headings, as in your present spreadsheet, it is better if the text can be right-justified or placed in the centre of the cell. This can be achieved through the **Format** command.

What you want to do is to make the headings at the top of the columns right-justified (cells A3 to F4). To do this type in:

/	to call up commands
F	to select **Format**
E	to specify **Entry**
A3.F4	to select entry required

Use the cursor keys to highlight the range if preferred

ENTER

T	to select **Text**
R	to select **Right**
Accept	to put changes into operation

The display should now show:

```
  | A    ||   B    ||   C    ||   D    ||   E    ||   F    ||   G    ||   H    |
1  Break Even Analysis
2  ---------------------------------------------------------------------------
3     Units    Fixed Variable    Total  Revenue  Profit/
4  Produced    Costs    Costs    Costs              Loss
5  ---------------------------------------------------------------------------
6         0    20000        0    20000        0   -20000
7      1000    20000     3000    23000     5000   -18000
8      2000    20000     6000    26000    10000   -16000
9      3000    20000     9000    29000    15000   -14000
10     4000    20000    12000    32000    20000   -12000
11     5000    20000    15000    35000    25000   -10000
12     6000    20000    18000    38000    30000    -8000
13     7000    20000    21000    41000    35000    -6000
14     8000    20000    24000    44000    40000    -4000
15     9000    20000    27000    47000    45000    -2000
16    10000    20000    30000    50000    50000        0
17    11000    20000    33000    53000    55000     2000
18    12000    20000    36000    56000    60000     4000
19    13000    20000    39000    59000    65000     6000
20    14000    20000    42000    62000    70000     8000
 TEMP1!G6
Width:  9  Memory:  180  Last Col/Row:F26
  1>
READY F1:Help  F3:Names  Ctrl-Backspace:Undo  Ctrl-Break:Cancel
```

Fig 6.8

The text could also have been **centred**, which would have positioned it in the middle of each cell. Try and do this now; the process will be the same as that for **Text Right** except that you will need to select **Centre** from the **Text** option instead of text right.

/	to call up commands
F	to select **Format**
E	to specify **Entry**
A3.F4	to select **Entry** required

Use the cursor keys to highlight the range if preferred

ENTER

T	to select **Text**
C	to select **Centre**
Accept	to put changes into operation

The display will now show the text in the centre of the cell instead of being right-justified.

```
    |    A    ||    B    ||    C    ||    D    ||    E    ||    F    ||    G    ||    H    |
 1  Break Even Analysis
 2  --------------------------------------------------------------------------------
 3    Units    Fixed    Variable   Total    Revenue  Profit/
 4   Produced  Costs     Costs     Costs              Loss
 5  --------------------------------------------------------------------------------
 6          0    20000         0    20000         0   -20000
 7       1000    20000      3000    23000      5000   -18000
 8       2000    20000      6000    26000     10000   -16000
 9       3000    20000      9000    29000     15000   -14000
10       4000    20000     12000    32000     20000   -12000
11       5000    20000     15000    35000     25000   -10000
12       6000    20000     18000    38000     30000    -8000
13       7000    20000     21000    41000     35000    -6000
14       8000    20000     24000    44000     40000    -4000
15       9000    20000     27000    47000     45000    -2000
16      10000    20000     30000    50000     50000        0
17      11000    20000     33000    53000     55000     2000
18      12000    20000     36000    56000     60000     4000
19      13000    20000     39000    59000     65000     6000
20      14000    20000     42000    62000     70000     8000
 TEMP1!G6
Width:  9  Memory:  180  Last Col/Row:F26
  1>
READY F1:Help  F3:Names  Ctrl-Backspace:Undo  Ctrl-Break:Cancel
```

Fig 6.9

The **Format** command can be used to alter the layout of text anywhere on the Spreadsheet and it can be returned to the original justification by using the **Text, Left** option. SuperCalc will allow you to alter either an **Entry, Row, Column** or **Global** (**Global** means the entire spreadsheet).

6.5 Adjusting numbers

The **Format** command can also be used to alter the format of cells containing numbers.

An explanation of each of the **Format** options was given in Lesson 2, when **Format** was used to widen a column. The majority of the other options relate to numeric entries. All of the **Format** options can be applied to a specific **Entry, Column, Row** or **Global**. The other two options of **User-Define** and **Hide-column** have slightly different uses and will be discussed later. The options affecting numeric entries are:

Integer	rounds off numbers to a whole number (eg: 10.23 as 10)
$ (or £)	displays numbers with two decimal places (eg:10.234 as 10.23)

Exponent	displays numbers in scientific notation (eg: 10 as E1)
General	numbers displayed as *best fit*
*****	displays numbers as a series of asterisk's (eg: 5 as *****) (used for very basic graphic displays)
User-Define	allows user to define layout
Hide	hides confidential numbers
RIght	right justifies numbers (default value)
Left	left justifies numbers
Center	justifies numbers in the centre of a cell
Default	reverts to original status
Text	selects options for justifying **Text**
Width	alters width of columns (default 9)

Many of these options are of little use in this Spreadsheet but you can quickly examine some of them. What you can do is to alter the format of the columns so that column A shows two decimal places, column B is left justified, column C is hidden and column D is shown as an exponential.

The first step is to call up **Format**. Designate the range required and then select the option. The procedure to format column A as $ (or £) is:

/	to call up commands
F	to select **Format**
C	to select **Column**
A	to specify column A
ENTER	
$(or £)	to select the $ (or £) (decimal format)
ENTER	
Accept	to put changes into operation

Column A will now show each numeric entry with two decimal places. This is not really required here but would be if the Spreadsheet was using smaller numbers and you wanted to include both **pounds** and **pence**.

The next thing to do is to make column B left-justified; the sequence to do this is:

/	to call up commands
F	to select **Format**
C	to select **Column**
B	to specify column B
ENTER	
L	to select left justification of numbers
ENTER	
Accept	to put changes into operation

The screen should then show:

```
   |   A    ||   B    ||   C    ||   D    ||   E    ||   F    ||   G    ||   H   |
1  Break Even Analysis
2  ----------------------------------------------------------------------------
3    Units    Fixed   Variable  Total    Revenue  Profit/
4  Produced  Costs    Costs    Costs              Loss
5  ----------------------------------------------------------------------------
6        .00 20000          0    20000         0  -20000
7    1000.00 20000       3000    23000      5000  -18000
8    2000.00 20000       6000    26000     10000  -16000
9    3000.00 20000       9000    29000     15000  -14000
10   4000.00 20000      12000    32000     20000  -12000
11   5000.00 20000      15000    35000     25000  -10000
12   6000.00 20000      18000    38000     30000   -8000
13   7000.00 20000      21000    41000     35000   -6000
14   8000.00 20000      24000    44000     40000   -4000
15   9000.00 20000      27000    47000     45000   -2000
16  10000.00 20000      30000    50000     50000       0
17  11000.00 20000      33000    53000     55000    2000
18  12000.00 20000      36000    56000     60000    4000
19  13000.00 20000      39000    59000     65000    6000
20  14000.00 20000      42000    62000     70000    8000
 TEMP1!G6
Width:  9  Memory:  180  Last Col/Row:F26
  1>
READY F1:Help  F3:Names  Ctrl-Backspace:Undo  Ctrl-Break:Cancel
```

Fig 6.10

You can make some further changes to format by using the other options. Column C should be hidden and column D shown in exponential format. Follow the sequences as given above but for column C select **Hide** and for column D select **Exponent** – you will have to do this as two separate operations.

If you have done it properly then the screen should show the following:

```
   |  A  ||  B  ||  C  ||  D  ||  E  ||  F  ||  G  ||  H  |
1  Break Even Analysis
2  ----------------------------------------------------------------
3    Units    Fixed               Total   Revenue  Profit/
4   Produced  Costs               Costs             Loss
5  ----------------------------------------------------------------
6         .00 20000                 2e4        0   -20000
7     1000.00 20000               2.3e4     5000   -18000
8     2000.00 20000               2.6e4    10000   -16000
9     3000.00 20000               2.9e4    15000   -14000
10    4000.00 20000               3.2e4    20000   -12000
11    5000.00 20000               3.5e4    25000   -10000
12    6000.00 20000               3.8e4    30000    -8000
13    7000.00 20000               4.1e4    35000    -6000
14    8000.00 20000               4.4e4    40000    -4000
15    9000.00 20000               4.7e4    45000    -2000
16   10000.00 20000                 5e4    50000        0
17   11000.00 20000               5.3e4    55000     2000
18   12000.00 20000               5.6e4    60000     4000
19   13000.00 20000               5.9e4    65000     6000
20   14000.00 20000               6.2e4    70000     8000
TEMP1!C6                       Form=A6*3
Width:  9  Memory:  180  Last Col/Row:F26
 1>
READY F1:Help  F3:Names  Ctrl-Backspace:Undo  Ctrl-Break:Cancel
```

Fig 6.11

Note that **Hide** will hide the entire contents of the column not just the numbers, to **Hide** numbers only you would have to specify **Entry** instead of **Column**.

However, if you move the cursor into column C, the contents of each cell will be shown on the *status line*, the Data is only hidden and is not deleted completely. this option will be used again in a later lesson but is useful where some Data is confidential and the firm do not want it to be seen by every user.

The various **Format** commands do not have to be used individually, it is possible to format a column that is formatted to be **left-justified**, show **two decimal places** and be **hidden**.

Unfortunately, this has made a mess of the Spreadsheet, but the original layout can easily be recovered by selecting the **Format, Default** option.

The obvious thing to do would be to select this as a **Global** option, but unfortunately, **Default** will not always work properly when used globally. The quickest way of reverting to the default layout will be to select the **Column** option and specify the range as columns A to E. The procedure for this is:

/	to call up commands
F	to select **Format**
C	to select **Column**

A.E	to specify columns A to E
ENTER	
D	to select **default** layout
ENTER	
Accept	to put changes into operation

The layout of the spreadsheet should then revert to what it was before you started altering the **Format** of the numeric cells.

6.6 Hiding columns

You may have noticed that when you select **Format** there are two options that do not relate to the **ranges** required, these are **Hide-column** and **User-Define**. The **Hide** option available from the main list of **Format** options has already been described so you can now examine the **Hide-column** option to see what the differences are.

Firstly, the **Hide** option can be used to hide a row, column, cell, block or even the entire Spreadsheet. But, it will still show a blank line on the screen or printout.

The **Hide-column** option will actually remove the column from the display altogether.

Select the following:

/	to call up commands
F	to select **Format**
H	to select **Hide-Column**
D	to select column D
ENTER	
Y	to select **Yes** for Hide

The screen will then change to the following:

```
      | A  ||  B  ||  C  ||  E  ||  F  ||  G  ||  H  ||  I  |
1   Break Even Analysis
2   ----------------------------------------------------------------------
3     Units    Fixed   Variable Revenue  Profit/
4    Produced  Costs    Costs             Loss
5   ----------------------------------------------------------------------
6          0   20000        0        0   -20000
7       1000   20000     3000     5000   -18000
8       2000   20000     6000    10000   -16000
9       3000   20000     9000    15000   -14000
10      4000   20000    12000    20000   -12000
11      5000   20000    15000    25000   -10000
12      6000   20000    18000    30000    -8000
13      7000   20000    21000    35000    -6000
14      8000   20000    24000    40000    -4000
15      9000   20000    27000    45000    -2000
16     10000   20000    30000    50000        0
17     11000   20000    33000    55000     2000
18     12000   20000    36000    60000     4000
19     13000   20000    39000    65000     6000
20     14000   20000    42000    70000     8000
TEMP1!C6                     Form=A6*3
Width:  9  Memory:  180  Last Col/Row:F26
  1>
READY F1:Help  F3:Names  Ctrl-Backspace:Undo  Ctrl-Break:Cancel
```

Fig 6.12

Column D has now been completely removed from the screen as if it had been deleted. If this option has been selected it is impossible to examine the contents of this column. This differs from the **Hide** option as the column is removed from the display.

To recover the column you simply repeat the procedure but select the option for **No**; the screen will now revert to the original display.

6.7 User-defined formats

SuperCalc will allow the user to define his or her own formats, within certain limits. A maximum of eight different styles can be selected from the **User-Define** option in **Format**. The options within **User-Define** are predominantly for use in accounting functions in.

To examine the additional layouts available press:

/	to call up commands
F	to select **Format**
U	to select **User-Define**

You will then be presented with two options: **Number and Date**; select **Number** first and the following screen will appear:

```
USER-DEFINE NUMBER FORMAT MENU

Format        Currently Defined Format                    Zero as  Scaling
 Set                                                        Blank   Factor
  1.   $-11,111,111.11                                       No       0
  2.   $-11,111,111.11                                       Yes      0
  3.   ($11,111,111.11)                                      No       0
  4.   ($11,111,111.11)                                      Yes      0
  5.   $-11111111                                            No       0
  6.   -11,111,111                                           No       0
  7.   (11,111,111)                                          No       0
  8.   -1111111111.11%                                       No       0


TEMP1!C6                    Form=A6$3
Quit  1  2  3  4  5  6  7  8  Zap
 28>/Format,User-define,Number,
MENU  Finished defining formats; return to /Format menu
```

Fig 6.13

This display shows the eight different formats already created, each line containing a different format. At present they should all be the same. In order to make a bit more sense of these formats you will have to select one of them. Press **1** and the choices on offer will be displayed at the bottom of the screen.

Each item on this menu relates to one of the additional layouts that can be selected. The **User-Define** format enables the user to accept as many of these options as are required.

The different functions are as follows:

Before enables the user to specify what character should be used as a prefix before numbers (usually a $ or £)

After enables the user to specify what character should be used after numbers

Thousands enables the user to specify that all figures should have a comma inserted every 3rd place left of the decimal point.

Minus enables the user to specify whether minus figures should be in brackets or prefixed by a minus sign.

Percent	enables the user to specify that figures should be multiplied by 100 and expressed as a percentage.
Decimal	enables the user to decide the number of decimal places required (with a maximum of 7).
Zero	enables the user to specify whether zero is shown as a blank or as 0.
Scaling	enables the user to scale figures down by factors of ten (factor 2 will display contents divided by 100 [hundreds]).

Your Spreadsheet would be improved if the numbers had embedded commas and minus figures were in brackets. Set **User-Define Format 1** to the following:

Floating $ (or £)	N
Embedded commas	Y
Minus in ()	Y
Zero as Blank	N
%	N
Decimal Places	0
Scaling Factor	0

When you have completed this select **Quit** to return to the spreadsheet.

This has only *defined* the layout that you require; you must now use the **Format** command to specify which cells you want to define.

In your Spreadsheet you will want the **User-Defined Format 1** to apply to all cells containing numbers (ie: the block A6 to F26). To do this type in:

/	to call up commands
F	to select **Format**
E	to select **Entry**
A6.F26	to specify the block A6 to F26
ENTER	
U	to select **User-Define**
1	to select User defined format 1
Accept	to accept changes

Your Spreadsheet should now show the following:

	A	B	C	D	E	F	G	H
1	Break Even Analysis							
2	----------							
3	Units	Fixed	Variable	Total	Revenue	Profit/		
4	Produced	Costs	Costs	Costs		Loss		
5	----------							
6	0	20,000	0	20,000	0	(20,000)		
7	1,000	20,000	3,000	23,000	5,000	(18,000)		
8	2,000	20,000	6,000	26,000	10,000	(16,000)		
9	3,000	20,000	9,000	29,000	15,000	(14,000)		
10	4,000	20,000	12,000	32,000	20,000	(12,000)		
11	5,000	20,000	15,000	35,000	25,000	(10,000)		
12	6,000	20,000	18,000	38,000	30,000	(8,000)		
13	7,000	20,000	21,000	41,000	35,000	(6,000)		
14	8,000	20,000	24,000	44,000	40,000	(4,000)		
15	9,000	20,000	27,000	47,000	45,000	(2,000)		
16	10,000	20,000	30,000	50,000	50,000	0		
17	11,000	20,000	33,000	53,000	55,000	2,000		
18	12,000	20,000	36,000	56,000	60,000	4,000		
19	13,000	20,000	39,000	59,000	65,000	6,000		
20	14,000	20,000	42,000	62,000	70,000	8,000		

```
TEMP1!C6              U1          Form=A6*3
Width:  9  Memory:  180  Last Col/Row:F26
  1>
READY F1:Help  F3:Names  Ctrl-Backspace:Undo  Ctrl-Break:Cancel
```

Fig 6.14

The **User-Define** option includes upto eight different **definitions** so that you can include a variety of different definitions in any one spreadsheet.

6.8 Break even graphs

Now that you have created the break even chart you should also be able to produce a line graph of this Data. The line graph will require two lines: the Revenue line and the Total Cost line, the point at which they intersect is the break even point.

In order to devise this graph you will have to use the **Graphics** command to specify the variables. Variable A will be the Total costs line and will be the range D6 to D26, Variable B will be the Income line and will be the range E6 to E26. Set these variables as follows:

//	to call up commands
V	to select **Graphics**
D	to select **Data**
D6.D26	to enter range for **Series Range 1**
ENTER	to move to next variable
E6.E26	to enter range for **Series Range 2**

ENTER

This would be sufficient to produce a graph, but you have not yet specified the type of graph required – SuperCalc will produce a bar chart if no graph type is selected. You will have to specify that you require a Line chart, so press **Esc** to return to the **Graphics** command options. To select a line graph type in the following:

T to select **Type**

L to select **Line**

If you then press **F10** you should have the following graph:

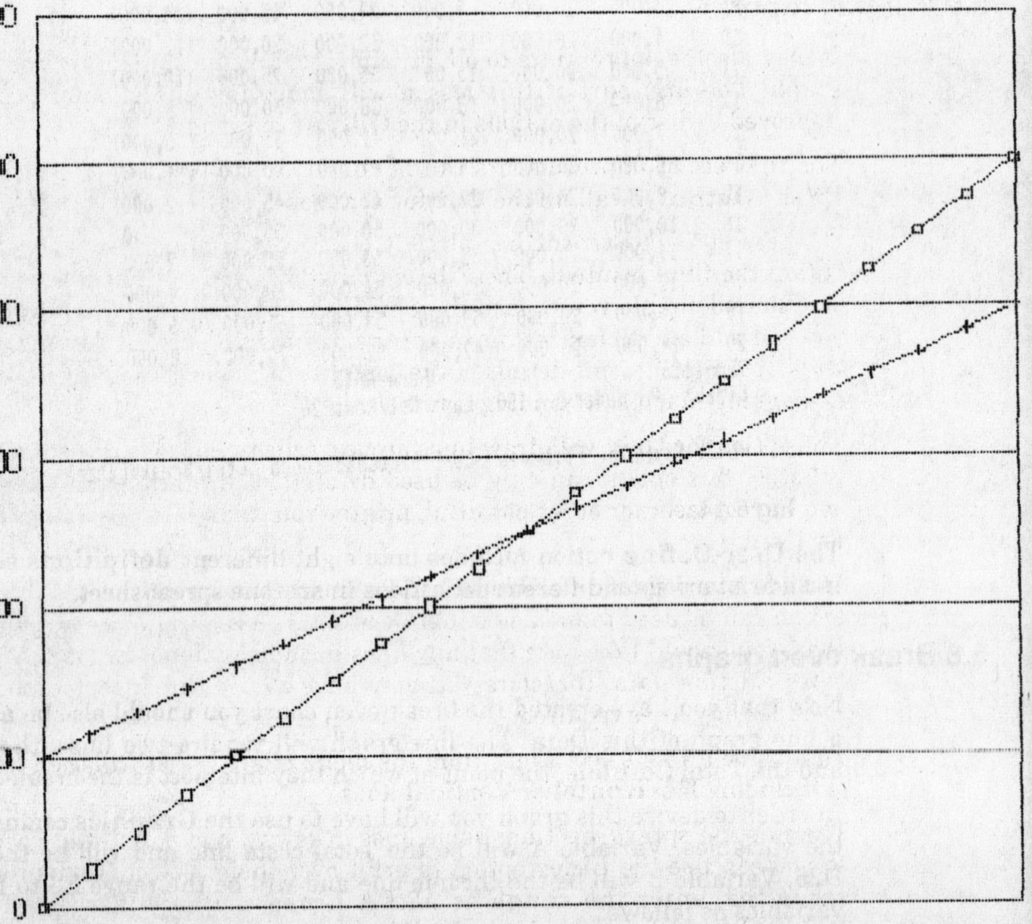

Fig 6.15

The graph would be improved by the use of labels and headings. See if you can set the labels and headings below on your own.

The **data labels** (ie: the lines) require the following labels: data series **1** is **Costs** and data series **2** is **Income**. Find which cell these appear in on the spreadsheet and use the **cell reference** as the data label.

The titles should include a **TOP TITLE** (main heading) which will be **Break Even Analysis**; again use the cell reference to enter this on the spreadsheet.

Check that your work is correct by pressing **F10** to view the graph. If you want a printout of your graph select **Plot** from the **Graphics** options or press **Alt** and **F10**. You can also practice the use of the **Graphics** options dealt with in Lessons 3 and 4.

6.9 Printing reports

It may also be appropriate to obtain a printout of the spreadsheet data as well as a graph. The last part of this lesson will show how the style of printouts can be improved by use of the options in the **Output** command.

The first set of improvements can be found on the first set of **Output** commands. Press / **Output** to call up the **Output** command.

Of these options **Printer** has already been used, and will be used again shortly to obtain the final printout. The **File** option allows you to print your report onto disk; this should enable you to load the Spreadsheet report onto a wordprocessor so that you can add additional text or insert the report into another document. The **Attributes** option prints out details of the contents of each cell and is primarily for use in *de-bugging* macros (ie: finding errors).

The option for **Grid** will draw lines around cells to improve presentation, but unfortunately this option can only be used by certain printers, mainly laser printers. If you have a laser, or other powerful, printer you can select this option and select **Yes** for **Grid**.

Most printers should be able to handle the remaining option which is **Lines**. This option can be used to include either horizontal or vertical lines on your report. However, you should take note that any lines included will not be *inserted* but will *overwrite* existing data, therefore you may have to use the **Insert** command to make room for any lines required.

To include a line select Lines from the menu offered. You will then have the choice of including **Horizontal** or **Vertical** lines.

The existing spreadsheet has some lines in rows 2 and 5, but these are *broken* lines so you can use the **Lines** option to print over them. Select **Horizontal** and, when requested, enter the **range** as A2.F2. **Lines** can be either **Single** or **Double** (although your printer may not be able to print double lines). Select **Single** for this line, and then select width as **3** – SuperCalc offers five different widths of line ranging from **1** (thin) to **5** (thick).

Your screen should now look like the one shown below:

```
  |  A  ||  B  ||  C  ||  D  ||  E  ||  F  ||  G  ||  H  |
1   Break Even Analysis
2   ______________________________________________
3    Units    Fixed  Variable  Total  Revenue  Profit/
4   Produced  Costs   Costs    Costs            Loss
5   ----------------------------------------------------
6          0  20,000        0  20,000       0  (20,000)
7      1,000  20,000    3,000  23,000   5,000  (18,000)
8      2,000  20,000    6,000  26,000  10,000  (16,000)
9      3,000  20,000    9,000  29,000  15,000  (14,000)
10     4,000  20,000   12,000  32,000  20,000  (12,000)
11     5,000  20,000   15,000  35,000  25,000  (10,000)
12     6,000  20,000   18,000  38,000  30,000  ( 8,000)
13     7,000  20,000   21,000  41,000  35,000  ( 6,000)
14     8,000  20,000   24,000  44,000  40,000  ( 4,000)
15     9,000  20,000   27,000  47,000  45,000  ( 2,000)
16    10,000  20,000   30,000  50,000  50,000         0
17    11,000  20,000   33,000  53,000  55,000     2,000
18    12,000  20,000   36,000  56,000  60,000     4,000
19    13,000  20,000   39,000  59,000  65,000     6,000
20    14,000  20,000   42,000  62,000  70,000     8,000
LESSON6A!C6          U1        Form=A6*3
Width:  9  Memory:  180  Last Col/Row:F26
  1>
READY F1:Help  F3:Names  Ctrl-Backspace:Undo  Ctrl-Break:Cancel
```

Fig 6.16

You can also include a line in row 5. Select **Output, Lines** again, and this time specify that you want a **Horizontal** line from **A5.F2**. Select **Double** as the type of line and **5** as the thickness.

Further exercises

The spreadsheet created uses formulae wherever possible which speeds up the process of creating the Spreadsheet. The disadvantage is that any major changes, such as change in selling price or variable cost, would mean that the formulae would need changing and then replicating all over again. This can be avoided if the selling price and variable costs are entered in a separate cell and *called up* by formulae.

For example, cell B6 contains the entry **20000**; if the **fixed costs** were increased to **24000** then you would have to type this in to cell B6 and then copy it to all other cells. However, if you had entered the fixed costs separately, say in cell D1, then they can be copied into cell B6 by simply typing **D1** as the formula. This can then be copied to all other cells in column B.

Retain the existing Spreadsheet but insert some new rows at the top of the Spreadsheet. Enter the following as text:

Variable cost: Fixed Cost: Selling Price:

Now enter the following figures for the respective headings:

15 (Variable cost) **50000** (Fixed Cost) **48** (Selling Price)

Now adjust the formula to *call up* the relevant figures from your new headings.

When you have successfully accomplished this task adjust the figures as follows and your Spreadsheet should automatically calculate the new break-even point.

47 (Variable cost) **90000** (Fixed Cost) **110** (Selling Price)

Lesson 7 *Stock control*

In this Lesson you will learn how SuperCalc can be used to perform simple stock control procedures. It will also demonstrate how SuperCalc can be configured to enable inexperienced staff to make use of its facilities.

At the end of this Lesson you should be able to:

a) **Protect** cells
b) **Unprotect** cells
c) use the **Global, Tab** command
d) use the **Global, Next** command
e) use the **Move** command
f) Create simple **Macros**

7.1 Designing the stock record card

Load SuperCalc as previously instructed. Your first task is to enter the headings across row 1, column A will be used to list the **Items** of stock. You don't know what the items will be yet but it is a reasonable assumption that they will require more than 9 characters of space, therefore you can widen column A to 18 spaces now (if you cannot remember how to do this refer back to Lesson 2 section 4).

You can now proceed to enter the other headings as shown below:

```
    |        A        || B || C || D || E || F || G |
  1 |ITEMS             |CAT NO. |PRICE    |QTY      |ORDER QTYORDER LVL|
  2
  3
  4
  5
  6
  7
  8
  9
 10
 11
 12
 13
 14
 15
 16
 17
 18
 19
 20
 TEMP1!G1                                                  TEXT
Width:  9  Memory:  184  Last Col/Row:F1
  1>
READY F1:Help  F3:Names  Ctrl-Backspace:Undo  Ctrl-Break:Cancel
```

Fig 7.1

The headings in columns E and F look untidy as they merge together. This can be improved by widening column E to 10 spaces – repeat the procedure you used for column A to widen column E.

Once you have widened column E you can underline the headings by using the **Repeating Text** key in A2.

```
   |        A         ||   B   ||   C   ||   D   ||   E   ||   F   ||   G   |
 1  ITEMS                CAT NO.  PRICE     QTY       ORDER QTY ORDER LVL
 2  --------------------------------------------------------------------------
 3
 4
 5
 6
 7
 8
 9
10
11
12
13
14
15
16
17
18
19
20
 TEMP1!A3
Width: 18  Memory:  184  Last Col/Row:F2
  1>
READY F1:Help  F3:Names  Ctrl-Backspace:Undo  Ctrl-Break:Cancel
```

Fig 7.2

7.2 Stock details

Data can now be entered on the spreadsheet, so move the cursor to cell A3 and enter the first item as **Desks**.

The catalogue number for desks is **123**, the price is **£145.75**, the current quantity in stock is **13**, the order quantity is **5** and the re-order level is **10**. Enter these figures under the appropriate heading.

This should complete your entries for the first item of stock, the second item is **Chairs**, enter this in cell A4.

The catalogue numbers run in sequence (ie: 123, 124, 125, etc) so you could enter this by means of a formula that can be **copied** rather than typing the number in each individual cell. Type in the formula which will **add** 1 to the figure in cell B3.

The screen should now show:

```
    |        A           ||   B    ||   C    ||   D    ||   E    ||   F    ||   G   |
 1  ITEMS               CAT NO.  PRICE     QTY       ORDER QTY ORDER LVL
 2  ------------------------------------------------------------------------------
 3  Desks                   123   145.75        13         5       10
 4  Chairs                  124
 5
 6
 7
 8
 9
10
11
12
13
14
15
16
17
18
19
20
 TEMP1!C4
Width:  9  Memory:  184  Last Col/Row:F4
  1>
READY F1:Help  F3:Names  Ctrl-Backspace:Undo  Ctrl-Break:Cancel
```

Fig 7.3

If you have entered the formula correctly then it can be **copied** to the other cells in column B. You will eventually have stock items down to row 7 so **copy** your formula to all cells up to and including cell B7 (if you cannot remember how to use **copy** then refer back to Lesson 2 section 1).

```
|        A        || B  || C  || D  || E  || F  || G  |
1  ITEMS           CAT NO.  PRICE    QTY     ORDER QTY ORDER LVL
2  ----------------------------------------------------------------
3  Desks              123   145.75     13         5      10
4  Chairs             124
5                     125
6                     126
7                     127
8
9
10
11
12
13
14
15
16
17
18
19
20
TEMP1!B4                 Form=B3+1
Width:  9  Memory:  184  Last Col/Row:F7
  1>
READY F1:Help  F3:Names  Ctrl-Backspace:Undo  Ctrl-Break:Cancel
```

Fig 7.4

You can now proceed to enter the remaining data for each stock item, making sure that you do not type anything else in column B as this will overwrite the formula. It may be a little tedious to have to type in the rest of the data, but unfortunately there is no short cut. You will discover when using your own spreadsheets that a spreadsheet can drastically reduce the time spent on calculating data and on amending figures but it will always be a time consuming job to enter the initial data.

The data is as follows:

```
   |        A        ||    B    ||    C    ||    D    ||    E    ||    F    ||    G    |

1  ITEMS              CAT NO.  PRICE      QTY       ORDER QTY ORDER LVL
2  ---------------------------------------------------------------------------
3  Desks                   123   145.75       13         5        10
4  Chairs                  124    45.75       20        11        10
5  Typewriters             125    55.75        5         3         5
6  Filing Cabinets         126   120.35        5         5        10
7  Waste Bins              127     5.99       20         5        20
8
9
10
11
12
13
14
15
16
17
18
19
20
 TEMP1!F8
Width:  9  Memory:  183  Last Col/Row:F7
  1>
READY F1:Help  F3:Names  Ctrl-Backspace:Undo  Ctrl-Break:Cancel
```

Fig 7.5

7.3 Inserting extra columns

You should now have a simple stock record card. There are some obvious improvements that can be made and you can now carry these out.

Firstly, there should be a column to show the **total value** of stock for each item. Use the **Insert** command to create a new column between **QTY** and **ORDER QTY** (*this is another command that you have used before so you should be able to do this without any instruction, if in doubt refer to Lesson 2 section 2*).

Your new column can now be given the heading **VALUE**, so enter this in cell E3. The next step is to calculate the total value of each item of stock – this will be the **PRICE** multiplied by the **QTY**. See if you can enter a suitable formula in cell E3 and then **copy** this formula to all other cells required.

```
   |        A         || B  ||  C   || D  ||  E   ||   F    ||  G  |
1  ITEMS              CAT NO.  PRICE    QTY     VALUE   ORDER QTY ORDER LVL
2  -----------------------------------------------------------------------
3  Desks                  123  145.75     13  1894.75         5        10
4  Chairs                 124   45.75     20      915        11        10
5  Typewriters            125   55.75      5   278.75         3         5
6  Filing Cabinets        126  120.35      5   601.75         5        10
7  Waste Bins             127    5.99     20    119.8         5        20
8
9
10
11
12
13
14
15
16
17
18
19
20
 TEMP1!E3                   Form=C3*D3
Width:  9  Memory:  183  Last Col/Row:G7
  1>
READY F1:Help  F3:Names  Ctrl-Backspace:Undo  Ctrl-Break:Cancel
```

Fig 7.6

An additional embellishment would be to add up the totals for **QTY** and the totals for **VALUE**. Move the cursor to cell E8 and enter an underline by typing and nine -s. You can then repeat this procedure to enter an underline in cell D8.

Now enter the **formula** to add the total **VALUE** and then the total **QTY**. This will provide the firm with some useful statistics concerning stock and will also be required as part of general accounting information.

```
   |     A       ||  B  ||  C  ||  D  ||  E  ||  F  ||  G  |
1   ITEMS          CAT NO.  PRICE   QTY     VALUE  ORDER QTY ORDER LVL
2   -----------------------------------------------------------------
3   Desks               123  145.75    13  1894.75         5        10
4   Chairs              124   45.75    20      915        11        10
5   Typewriters         125   55.75     5   278.75         3         5
6   Filing Cabinets     126  120.35     5   601.75         5        10
7   Waste Bins          127    5.99    20    119.8         5        20
8                                   -----------------
9                                      63  3810.05
10
11
12
13
14
15
16
17
18
19
20
 TEMP1!D9                   Form=SUM(D3:D7)
Width:  9  Memory:  183  Last Col/Row:G9
 1>
READY F1:Help  F3:Names  Ctrl-Backspace:Undo  Ctrl-Break:Cancel
```

Fig 7.7

7.4 Protecting cells

So far in this lesson you have only repeated **commands** that were used in previous lessons. From now on you will be using some new commands.

You have completed your record card, but the problem with this sort of application is that the data will be subject to constant alteration as the firm issues and receives supplies of each stock item.

Your stock system is quite small but it still suffers from the disadvantage that anybody who wants to amend stock details will firstly need some instruction in how to use SuperCalc. Furthermore, the main figures that will need amending are just the entries for **QTY** and **PRICE**.

The use of the stock record system can be simplified but this will involve the use of the **Protect** and **Global** commands.

As most of the entries will not alter they can be **protected** to ensure that they are not accidentally overwritten. If you examine the screen you should hopefully be able to see that the only cells that will regularly require updating are those for **PRICE** and **QTY** which form the block C3.D7.

Therefore, if you **protect** all other cells around this block you will ensure that the other cells cannot be accidentally overwritten. The method of protecting cells is:

/	to call up commands
P	to select Protect
A1.G2	to designate the block

ENTER

This will **protect** the top 2 rows of your spreadsheet. The next step is to **protect** the cells to the left and to the right of the block. The sequences required are as follows (if you enter the range with the cursor keys then it will make it much clearer which cells are being protected):

/	to call up commands
P	to select **Protect**
A3.B9	to designate the block
ENTER	

Followed by:

/	to call up commands
P	to select **Protect**
E3.G9	to designate the block
ENTER	

On some screens there will be no apparent difference to your screen, but most screens will show the protected area in a different colour or intensity (this depends entirely upon your computer and monitor). You can still move the cursor onto the protected cells, but the letter **P** should appear before the entry on the *status line.*

Protect is only obvious when you try to alter a cell that is protected, move the cursor to cell A1 and try to type in your name.

SuperCalc will not accept any alteration and displays the message that this cell is a protected entry.

```
   |        A         ||   B   ||   C   ||   D   ||   E   ||   F   ||   G   |
1  ITEMS                CAT NO.  PRICE     QTY      VALUE    ORDER QTY ORDER LVL
2  ---------------------------------------------------------------------------
3  Desks                    123   145.75      13   1894.75         5        10
4  Chairs                   124    45.75      20       915        11        10
5  Typewriters              125    55.75       5    278.75         3         5
6  Filing Cabinets          126   120.35       5    601.75         5        10
7  Waste Bins               127     5.99      20     119.8         5        20
8                                          ------------------
9                                                 63   3810.05
10
11
12
13
14
15
16
17
18
19
20
 TEMP1!A1                   P Text="ITEMS                        Protected data
Width: 18  Memory:  183  Last Col/Row:G9
 1>
READY F1:Help  F3:Names  Ctrl-Backspace:Undo  Ctrl-Break:Cancel
```

Fig 7.8

7.5 Unprotecting cells

There will be occasions when it is necessary to **unprotect** cells, for example if the details of a product need to be updated. This can be achieved in two ways: if the cells will not require **protecting** at all in future then the **Unprotect** command can be used. This is selected by **/ U** and the required range is entered in the same way as for **Protect**.

However, it will be more likely that a cell will only require temporary suspension of the **Protect** command so that minor adjustments can be made. In this case the **Global, Protection** command is more useful.

Suppose that your firm has been informed that the stock item **Desks** should have an **ORDER QTY** of **7** units instead of **5**. You only want to adjust this item and leave all others **protected.**

To amend this item and temporarily suspend **Protect** enter the following:

/	to call up commands
G	to select **Global**
P	to select **Protect**

You should now be able to alter the figure for **ORDER QTY** to **7.**

```
     |        A       ||    B   ||    C   ||    D   ||    E   ||    F   ||    G   |
 1    ITEMS               CAT NO.   PRICE       QTY     VALUE   ORDER QTY ORDER LVL
 2    ---------------------------------------------------------------------------
 3    Desks                   123    145.75       13   1894.75          7        10
 4    Chairs                  124     45.75       20       915         11        10
 5    Typewriters             125     55.75        5    278.75          3         5
 6    Filing Cabinets         126    120.35        5    601.75          5        10
 7    Waste Bins              127      5.99       20     119.8          5        20
 8                                               -----------------
 9                                                63   3810.05
10
11
12
13
14
15
16
17
18
19
20
  TEMP1!F4                           P Form=11
 Width: 10  Memory:  183  Last Col/Row:G9
  1>
 READY F1:Help  F3:Names  Ctrl-Backspace:Undo  Ctrl-Break:Cancel
```

Fig 7.9

The **Global, Protection** command has temporarily suspended *all* protection and to reinstate the **Protect** command you must repeat the **Global, Protection** command as above. Like most of the **Global** commands this is a *toggle* command: the first time you press it the protection is **off**; the second time you press it it is in **on**. Select **Global, Protection** again now to switch **Protect** back on.

When you are using SuperCalc to create some spreadsheets of your own it will not matter too much if you forget to reinstate **Protect** as the **Global, protection** command will only be valid for the current work session.

7.6 Automatic cursor movement

The **Protect** command is a good way of preventing accidental loss of data, but it is probably more useful in that it can allow you to make the cursor move to the required cells only.

It was stated earlier that the only cells that would require constant updating would be those relating to **price** and **quantity**. These are the only cells on your spreadsheet that contain an entry and are not **protected**.

The **Global, Tab** command can be used to automatically move the cursor to the next available **unprotected** cell. The advantage of this is that it means that a relatively inexperienced user can operate your stock record system.

Now move the cursor one cell to the *right* (this should ensure that the direction of movement is *right*). then move to cell A1 using either the **GoTo** command or the **HOME** key.

Now select the **Global, Tab** command as follows:

/	to call up the commands
G	to select **Global**
T	to select **Tab**

Nothing has happened yet, but if you now press **ENTER** the cursor should move straight to cell C3.

If you continue to press **ENTER** the cursor should move through the columns for **price** and **quantity** only. To repeat the sequence move to *A1* using **GoTo** or **HOME** and start all over again.

Change the price for **Desks** to **£180.75**, and for **Chairs** to **£55.75**. Alter the quantities of **Typewriters** to **7** and **Waste-bins** to **18**. The totals should be re-calculated automatically.

```
   |    A           ||  B    ||   C    ||  D    ||   E    ||   F    ||   G    |
1  ITEMS            CAT NO.  PRICE     QTY      VALUE    ORDER QTY ORDER LVL
2  ---------------------------------------------------------------------------
3  Desks                123   180.75     13   2349.75         7        10
4  Chairs               124    55.75     20      1115        11        10
5  Typewriters          125    55.75      7    390.25         3         5
6  Filing Cabinets      126   120.35      5    601.75         5        10
7  Waste Bins           127     5.99     18    107.82         5        20
8                                        ----------------
9                                        63   4564.57
10
11
12
13
14
15
16
17
18
19
20
 TEMP1!D8                  Text="---------
Width:  9  Memory:  183  Last Col/Row:G9
  1>
READY F1:Help  F3:Names  Ctrl-Backspace:Undo  Ctrl-Break:Cancel
```

Fig 7.10

The **Global, Tab** option suspends the full use of the cursor keys and will only allow the user to go to non-protected cells. It is another *toggle* command and if you press / **G T** again you switch the normal cursor movement back on.

If your screen is powerful enough to show the protected cells in a different colour/intensity then the same colour/intensity will be used to highlight those toggle commands which are currently switched **off** in the **Global** command. If you select the **Global** command again you should be able to identify which options are currently switched **on**.

One option which should be switched on at present is the **Global, Next** option. This option can be used to decide whether you want the cursor to move to the **next** cell when the **ENTER** key is pressed. Switch this off now by selecting **Next**.

Move the cursor back into cell A1 by pressing the **HOME** key. If you press **ENTER** now nothing will happen, however you can still move the cursor by using the cursor movement keys.

The **Global, Next** command is not just intended for use with the **Global, Tab** option but can be used to prevent the cursor automatically moving to the next cell in any spreadsheet. This may be useful if you are entering a series of very complex formulae and want to check them before continuing.

7.7 Deleting data

This file will be used in later lessons so you can **save** your spreadsheet now as **LESSON7**.

Most people will devise a spreadsheet as they go along, and this frequently means that alterations will need to be made to insert new columns/rows or widen columns. It may also mean that it is decided that a certain entry is no longer required or is in the wrong place. This section will demonstrate how to delete entries.

Firstly, select **Global, Protection** again so that you can alter the protected cells.

Let us assume that some entries are not required, for example the entry in cell A3 (ie: **Desks**) can be assumed to be unnecessary. The best command to delete this entry will be the **Blank** command. To use this command press / and then select **Blank**. Use the cursor to highlight cell A3 and then press **ENTER**.

```
     |          A          ||   B    ||   C   ||   D   ||   E    ||    F    ||   G    |
 1   ITEMS                  CAT NO.  PRICE     QTY      VALUE     ORDER QTY ORDER LVL
 2   -------------------------------------------------------------------------------
 3                              123   180.75       13  2349.75           7        10
 4   Chairs                     124    55.75       20     1115          11        10
 5   Typewriters                125    55.75        7   390.25           3         5
 6   Filing Cabinets            126   120.35        5   601.75           5        10
 7   Waste Bins                 127     5.99       18   107.82           5        20
 8                                             -----------------
 9                                                 63  4564.57
10
11
12
13
14
15
16
17
18
19
20
 LESSON7!A3
Width: 18  Memory:  182  Last Col/Row:G9
  1>
READY F1:Help  F3:Names  Ctrl-Backspace:Undo  Ctrl-Break:Cancel
```

Fig 7.11

The entry in cell A3 should now be deleted. The **Blank** command is very useful for deleting single entries or small ranges (eg: A1 to D4), but is not very quick if you want to delete an entire row or column.

If your computer has sufficient memory (and if it has been configured correctly with **Global, Options**) then you can use the **Undo** command to reverse the effect of any command. This is especially useful if you delete the wrong entry by mistake.

Clearly, cell A3 should not have been **blanked** as there is now no heading for this row. If you press the **Ctrl** and **BACKSPACE** keys this should (on most computers) *undo* the previous command. *The BACKSPACE key is the key used for deleting entries to the left of the cursor.*

The other command used for deleting entries is, not surprisingly, the **Delete** command. Press / again and then select **Delete**. The options available with this command are:

Row	to delete one or more rows
Column	to delete one or more columns
Block	to delete a specified block/range
File	to delete a file currently saved on disk
Page	to delete one or pages (on large spreadsheets)

You can select **Row** and highlight rows 3 and 4, then press **ENTER** to accept this command.

```
   |         A        ||   B   ||   C   ||   D   ||   E   ||   F   ||   G  |
 1  ITEMS              CAT NO.  PRICE     QTY     VALUE    ORDER QTY ORDER LVL
 2  --------------------------------------------------------------------------
 3  Typewriters          ERROR    55.75      7   390.25          3         5
 4  Filing Cabinets      ERROR   120.35      5   601.75          5        10
 5  Waste Bins           ERROR     5.99     18   107.82          5        20
 6                                      ------------------
 7                                         30  1099.82
 8
 9
10
11
12
13
14
15
16
17
18
19
20
  LESSON7!A3                     P Text="Typewriters
Width: 18  Memory:  183  Last Col/Row:G7
  1>
READY F1:Help  F3:Names  Ctrl-Backspace:Undo  Ctrl-Break:Cancel
```

Fig 7.12

The entries in column B now appear as **ERROR.** If you move the cursor onto cell B3 you will notice that the problem is because the formula in this cell reads **ERROR+1**. This is because this formula was copied from the original cell B3 and as the other rows have moved up to fill the gap left when rows 3 and 4 were deleted the formula is now incorrect.

The **Undo** command can be used to reverse the effect of the **Delete** command as well, try this now. Note that the **Undo** command will only undo the last thing that you did, including cursor movements.

7.8 Deleting files

One of the additional options available with the **Delete** command is to delete files. This is useful if your disk is getting full and you realise that there are some files that you no longer require; deleting these files will increase the amount of space on your disk.

Your spreadsheet should now show the same information as it did before you started the last session. Therefore you no longer need the **saved** version of your file LESSON7, so this can be deleted quite simply and quickly by using the **Delete** command.

Call up the **Delete** command by pressing / then select **Delete**. This time the option that you require is **File**, so select this option now. The screen should show the following:

```
   |         A         || B  ||  C   ||  D  ||   E   ||    F    ||   G   |
 1  ITEMS              CAT NO.  PRICE     QTY      VALUE    ORDER QTY ORDER LVL
 2  -------------------------------------------------------------------------
 3  Desks                  123   180.75     13  2349.75          7        10
 4  Chairs                 124    55.75     20     1115         11        10
 5  Typewriters            125    55.75      7   390.25          3         5
 6  Filing Cabinets        126   120.35      5   601.75          5        10
 7  Waste Bins             127     5.99     18   107.82          5        20
 8                                        ------------------
 9                                          63  4564.57
10
11
12
13
14
15
16
17
18
19
20
  LESSON7!A3                         P Text="Desks
Enter Filename
 23>/Delete,File,a:lesson7
FILE  F1:Help  F2:Edit  F3:File list  Ctrl-Break:Cancel
```

Fig 7.13

The program has remembered that the last file you **Saved** was called **LESSON7** and has assumed that this is the file that you want to delete. If you wanted to delete this file now you could simply press **ENTER**. However, let us assume that this is not the file you want deleted and that you want to see what other files are stored on the disk. If you glance at the bottom of the screen you should see that the HELP prompts include a prompt for a **File List**, which can be obtained by pressing **F3** (one of the *function* keys found on either the right hand side or top of the keyboard).

Press **F3** and the screen should display all files on the **default disk** (this may be drive C: or A:) depending upon how your machine has been configured). If you want to examine the other disk drive press **F2** for **Edit**. The cursor will then skip to the top part of the screen which shows the data directory. Normally all data files should be stored on drive A:, to examine the files on this drive press the **Ins** key (to activate the **Insert** command) and then type **A:** (or **C:**). The data directory should then read **A:*.CAL**. This means that the display will include all files on drive A that have the suffix of **CAL**. Press **ENTER** and the display will change to show the files contained on drive A: (don't worry if your disk contains different files)

```
FILE LIST
Directory displayed is A:\
Data directory is A:\

*.CAL

<DIRECTORIES> ASST    .cal BACKUP  .cal LESSONA .cal LESSON1B.cal
 LESSON10.cal LESSON11.cal LESSON2 .cal LESSON4 .cal LESSON5 .cal
 LESSON6 .cal LESSON7 .cal LESSON7A.cal LESSON9 .cal P       .cal
 PAY1    .cal Q       .cal TAX1    .cal UPDATE  .cal W       .cal
```

Fig 7.14

If you use the arrow keys you can move the cursor onto the file that you want deleted, move the cursor onto the file **LESSON7** and then press **ENTER**. The file will not be deleted immediately as there is an extra prompt just to make sure that you do not erase files accidentally. As you will need this file for the Further Exercises you can select **No** to avoid deleting the file.

7.9 Simple macros

A **macro** is a term used to describe a single instruction which replaces a sequence of commands. Macros are used in most spreadsheet packages and a number of word-processor and database packages.

The object in designing a macro is that it is much easier for a user to remember to press one or two keys than it is to remember a whole sequence of commands. This is especially useful in designing spreadsheets such as the one created in this lesson as it means that any user only needs to know the macro keys and does not need extensive training in SuperCalc before operating the stock control spreadsheet.

This session will provide a very brief introduction to macros which will be expanded on in future lessons.

Firstly, you need to decide what you want the macro to do. In this example you want the user to **load** the stock Control file, make any amendments and then **save** the revised version of the file.

The first part of this operation is to **load** the file. This can be done automatically whilst loading SuperCalc. You should still have the file **LESSON7** on disk, you can check this by selecting / then **Load** and pressing **F3** to get a display of files (you may have to use **F2** to change the disk drive) – if the file is listed press **Ctrl** and **Break** to return to the spreadsheet.

In order to demonstrate how files can be automatically loaded you will first have to **quit** SuperCalc. Select / then **Quit** and answer either **Yes** or **DOS** (this last option temporarily suspends operation of SuperCalc until **Exit** is typed – you will have to use this if your system does not allow you access to the system prompt).

The screen should now display the system prompt (either **C:** or **A:**). To load SuperCalc you simply type in **SC5**; however, by typing **SC5 A:LESSON7** (don't miss out the space), SuperCalc will load and will also load your file **LESSON7** at the same time. Try this now.

```
Select <DIRECTORIES> to list subdirectories        35840 bytes free
 23>/Delete,File,a:lesson7
FILE  F2:Edit  F4:Update or F5:Clear data directory  F6:Toggle details




C>sc5 A:lesson7
```

Fig 7.15

This makes things much easier for an inexperienced user as you can now give them a one line instruction for **loading** the stock control spreadsheet. The **Global, Tab** command has already made it impossible to alter any items other than those affecting price and quantity, so the only remaining problem for a new user is how to **save** or **quit** the amended spreadsheet. As the **Quit** command has an option to save your file it will probably be easier to create a macro that saves data by using **Quit** instead of having to use **Save** followed by **Quit** to exit the program.

You will shortly create a macro to do this but before attempting to create the macro you need to understand what commands are used in the **Quit** operation. You can **quit** your spreadsheet again now and you should find that you follow this sequence exactly:

/Q	to call up the **Quit** command
S	to select the **Save** option from the **Quit** options
O	to **Overwrite** the existing file for LESSON7

Notice that all commands were activated as soon as you pressed the appropriate letter. These two sequences can now be used to create a macro that will select the chain of items automatically.

This sequence of commands is possibly the most important in the macro that you are going to create, but it is still going to be confusing for someone who has never used SuperCalc before as he or she will be presented with a strange screen and no instructions. Therefore this macro, whilst still remaining very simple, will attempt to introduce a few tips for making data entry easier.

7.9.1 Moving data

First, **reload** the file LESSON7. The most important thing to do first is to provide the user with some very basic instructions, so these should be the first thing that appears on the screen. In order to do this you will have to move the existing stock record data to another portion of the screen.

In order to do this and enter the other instructions you will have to turn the **Global, Protection** and **Global, Tab** options off first; do this now.

The **Copy** command can be used to move the data but this would affect the formulae used; a more appropriate command would be the **MOVE** command. This can be used to move the entire block to another part of the screen. The block only needs to be moved off the opening screen so it will be acceptable to move it to cell A21, just off the opening screen.

To move the block select the following:

/	to call up commands
M	to select **Move**
B	to select **Block**
A1.G9	to select the range required
(use the cursor key if you prefer)	
A21	to select the new starting point

```
   |       A       || B || C || D || E || F || G |
21 ITEMS           CAT NO.  PRICE   QTY    VALUE   ORDER QTY ORDER LVL
22 -------------------------------------------------------------------
23 Desks               123  180.75    13  2349.75         7        10
24 Chairs              124   55.75    20     1115        11        10
25 Typewriters         125   55.75     7   390.25         3         5
26 Filing Cabinets     126  120.35     5   601.75         5        10
27 Waste Bins          127    5.99    18   107.82         5        20
28                                ------------------
29                                    63  4564.57
30
31
32
33
34
35
36
37
38
39
40
  LESSON7!C25                  Form=55.75
Width:  9  Memory:  182  Last Col/Row:G29
  1>
READY F1:Help  F3:Names  Ctrl-Backspace:Undo  Ctrl-Break:Cancel
```

Fig 7.16

The initial part of the screen can now be used to enter some simple instructions for new users. Most firms would also include some statement as to the nature and ownership of the program. Enter the text shown in Fig 7.17 as the opening instructions – the exact position does not matter too much.

```
      |     A      ||  B  ||  C  ||  D  ||  E  ||    F    ||  G  |
 1
 2
 3                  ABC LIMITED
 4                  STOCK CONTROL PROGRAM
 5
 6
 7                  Press the Alt and S keys together to
 8                  start the program.
 9
10                  Enter alterations to stock items by
11                  using the cursor keys or ENTER and
12                  select Function key 8 (F8) when complete.
13
14
15
16
17
18
19
20
  LESSON7!B12              Text="select Function key 8 (F8) when comp TEXT
Width:  9  Memory:  182  Last Col/Row:G29
  1>
READY F1:Help  F3:Names  Ctrl-Backspace:Undo  Ctrl-Break:Cancel
```

Fig 7.17

You may notice that the instructions state that the user should press **Alt** and **S** to start the program. This is the command that will be used to start up the macro (S for **stock**. or **start**). You can now move the cursor to cell I1 ready to start entering the macro details.

7.9.2 Macro layout

The simplest macros will merely be a sequence of commands, but the problem with such macros is that it is often very difficult to edit them at a later date. SuperCalc allows you to create macros that occupy three columns which have the following format:

Column 1	**Column 2**	**Column 3**
Macro title	*Macro commands*	*Comments*

Column 1 is important as the title is also usually used to start the macro – most macros are selected by pressing the **Alt** key in conjunction with the macro name (**S** in this example).

Column 2 actually contains the most important information: the sequence of commands that make up the macro. This column will usually involve a number of different actions on consecutive lines.

Column 3 is optional and allows the writer of the macro to include some brief comments as a reminder of what each line of the macro is intended to do.

You can enter **S** in cell I1, which signifies the macro title and allows you to press **Alt** and **S** to start running the macro.

The cells **J1** to **J7** will contain the actual macro instructions. Before you start entering these there are a few things that you need to know about entering commands.

7.9.3 Macro contents

Virtually any command that you use in SuperCalc 5 can be included as part of a macro, provided certain rules are observed. Any command that would normally be entered by pressing / must be preceded by " when being included in a macro – failure to do so will mean that the command will be instigated immediately.

Other commands that use characters from the keyboard, such as cursor movement keys, can be entered by typing in the appropriate key name within the { } brackets (eg: {PGUP}). The range of commands for use within macros is quite extensive and will be examined in more detail in future lessons.

Enter the following details for your macro, and remember that commands that begin with / must be preceded by the symbol, even though the will not appear on the screen.

```
      |  G  ||  H  ||  I  ||      J      ||  K  ||  L  ||  M  ||  N  |
 1                     \s     {ENTRYOFF}   Turns off entry line
 2                            {PANELOFF}   Turns off prompt and status line
 3                            /GB          Removes screen border
 4                            {PGDN}       Page down (to cell a21)
 5                            /GT          Global Tab
 6                            {SUSPEND}    Suspend macro while data entered
 7                            /QSO         Quit and Save
 8
 9
10
11
12
13
14
15
16
17
18
19
20
 LESSON7!K6              P Text="Suspend macro while data entered      TEXT
Width:  9  Memory:  181  Last Col/Row:K30
  1>
READY F1:Help  F3:Names  Ctrl-Backspace:Undo  Ctrl-Break:Cancel
```

Fig 7.18

Column K has been used to provide comments explaining what each command will do. The only items that should be new to you are **{SUSPEND}** – one of the keyboard control commands for use in macros, and temporarily halts the sequence of commands whilst data is entered – pressing **F8** will resume operation of the macro; and **{ENTRYOFF}**– removes the entry line display to make the screen less congested.

Column J has been widened to 11 characters in this example but this is not essential.

7.9.4 Naming macros

The macro is now complete and ready to save. More powerful macros would probably be devised using the options available in the **//MACRO** command, but this is a very straightforward macro and it is not necessary to use this option at this stage. All that is required now is that the macro is stored as a **Named range,** which is achieved by using the **Name** command.

Select **Name** and then choose the option for **Create**. This option will ask for a **Name**, so enter **S** as the range name. The prompt will then ask for the range required. Although the range title appears in cell I1 the macro itself appears in the range **J1.J7** and this is the range required. This is worth remembering as most first attempts at creating macros fail because the range has been entered incorrectly. The screen should show the following:

```
  |  G  ||  H  ||  I  ||     J     ||  K  ||  L  ||  M  ||  N  |
1                    \s   {ENTRYOFF}  Turns off entry line
2                         {PANELOFF}  Turns off prompt and status line
3                         /GB         Removes screen border
4                         {PGDN}      Page down (to cell a21)
5                         /GT         Global Tab
6                         {SUSPEND}   Suspend macro while data entered
7                         /QSO        Quit and Save
8
9
10
11
12
13
14
15
16
17
18
19
20
 LESSON7!J7                 P Text="/QSO                 Redefines all synonyms
Enter new range
 22>/Name,Create,\s,J1:J7
POINT F1:Help F2:Edit F3:Names Home:1st End-Arrow:last Ctrl-Break:Cancel
```

Fig 7.19

Your macro should now be ready to use. **Save** the file **LESSON7** again and then **quit** SuperCalc.

7.9.5 Running macros

The whole object in creating this macro was to make data entry as easy as possible for inexperienced SuperCalc 5 users.

If this macro works properly then the only instructions that the user requires should be the command **SC5 A:LESSON7** to load the file. The opening screen will tell them to press **Alt** and **S** to start the macro, and this will enable them to enter revised data on prices and stock levels, the macro will then automatically quit and save the revised data once either **F8** is pressed or the end of the data is reached.

Try this now to check for yourself if it works. If there is a need to change any items then the spreadsheet can still be used normally by simply **not** pressing **Alt** and **s.**

Further exercises

There are still a number of improvements that could be made to your spreadsheet. Firstly, use **Global, Protection** to temporarily remove the **Protect** command on all cells so that you can alter the **Formats.**

Carry out the following improvements:

1) Use the **Format** command to right-justify all headings.
2) The heading **Item** is out of line, so reformat this heading only as text-centred.
3) The heading **Order Lvl** should really be **Re-Order Lvl,** so enter this and shorten all other columns to the minimum possible spacing.
4) Use the **User-Define** option to configure the spreadsheet so that all monetary figures are prefixed by the $ (or £) sign.
5) Remove the screen border and obtain a printout.
6) Produce a stacked bar graph to show the **prices** and **values** of each item.

Lesson 8 *Payroll*

This lesson is designed to show how SuperCalc can be used for simple payroll calculations. payroll is slightly more complex than the other exercises as it calculates pay and tax due. In the UK tax is calculated on a *cumulative* basis, where each week's pay is added to that earned in previous weeks. Therefore, any spreadsheet designed to calculate payroll must be capable of taking into account this cumulative effect.

This lesson will introduce some new commands and also some more options for commands used in previous lessons. At the end of this lesson you will be able to:

a) **Move** rows or columns
b) **Arrange** rows or columns into order
c) use **LOOKUP** statements to find data from tables
d) Use **IF** statements to perform calculations
e) **Copy** formulae with adjustments
f) Use **DATE** functions

8.1 Designing the layout

The spreadsheet will require headings to be entered for the various columns. The columns will also require re-formatting as some need to be wider and some narrower.

Load SuperCalc and use the **Format** command to alter the column widths (see Lesson 2 section 2.4) as follows:

Column	A	B	C	D	E	F	G
Width	5	15	15	9	7	6	7

Now enter the headings as shown in Fig 8.1 note that some are actually on two rows (eg: **O/T Hours**). Insert an underline using the **Repeating Text** key.

A	B	C	D	E	F	G	H	I	J	K	L	M	N	O
No:	SURNAME	FIRST NAME	GRADE	BASIC	O/T Hours	O/T Amount	GROSS PAY	TAX CODE	PAY TO DATE	FREE PAY	TAXABLE PAY	TAX DUE	NET PAY	TAX DEDUCTED

Fig 8.1

As most of the entries under these headings will be numerical you can use the **Format** command to make the text centred (see Lesson 5).

You can now start to enter the data relating to the employees: each employee has a **payroll number**, and you need to enter this along with each employee's surname and Christian name.

The details are as follows:

```
     | A ||      B       ||       C       ||  D   || E  || F || G  ||  H  |
1    No:    SURNAME          FIRST NAME    GRADE   BASIC  O/T   O/T    GROSS
2                                                       Hours Amount   PAY
3    -------------------------------------------------------------------------
4    101 Clough          Nigel
5    104 Charlton        Jack
6    107 Best            George
7    109 Moore           Bobby
8    113 Robson          Bryan
9    130 Stiles          Nobby
10   133 Hoddle          Glenn
11   135 Clough          Brian
12   148 Shilton         Peter
13   165 Adams           Tony
14   170 Charlton        Bobby
15   180 Robson          Bobby
16   181 Keegan          Kevin
17   208 Beardsley       Peter
18   210 Sansom          Kenny
19   290 Anderson        Viv
20   319 Barnes          John
LESSON7A!A4                 Form=101
Width:  5  Memory:  181  Last Col/Row:P30
  1>
READY F1:Help  F3:Names  Ctrl-Backspace:Undo  Ctrl-Break:Cancel
```

Fig 8.2

The reason that the payroll numbers do not follow a set sequence is that each employee is given the next available number on starting with the firm, but some of the other employees will leave the firm and so **gaps** will appear in the sequence.

On the display shown, the payroll numbers in column A have been **formatted** to **the left**; this stops them from merging with the employee name – you are advised to do the same on your display.

8.2 Moving data

The data is at present in **payroll number** order. This is the way that most organisations would store their data, but there may be occasions when it is preferable to have the data in **alphabetical** order according to the surnames.

SuperCalc will allow you to manipulate data in two ways; the first is to use the **Move** command. If you examine the spreadsheet you should see that if the data were in alphabetical surname order, then Jack Charlton ought to come before Bobby Robson in the list. The entire row relating to Jack Charlton can be **moved** quite easily. Type in the following sequence:

/	to call up commands
M	to select **Move**

R	to specify a **row**
5	to select the row to be moved
4	to specify the row to move it to

The screen should now show:

```
    | A ||     B      ||     C      ||  D  ||  E  || F || G ||  H  |
1   No:    SURNAME        FIRST NAME   GRADE   BASIC  O/T   O/T   GROSS
2                                                     Hours Amount  PAY
3   ----------------------------------------------------------------------
4   104 Charlton      Jack
5   101 Clough        Nigel
6   107 Best          George
7   109 Moore         Bobby
8   113 Robson        Bryan
9   130 Stiles        Nobby
10  133 Hoddle        Glenn
11  135 Clough        Brian
12  148 Shilton       Peter
13  165 Adams         Tony
14  170 Charlton      Bobby
15  180 Robson        Bobby
16  181 Keegan        Kevin
17  208 Beardsley     Peter
18  210 Sansom        Kenny
19  290 Anderson      Viv
20  319 Barnes        John
LESSON7A!A4                    Form=104
Width:  5  Memory:  181  Last Col/Row:P30
  1>
READY F1:Help  F3:Names  Ctrl-Backspace:Undo  Ctrl-Break:Cancel
```

Fig 8.3

If you examine the screen now, the row for Jack Charlton has moved to the top of your data and the previous row number 4 has now become row 5. However, if you examine as far down as row 6, you can see that this row should be before that for Jack Charlton. You can move this row as follows:

/	to call up commands
M	to select **Move**
R	to specify a **row**
6	to select the row to be moved
4	to specify the row to move it to

The screen will now show:

```
  | A ||       B        ||      C       ||   D   ||  E  || F ||  G  ||  H  |
1  No:     SURNAME          FIRST NAME    GRADE   BASIC   O/T    O/T    GROSS
2                                                         Hours Amount   PAY
3  -------------------------------------------------------------------------
4    107 Best            George
5    104 Charlton        Jack
6    101 Clough          Nigel
7    109 Moore           Bobby
8    113 Robson          Bryan
9    130 Stiles          Nobby
10   133 Hoddle          Glenn
11   135 Clough          Brian
12   148 Shilton         Peter
13   165 Adams           Tony
14   170 Charlton        Bobby
15   180 Robson          Bobby
16   181 Keegan          Kevin
17   208 Beardsley       Peter
18   210 Sansom          Kenny
19   290 Anderson        Viv
20   319 Barnes          John
 LESSON7A!A6                       Form=101
Width:  5  Memory:  181  Last Col/Row:P30
  1>
READY F1:Help  F3:Names  Ctrl-Backspace:Undo  Ctrl-Break:Cancel
```

Fig 8.4

The entire row can be sorted into order by using the **Move** command, but it would be a very tedious process. The **Move** command is more often used to rectify errors or change the layout of the spreadsheet rather than for sorting data. A better use for the **Move** command would be to move column C to become column B, this way the Christian names would appear before the Surnames. See if you can do this on your own.

You should have followed the sequence below:

/	to call up commands
M	to select **Move**
C	to specify a **column**
C	to select the column to be moved
B	to specify the column to move it to

When you have done this the screen should appear as in Fig 8.5.

```
   | A ||      B      ||      C      ||  D  ||  E || F || G ||  H  |
 1  No:    FIRST NAME      SURNAME       GRADE   BASIC   O/T    O/T    GROSS
 2                                                       Hours  Amount  PAY
 3  ---------------------------------------------------------------------------
 4  107 George          Best
 5  104 Jack            Charlton
 6  101 Nigel           Clough
 7  109 Bobby           Moore
 8  113 Bryan           Robson
 9  130 Nobby           Stiles
10  133 Glenn           Hoddle
11  135 Brian           Clough
12  148 Peter           Shilton
13  165 Tony            Adams
14  170 Bobby           Charlton
15  180 Bobby           Robson
16  181 Kevin           Keegan
17  208 Peter           Beardsley
18  210 Kenny           Sansom
19  290 Viv             Anderson
20  319 John            Barnes
 LESSON7A!A6                    Form=101
Width:  5  Memory:  181  Last Col/Row:P30
  1>
READY F1:Help  F3:Names  Ctrl-Backspace:Undo  Ctrl-Break:Cancel
```

Fig 8.5

8.3 Arranging data

You still haven't sorted the data into alphabetical order. The best command for this type of operation is the **Arrange** command. This command will sort data into either alphabetical order or number order. The spreadsheet will need to be sorted into alphabetical order in the column containing surnames (column C); to do this type in:

/	to call up commands
A	to select **Arrange**
C	to specify **Column**
C	to select the column to be arranged
ENTER	

This should produce the screen shown below.

```
    | A ||      B       ||      C       ||  D  || E || F || G || H |
1    165 Tony           Adams
2    290 Viv            Anderson
3    319 John           Barnes
4    208 Peter          Beardsley
5    107 George         Best
6    104 Jack           Charlton
7    170 Bobby          Charlton
8    101 Nigel          Clough
9    135 Brian          Clough
10   133 Glenn          Hoddle
11   181 Kevin          Keegan
12   109 Bobby          Moore
13   113 Bryan          Robson
14   180 Bobby          Robson
15   210 Kenny          Sansom
16   148 Peter          Shilton
17   130 Nobby          Stiles
18   No:    FIRST NAME      SURNAME      GRADE   BASIC   O/T    O/T     GROSS
19                                                      Hours  Amount   PAY
20   ------------------------------------------------------------------------
 LESSON7A!A6                       Form=104
Width:  5  Memory:  181  Last Col/Row:P30
  1>
READY F1:Help  F3:Names  Ctrl-Backspace:Undo  Ctrl-Break:Cancel
```

Fig 8.6

Unfortunately there are two problems:

i) You have **arranged** the entire column, including the headings, therefore the whole spreadsheet is now out of sequence.

ii) SuperCalc is unable, at present, to differentiate between the two Charltons, the two Cloughs and the two Robsons. To sort them properly you need to use the **Christian name** column as part of the sort.

This is a deliberate mistake that has been included with the object of demonstrating how careful you must be when using **Arrange**. If you make the slightest error with this command then you can waste a lot of time re-designing the spreadsheet. You are strongly advised to **save** your spreadsheet *before* using the **Arrange** command then, if the resulting spreadsheet is a mess, you can simply reload your original version.

The first problem can easily be rectified by using the **Move** command to move the headings back to row 1. See if you can do this on your own by referring back to the previous section; if you have difficulty the sequence is:

/	to call up commands
M	to select **Move**
C	to specify a row
18.20	to select the rows to be moved

1	to specify where to move them to

It is possible to specify the range that needs to be arranged, to ensure that the headings are not moved again. Type in:

/	to call up commands
A	to select **Arrange**
C	to specify **Column**
C	to select the column to be arranged
,	to select **Arrange options**
A4.G20	to select range required
ENTER	

The second mistake, ie not sorting the Charltons etc, has arisen because the initial command was incomplete. It is possible to include a second column as part of the **Arrange** command to act as a *tie-breaker* (eg: where surnames are the same). Type in the following:

A	to specify sort into **Ascending** order
N	to specify **No adjustment**
,	to select options again
B	to specify **Secondary** column
A	to specify sort into **Ascending** order

This should now produce the following display:

```
     | A ||      B      ||      C      ||   D   ||  E  ||  F ||   G  ||   H   |
1    No:    FIRST NAME      SURNAME        GRADE  BASIC   O/T    O/T    GROSS
2                                                        Hours Amount   PAY
3    -------------------------------------------------------------------------
4    165 Tony          Adams
5    290 Viv           Anderson
6    319 John          Barnes
7    208 Peter         Beardsley
8    107 George        Best
9    170 Bobby         Charlton
10   104 Jack          Charlton
11   135 Brian         Clough
12   101 Nigel         Clough
13   133 Glenn         Hoddle
14   181 Kevin         Keegan
15   109 Bobby         Moore
16   180 Bobby         Robson
17   113 Bryan         Robson
18   210 Kenny         Sansom
19   148 Peter         Shilton
20   130 Nobby         Stiles
 LESSON7A!A6                 Form=319
Width:  5  Memory:  181  Last Col/Row:P30
  1>
READY F1:Help  F3:Names  Ctrl-Backspace:Undo  Ctrl-Break:Cancel
```

Fig 8.7

As you can see the option of including a **secondary** column means that you can ensure that there is a tie-breaker where entries in the main range are identical. The option asking for **No adjustment** relates to formula cells and must be used with great caution. If you **arrange** a column of formulae you are quite likely to produce an **iteration** situation; this is where (because formulae automatically adjust on being re-arranged) a cell is multiplying its own contents over and over again.

8.4 LOOKUP using tables

You can now proceed to enter the remainder of the data required in the spreadsheet. The column headed GRADE indicates the salary grade of the employee's, this firm has five different grades of pay categorised from 1 to 5. Enter the grades for staff as shown in Fig 8.8.

```
     | A ||      B       ||      C      ||   D   || E || F || G  ||  H  |
2                                                   Hours Amount   PAY
3   ----------------------------------------------------------------------
4     165 Tony          Adams              1
5     290 Viv           Anderson           4
6     319 John          Barnes             2
7     208 Peter         Beardsley          1
8     107 George        Best               4
9     170 Bobby         Charlton           2
10    104 Jack          Charlton           3
11    135 Brian         Clough             5
12    101 Nigel         Clough             1
13    133 Glenn         Hoddle             1
14    181 Kevin         Keegan             5
15    109 Bobby         Moore              3
16    180 Bobby         Robson             2
17    113 Bryan         Robson             3
18    210 Kenny         Sansom             1
19    148 Peter         Shilton            4
20    130 Nobby         Stiles             2
21
 LESSON7A!D21
Width:  9  Memory:  181  Last Col/Row:P30
  1>
READY F1:Help  F3:Names  Ctrl-Backspace:Undo  Ctrl-Break:Cancel
```

Fig 8.8

The next column is for the basic salary, but it is pointless to type in each of the amounts separately as all staff on Grade 1 will receive the same amount, all staff on Grade 2 will receive the same amount, and so on. SuperCalc can enter the correct salary for you by using a **LOOKUP** statement.

The first step in this procedure is to enter a table to show the grades and salary for each grade. Move the cursor off the present screen to cell D25 and type the following in the block between cells D25 and E30:

Column:		D	E
Row	**25**	Grade	Basic
	26	1	400
	27	2	480
	28	3	530
	29	4	780
	30	5	1300

This is the table that can be referred to from the main payroll. Move the cursor back to cell E4; this cell should show the **Basic** salary for Grade 1 – SuperCalc will enter this for you if you use a LOOKUP statement.

The LOOKUP statement will literally *look up* a cell reference and find the corresponding value from a LOOKUP table. Type the following statement in cell E4:

LOOKUP(D4,D26.D30)

ENTER

The program will now check what the figure is in cell D4 (ie: 1), and then it will examine the table in the range D26.D30 to find the same value in that table (ie: cell D26); it then takes the value from the adjacent cell (ie: E26: 400) and inserts that as the value in cell E4.

A further benefit of using the LOOKUP statement is that this can now be copied for all of the other employee's. **Copy** this formula now as follows:

/	to call up commands
C	to select **Copy**
E4	to select cell to copy from
ENTER	
E5.E20	to select cells to copy to
ENTER	

The screen will now show:

```
   | A ||      B       ||      C       ||  D  ||  E  ||  F ||  G  ||  H  |
1   No:    FIRST NAME       SURNAME       GRADE  BASIC   O/T   O/T    GROSS
2                                                       Hours Amount   PAY
3  ------------------------------------------------------------------------
4   165 Tony           Adams               1     400
5   290 Viv            Anderson            4     780
6   319 John           Barnes              2     N/A
7   208 Peter          Beardsley           1     N/A
8   107 George         Best                4     N/A
9   170 Bobby          Charlton            2       0
10  104 Jack           Charlton            3       0
11  135 Brian          Clough              5       0
12  101 Nigel          Clough              1       0
13  133 Glenn          Hoddle              1       0
14  181 Kevin          Keegan              5       0
15  109 Bobby          Moore               3       0
16  180 Bobby          Robson              2       0
17  113 Bryan          Robson              3       0
18  210 Kenny          Sansom              1       0
19  148 Peter          Shilton             4       0
20  130 Nobby          Stiles              2       0
 LESSON7A!F4
Width:  6  Memory:  181  Last Col/Row:P30
  1>
READY F1:Help  F3:Names  Ctrl-Backspace:Undo  Ctrl-Break:Cancel
```

Fig 8.9

8.5 Copy using adjustment

Unfortunately this has not worked properly as a number of cells have **N/A** instead of the appropriate amount. The statement N/A is used by SuperCalc when the answer to a cell is **not available**.

If you move the cursor into one of these cells you may be able to see why the answer is not available. The reason is that the **Copy** command has automatically adjusted the LOOKUP formula as it has moved down the columns. This is not what is desired as the LOOKUP table itself has not moved from the block D26:E30.

The solution is to use the **Copy** command, but to request that the formula is only partly adjusted as it is copied to the new cells. Type in the following:

/	to call up commands
C	to select **Copy**
E4	to select cell to copy from
ENTER	
E5.E20	to select cells to copy to
,	to request **Options**

This will enable you to specify which parts of the formula will need updating and which should remain fixed. The formula that you are about to copy is:

LOOKUP(D4,D26.D30)

When the formula is **copied** SuperCalc will update all of the cell references; therefore, when this is copied to cell E5 the formula **will** be amended to:

LOOKUP(D5,D27.D31)

The first part is correct in that the value for the grade to be looked-up will be in cell D5, *but the LOOKUP table itself is still in the range D26.D30 and has not moved down one row to D27.D31*. So, when the formula is copied you want the first cell reference to be updated, but the range must remain as D26.D30. Asking for an **adjustment** will allow you to do this.

The *prompt line* should now be stating:

Source cell E4 – adjust D4 (Y/N)

This is asking if you want the first cell updated and the answer is **yes**, so press **Y**. This means that when you **copy** the formula, this part of the formula will change to show the new cell.

The *prompt line* will now ask:

Source cell E4 – adjust D26 (Y/N)

This is the first cell in the LOOKUP table and will not require updating so press **N** for **no**. This will not need altering as the LOOKUP table will not move from its present position; you are copying the **formula** not the **LOOKUP table**.

The *prompt line* will now ask:

Source cell E4 – adjust D30 (Y/N)

Again, this is referring to the LOOKUP table so does not require updating, so press is **N** for **no**.

The screen will now show:

```
   | A ||      B       ||        C        ||  D  ||  E  || F || G  ||  H  |
1   No:    FIRST NAME        SURNAME        GRADE   BASIC  O/T   O/T   GROSS
2                                                         Hours Amount  PAY
3  ---------------------------------------------------------------------------
4   165 Tony            Adams                  1     400
5   290 Viv             Anderson               4     780
6   319 John            Barnes                 2     480
7   208 Peter           Beardsley              1     400
8   107 George          Best                   4     780
9   170 Bobby           Charlton               2     480
10  104 Jack            Charlton               3     530
11  135 Brian           Clough                 5    1300
12  101 Nigel           Clough                 1     400
13  133 Glenn           Hoddle                 1     400
14  181 Kevin           Keegan                 5    1300
15  109 Bobby           Moore                  3     530
16  180 Bobby           Robson                 2     480
17  113 Bryan           Robson                 3     530
18  210 Kenny           Sansom                 1     400
19  148 Peter           Shilton                4     780
20  130 Nobby           Stiles                 2     480
 LESSON7A!F4
Width:  6  Memory:  180  Last Col/Row:P30
  1>
READY F1:Help  F3:Names  Ctrl-Backspace:Undo  Ctrl-Break:Cancel
```

Fig 8.10

8.6 IF statements

The next column on the spreadsheet is for **overtime hours**, and the column after this will be for the **overtime payment**. Most organisations pay overtime at a number of rates, such as time and a half for the first six hours and then double time thereafter.

To keep our payroll nice and simple we will assume that overtime is paid at £2.00 per hour for periods up to five hours and then £2.75 per hour for any hours over five. Even though this is quite simple it requires some thought as to how it can be included as a formula.

First of all you can enter the details of overtime hours worked; these are as shown in Fig 8.11 and can simply be typed in.

```
   | A ||     B      ||     C      ||  D  || E || F || G ||  H |
2                                                Hours Amount  PAY
3  ---------------------------------------------------------------
4    165 Tony          Adams           1    400    0
5    290 Viv           Anderson        4    780   10
6    319 John          Barnes          2    480    2
7    208 Peter         Beardsley       1    400    0
8    107 George        Best            4    780    5
9    170 Bobby         Charlton        2    480    3
10   104 Jack          Charlton        3    530    2
11   135 Brian         Clough          5   1300    0
12   101 Nigel         Clough          1    400   15
13   133 Glenn         Hoddle          1    400    8
14   181 Kevin         Keegan          5   1300    0
15   109 Bobby         Moore           3    530    4
16   180 Bobby         Robson          2    480    0
17   113 Bryan         Robson          3    530    7
18   210 Kenny         Sansom          1    400  8.5
19   148 Peter         Shilton         4    780   10
20   130 Nobby         Stiles          2    480  4.5
21
 LESSON7A!F21
Width:  6  Memory:  180  Last Col/Row:P30
  1>
READY F1:Help  F3:Names  Ctrl-Backspace:Undo  Ctrl-Break:Cancel
```

Fig 8.11

The next column is for the overtime amounts, and is where the formula will have to be used to calculate the amounts. This formula is more complex than any others used so far.

The solution is to use an **IF** statement (these were used in Lesson 1). If you break the problem down you have three parts:

1) If no overtime is worked no overtime payment is made.

2) If less than five hours are worked then overtime is paid at a rate of £2.00 per hour.

3) If more than four hours are worked then the first four hours are paid at £2.00 per hour and the remainder at £2.75 per hour.

The most important part of the equation is determining if less than five hours are worked. This can be calculated by a simple **IF** statement such as:

IF *cell reference*<5

The next part of the statement will be the instructions to be carried out if this is correct (ie: if the cell is less than 5). The formula for this will be:

***cell reference* * 2**

Note that this also solves the problem of those staff who haven't done any overtime, as nil hours multiplied by £2.00 is still nil.

The only other problem is dealing with those staff who have done more than five hours overtime; the formula for these will be:

10 + ((*cell reference* – 5) * 2.75)

This starts with 10 as this part of the formula will only relate to employees working more than five hours overtime, and will therefore all start with £10.00 (5 hours * £2.00). The second part of the formula (in brackets) is used to calculate the overtime payment for the hours worked in excess of five hours, hence the deduction of five.

If the separate parts are now combined and the appropriate cell reference included the final formula will be:

IF(F4<5,F4*2,10+((F4-5)*2.75))

Note: make sure that all brackets are closed otherwise you will get an error message.

This formula can now be copied to the other cells for employee's. You should be able to do this on your own by now.

	A	B	C	D	E	F	G	H
1	No:	FIRST NAME	SURNAME	GRADE	BASIC	O/T	O/T	GROSS
2						Hours	Amount	PAY
3	----	----	----	----	----	----	----	----
4	165	Tony	Adams	1	400	0	0	
5	290	Viv	Anderson	4	780	10	23.75	
6	319	John	Barnes	2	480	2	4	
7	208	Peter	Beardsley	1	400	0	0	
8	107	George	Best	4	780	5	10	
9	170	Bobby	Charlton	2	480	3	6	
10	104	Jack	Charlton	3	530	2	4	
11	135	Brian	Clough	5	1300	0	0	
12	101	Nigel	Clough	1	400	15	37.5	
13	133	Glenn	Hoddle	1	400	8	18.25	
14	181	Kevin	Keegan	5	1300	0	0	
15	109	Bobby	Moore	3	530	4	8	
16	180	Bobby	Robson	2	480	0	0	
17	113	Bryan	Robson	3	530	7	15.5	
18	210	Kenny	Sansom	1	400	8.5	19.625	
19	148	Peter	Shilton	4	780	10	23.75	
20	130	Nobby	Stiles	2	480	4.5	9	

```
LESSON7A!G4              Form=IF(F4<5,F4*2,10+((F4-5)*2.75))
Width:  7  Memory:  180  Last Col/Row:P30
  1>
READY F1:Help  F3:Names  Ctrl-Backspace:Undo  Ctrl-Break:Cancel
```

Fig 8.12

The next column is for **GROSS PAY**, and will be the total of the BASIC column and the OVERTIME column; enter a suitable formula (E4+G4) and **copy** down the entire column.

The column headed CODES is for the *tax code numbers* of employees, and is used to determine how much Income Tax is deducted from salaries. The tax codes vary from person to person so you will have to type these in as follows:

```
   |      B      ||      C      ||  D  ||  E  || F ||  G  ||   H   |
2                                              Hours Amount    PAY
3  ----------------------------------------------------------------
4  Tony          Adams              1    400     0       0      400
5  Viv           Anderson           4    780    10   23.75   803.75
6  John          Barnes             2    480     2       4      484
7  Peter         Beardsley          1    400     0       0      400
8  George        Best               4    780     5      10      790
9  Bobby         Charlton           2    480     3       6      486
10 Jack          Charlton           3    530     2       4      534
11 Brian         Clough             5   1300     0       0     1300
12 Nigel         Clough             1    400    15    37.5    437.5
13 Glenn         Hoddle             1    400     8   18.25   418.25
14 Kevin         Keegan             5   1300     0       0     1300
15 Bobby         Moore              3    530     4       8      538
16 Bobby         Robson             2    480     0       0      480
17 Bryan         Robson             3    530     7    15.5    545.5
18 Kenny         Sansom             1    400   8.5  19.625  419.625
19 Peter         Shilton            4    780    10   23.75   803.75
20 Nobby         Stiles             2    480   4.5       9      489
21
 LESSON7A!H21
Width:  9  Memory:  179  Last Col/Row:P30
  1>
READY F1:Help  F3:Names  Ctrl-Backspace:Undo  Ctrl-Break:Cancel
```

Fig 8.13

As stated at the beginning of this lesson, payroll needs to be cumulative, which means that the previous month's figures will need to be added to the current month's figures. You can assume that this is the first month of the year and that there are no previous figures to include. This means that the **pay to date** will be the same as the **gross pay**; if you type **H4** in cell **J4** the amount should be copied. This will need copying to all of the other cells in column J, so do this now.

8.7 Using the date functions

The next column is for **FREE PAY**, which is the amount that each employee can earn before paying tax. It is also a cumulative amount and is calculated from the tax code number.

The tax code numbers in column I are the tax free amounts that each employee can earn, but they have all been divided by 10. Therefore, the tax code 242 is in fact equal to £2,420.

In addition, each tax free amount is divided into monthly or weekly amounts. Consequently, someone with a tax code of 242 can earn £201.66 in the first month of the year before paying any tax (£2,420 * 1/12 months).

This is also cumulative so in month 2 that same employee can have *total earnings for the year* of £403.23 before paying tax (£2,420 * 2/12 months). It is important that you understand this formula.

This would normally be a problem because, although this can be entered as a formula, the number of months will need to be amended every month. SuperCalc has a statement which can be used for entering dates, and this can be used as part of the formula.

Your spreadsheet does not have a heading yet and it will also be necessary to state which month this spreadsheet relates to. Use the **Insert** command to insert an additional two rows at the very top of the spreadsheet.

In A1 you can enter the heading as **PAYROLL** and enter **DATE** in cell C1. Move the cursor to cell D1 and type in the date as:

30/04/91

ENTER

The screen should now show:

```
    | A ||      B      ||      C       ||   D    || E || F || G  ||   H   |
1   PAYROLL            DATE             .0824176
2
3    No:    FIRST NAME      SURNAME      GRADE   BASIC   O/T   O/T    GROSS
4                                                       Hours Amount   PAY
5   ----------------------------------------------------------------------
6    165 Tony           Adams                1    400     0      0      400
7    290 Viv            Anderson             4    780    10  23.75   803.75
8    319 John           Barnes               2    480     2      4      484
9    208 Peter          Beardsley            1    400     0      0      400
10   107 George         Best                 4    780     5     10      790
11   170 Bobby          Charlton             2    480     3      6      486
12   104 Jack           Charlton             3    530     2      4      534
13   135 Brian          Clough               5   1300     0      0     1300
14   101 Nigel          Clough               1    400    15   37.5    437.5
15   133 Glenn          Hoddle               1    400     8  18.25   418.25
16   181 Kevin          Keegan               5   1300     0      0     1300
17   109 Bobby          Moore                3    530     4      8      538
18   180 Bobby          Robson               2    480     0      0      480
19   113 Bryan          Robson               3    530     7   15.5    545.5
20   210 Kenny          Sansom               1    400   8.5 19.625  419.625
LESSON7A!E1
Width:  7  Memory:  178  Last Col/Row:P32
  1>
READY F1:Help  F3:Names  Ctrl-Backspace:Undo  Ctrl-Break:Cancel  CAPS
```

Fig 8.14

There is obviously an error. This is because SuperCalc has interpreted the date as formula:

31 divided by 4, divided by 88

If you want to enter dates on a spreadsheet you have to prefix the date with " to make it text, or use the **DATE** statement. If the date is to be used in formulae then you must use the DATE statement. Type the following as the entry for cell D1:

DATE(04,30,88)

It is worth remembering that SuperCalc uses the USA layout for dates (ie: month, day, year) rather than the European layout (ie: day, month, year), and also that the dates are subdivided by a comma not a /, hence the formula shown above.

The date can be *entered* in European style (ie: day, month, year) by using the formula **EDAT(dd,mm,yy)** instead of **DATE(mm,dd,yy)** but the display will still revert to the USA style.

However, the *display* of the date can be altered by using the **Format** command and the **User-Define** options. Call up **Format** and select **User-Define** from the options listed.

The next prompt will show **Number** and **Date**; the **number** options were demonstrated in Lesson 5: This time you want the **Date** option, so select this and you should be presented with the following screen:

```
USER-DEFINE DATE FORMAT MENU

     Format                 Example (using March 8, 1980  7:09:10 AM)
1.   _BM/BD/YYYY                  3/ 8/1980
2.   DD-MMM-YY                   08-Mar-80
3.   DD-MMM                      08-Mar
4.   MMM-YY                      Mar-80
5.   MM/DD/YY                    03/08/80
6.   MM/DD                       03/08
7.   YY-MM-DD                    80-03-08
8.   DD.MM.YY                    08.03.80
T.   BH:TT:SS_AM/PM               7:09:10 AM

     Use M, BM, MM, MMM, MMMM or R  for month
     Use D, BD, DD,                 for day
     Use Y, YY, YYYY                for year
     Use WWW, WWWW                  for weekday
     Use BH, HH                     for hour
     Use BT, TT                     for minute
     Use BS, SS                     for second
     Use A/P, a/p, AM/PM, am/pm     for clock
LESSON7A!C1              Text="DATE
Quit  1  2  3  4  5  6  7  8  T  Zap
 26>/Format,User-define,Date,
MENU  Finished defining formats; return to /Format menu          CAPS
```

Fig 8.15

This menu gives you up to nine different formats for presenting dates – the bottom half of the screen explains what the abbreviations stand for. The format closest to that required is number 8, but this shows day, month and year divided by a full stop. You could amend this to show a / instead, but number 2 is a better format and does not require any alteration, so you can simply select **Quit**. (Amendments can be made to any format by pressing **F2** and then typing in the desired format.)

To include the new format you will have to select the following:

E	to select the category **Entry**
D1	to select the range required
U	to select **User-Define**
D	to select **Date**
2	to select date format **2**
A	to select the new format

The screen will now show the following:

```
   | A ||      B          ||      C        ||   D   || E  || F || G  ||   H   |
 1  PAYROLL                 DATE             30-Apr-91
 2
 3  No:   FIRST NAME          SURNAME          GRADE  BASIC   O/T    O/T     GROSS
 4                                                          Hours  Amount    PAY
 5  ------------------------------------------------------------------------------
 6   165 Tony               Adams                1    400     0       0      400
 7   290 Viv                Anderson             4    780    10   23.75   803.75
 8   319 John               Barnes               2    480     2       4      484
 9   208 Peter              Beardsley            1    400     0       0      400
10   107 George             Best                 4    780     5      10      790
11   170 Bobby              Charlton             2    480     3       6      486
12   104 Jack               Charlton             3    530     2       4      534
13   135 Brian              Clough               5   1300     0       0     1300
14   101 Nigel              Clough               1    400    15    37.5    437.5
15   133 Glenn              Hoddle               1    400     8   18.25   418.25
16   181 Kevin              Keegan               5   1300     0       0     1300
17   109 Bobby              Moore                3    530     4       8      538
18   180 Bobby              Robson               2    480     0       0      480
19   113 Bryan              Robson               3    530     7    15.5    545.5
20   210 Kenny              Sansom               1    400   8.5  19.625  419.625
LESSON7A!C1                      Text="DATE
Width: 15  Memory:  178  Last Col/Row:P32
  1>
READY F1:Help  F3:Names  Ctrl-Backspace:Undo  Ctrl-Break:Cancel  CAPS
```

Fig 8.16

Now move the cursor to cell I2 and type in **MONTH:**. Although the actual month is April (month 4) it is still only month 1 in the tax year, so the entry alongside **MONTH** should show **1** not 4. As you will be updating the spreadsheet each month it would be an improvement if the month was calculated for you. SuperCalc can do this by referring back to the date in cell D1.

Move the cursor to cell J2 and type in:

MONTH(D1)-3 ENTER

This will extract the month value from the DATE in cell D1 and subtract 3 (ie: 4 - 3 = 1).

	C	D	E	F	G	H	I	J
1	DATE	30-Apr-91						
2							MONTH:	1
3	SURNAME	GRADE	BASIC	O/T	O/T	GROSS	TAX	PAY TO
4				Hours	Amount	PAY	CODE	DATE
5	------------------------	--------	--------	--------	--------	--------	--------	--------
6	Adams	1	400	0	0	400	242	400
7	Anderson	4	780	10	23.75	803.75	315	803.75
8	Barnes	2	480	2	4	484	242	484
9	Beardsley	1	400	0	0	400	180	400
10	Best	4	780	5	10	790	412	790
11	Charlton	2	480	3	6	486	242	486
12	Charlton	3	530	2	4	534	355	534
13	Clough	5	1300	0	0	1300	242	1300
14	Clough	1	400	15	37.5	437.5	355	437.5
15	Hoddle	1	400	8	18.25	418.25	195	418.25
16	Keegan	5	1300	0	0	1300	242	1300
17	Moore	3	530	4	8	538	387	538
18	Robson	2	480	0	0	480	355	480
19	Robson	3	530	7	15.5	545.5	410	545.5
20	Sansom	1	400	8.5	19.625	419.625	169	419.625

```
LESSON7A!C6              Text="Adams
Width: 15  Memory:  177  Last Col/Row:O32
  1>
READY F1:Help  F3:Names  Ctrl-Backspace:Undo  Ctrl-Break:Cancel  CAPS
```

Fig 8.17

If you have used DATE as a means of entering a date then you can also use DAY, YEAR, WDAY (for the day of the week), and JDATE (for the date in the Julian calendar) to extract details from that cell in the same way as you have just used MONTH.

You can now enter the formula to calculate **free pay** in cell J6. As explained previously, the tax code needs to be multiplied by 10 and then multiplied again by the month number divided by 12. There are a number of ways of entering this formula, but it is recommended that you type in the following:

(I6*10)*(J2/12)

The reference J2 is used to call up the month number – in the next lesson you will change the month number in cell J2 and this formula will update accordingly.

This formula will also need **copying** to all of the other cells used in column K. If you examine the formula then it should become apparent that you will have a similar problem to that experienced when copying the LOOKUP formula earlier in this lesson. The problem is that of the two cell references used in this formula, one (I6) will need adjusting as it is copied, whereas the other (J2) needs to remain fixed. See if you can **copy** the formula and make the necessary adjustments, the correct method is outlined below.

/	to call up commands
C	to select **Copy**
K6	to select cell to copy from
ENTER	
K7.K22	to select cells to Copy to
,	to request **Options**
A	to ask for **Adjustment**
Y	to request that cell I6 be adjusted
N	to request that cell J2 is not adjusted

```
  |   D   ||  E  ||  F ||  G  ||    H    ||   I   ||   J   ||   K   ||   L   |
1  30-Apr-91
2                                           MONTH:            1
3   GRADE  BASIC   O/T   O/T     GROSS      TAX     PAY TO    FREE   TAXABLE
4                Hours Amount     PAY       CODE     DATE      PAY     PAY
5  ---------------------------------------------------------------------------
6       1    400     0      0       400      242       400 201.6667
7       4    780    10  23.75    803.75      315    803.75    262.5
8       2    480     2      4       484      242       484 201.6667
9       1    400     0      0       400      180       400      150
10      4    780     5     10       790      412       790 343.3333
11      2    480     3      6       486      242       486 201.6667
12      3    530     2      4       534      355       534 295.8333
13      5   1300     0      0      1300      242      1300 201.6667
14      1    400    15   37.5     437.5      355     437.5 295.8333
15      1    400     8  18.25    418.25      195    418.25    162.5
16      5   1300     0      0      1300      242      1300 201.6667
17      3    530     4      8       538      387       538    322.5
18      2    480     0      0       480      355       480 295.8333
19      3    530     7   15.5     545.5      410     545.5 341.6667
20      1    400   8.5 19.625   419.625      169   419.625 140.8333
 LESSON8!L6
Width:  9  Memory:  177  Last Col/Row:032
   1>
READY F1:Help  F3:Names  Ctrl-Backspace:Undo  Ctrl-Break:Cancel  CAPS
```

Fig 8.18

See if you can enter the formula for the remaining four columns: TAXABLE PAY is calculated as PAY TO DATE minus FREE PAY; TAX DUE is 25% of the TAXABLE PAY; NET PAY is PAY TO DATE less TAX DUE; and TAX DEDUCTED is (for this month) the same as TAX DUE. See if you can enter the formula for these items and then **copy** the results to the remainder of the columns.

	H	I	J	K	L	M	N	O
1								
2		MONTH:	1					
3	GROSS	TAX	PAY TO	FREE	TAXABLE	TAX	NET	TAX
4	PAY	CODE	DATE	PAY	PAY	DUE	PAY	DEDUCTED
5	----------	----------	----------	----------	----------	----------	----------	----------
6	400	242	400	201.6667	198.3333	49.58333	350.4167	49.58333
7	803.75	315	803.75	262.5	541.25	135.3125	668.4375	135.3125
8	484	242	484	201.6667	282.3333	70.58333	413.4167	70.58333
9	400	180	400	150	250	62.5	337.5	62.5
10	790	412	790	343.3333	446.6667	111.6667	678.3333	111.6667
11	486	242	486	201.6667	284.3333	71.08333	414.9167	71.08333
12	534	355	534	295.8333	238.1667	59.54167	474.4583	59.54167
13	1300	242	1300	201.6667	1098.333	274.5833	1025.417	274.5833
14	437.5	355	437.5	295.8333	141.6667	35.41667	402.0833	35.41667
15	418.25	195	418.25	162.5	255.75	63.9375	354.3125	63.9375
16	1300	242	1300	201.6667	1098.333	274.5833	1025.417	274.5833
17	538	387	538	322.5	215.5	53.875	484.125	53.875
18	480	355	480	295.8333	184.1667	46.04167	433.9583	46.04167
19	545.5	410	545.5	341.6667	203.8333	50.95833	494.5417	50.95833
20	419.625	169	419.625	140.8333	278.7917	69.69792	349.9271	69.69792

```
 LESSON7A!O6                    Form=M6
Width:  9  Memory:  177  Last Col/Row:O32
  1>
READY F1:Help  F3:Names  Ctrl-Backspace:Undo  Ctrl-Break:Cancel  CAPS
```

Fig 8.19

As this lesson forms the basis for Lesson 9, it is essential that you save it onto disk. Follow the instructions given previously for **saving** spreadsheets and call it LESSON8.

Further exercises

A firm has an unusual system for paying commission to sales staff. The various rates have been greatly amended over a number of years and there is no longer any clear mathematical relationship between most rates of commission.

See if you can devise a spreadsheet incorporating a LOOKUP table, an IF statement and making reference to the DATE.

The sales figures for the month ending July 1989 are as follows:

Rep:	Sales:
Joe	£12,000
Fred	£7,600
Anne	£4,890
Dalbir	£9,020
Ken	£2,705
Sue	£5,400

Commission is paid at the following rates:

Basic rate:

Joe	£200
Fred	£280
Anne	£220
Dalbir	£245
Ken	£170
Sue	£190

In addition to this, all staff are paid a bonus of 5% on sales up to £5,000, and an additional 3% on sales in excess of £5,000 (ie: 8% on anything over £5,000).

NB: To *look up* text items the text must be enclosed by quotes (eg: "Joe").

Lesson 9 *Advanced payroll*

The previous lesson demonstrated how SuperCalc can be used for simple payroll calculations. This lesson will take things a step further by showing how SuperCalc can devise a *cumulative* spreadsheet. One of the main problems in devising payroll programs is that the previous weeks' or months' data will need to be added to the current week's or month's figures.

In order to enable the previous weeks' figures to be added to the current week it will be necessary to save and then reload them. This will require the use of some new aspects of both the **Save** and the **Load** commands. By the end of this lesson you should be able to:

a) **load** parts of files
b) **save** parts of files
c) **add** files together
d) use **Macro** commands to make data entry easier
e) **delete** files
f) **move** columns

9.1 Moving columns

Before starting this exercise properly it will be necessary to alter the design of your existing spreadsheet. The spreadsheet to be used is **LESSON8**, so reload this now.

This spreadsheet was only designed for one month's figures, so the layout needs to be changed before you can enter another month's figures. You will need two extra columns – one for **PAY TO DATE** and one for **TAX TO DATE**.

The column showing **NET PAY** – (column N) can be moved to column P. The **Move** command was used in the last lesson to move a row, and you can use it now to move a column. To do this type:

/	to call up commands
M	to select **Move**
C	to select **Column**
N	to specify column **N** as column to be moved
P	to designate column to move to

Once you have done this you can then change the heading for the new column N from **TAX DEDUCTED** to **TAX TO DATE**.

The heading TAX DEDUCTED can now be entered as the heading for Column O. This is to give an extra column for recording tax paid in previous months.

As you can assume that this is month 1, then the tax deducted to date is nil; change the first entry in this column to **0** and then use the **Copy** command to copy it to all other cells in this column.

The screen should now show the following:

```
   |    I   ||    J    ||    K    ||    L    ||    M    ||    N    ||    O    ||    P    |
1
2  MONTH:           1
3     TAX      PAY TO     FREE    TAXABLE     TAX        TAX        TAX       NET
4     CODE      DATE      PAY       PAY       DUE      TO DATE   DEDUCTED     PAY
5  --------------------------------------------------------------------------------
6        242       400 201.6667 198.3333 49.58333 49.58333            0 350.4167
7        315    803.75    262.5   541.25 135.3125 135.3125            0 668.4375
8        242       484 201.6667 282.3333 70.58333 70.58333            0 413.4167
9        180       400      150      250     62.5     62.5            0    337.5
10       412       790 343.3333 446.6667 111.6667 111.6667            0 678.3333
11       242       486 201.6667 284.3333 71.08333 71.08333            0 414.9167
12       355       534 295.8333 238.1667 59.54167 59.54167            0 474.4583
13       242      1300 201.6667 1098.333 274.5833 274.5833            0 1025.417
14       355     437.5 295.8333 141.6667 35.41667 35.41667            0 402.0833
15       195    418.25    162.5   255.75  63.9375  63.9375            0 354.3125
16       242      1300 201.6667 1098.333 274.5833 274.5833            0 1025.417
17       387       538    322.5    215.5   53.875   53.875            0  484.125
18       355       480 295.8333 184.1667 46.04167 46.04167            0 433.9583
19       410     545.5 341.6667 203.8333 50.95833 50.95833            0 494.5417
20       169   419.625 140.8333 278.7917 69.69792 69.69792            0 349.9271
LESSON8!O6                  Form=0
Width:  9  Memory:  175  Last Col/Row:P32
  1>
READY F1:Help  F3:Names  Ctrl-Backspace:Undo  Ctrl-Break:Cancel  CAPS
```

Fig 9.1

9.2 Saving parts of files

These changes to headings will mean that it is also necessary to include some additional formulae to calculate the revised pay and tax figures.

The figure for TAX DEDUCTED will be column M minus column N. Move the cursor to cell O6 and enter the new formula as:

M6-N6

You can now **copy** this to all other cells in column N; this will not result in any immediate changes to values.

The NET PAY will now be GROSS PAY less TAX DEDUCTED, which means that the formula in column P will be column J minus column O (examine the screen to make sure that you are following this). Move the cursor to cell P6 and enter the formula as:

J6–O6

This formula can then be copied to all other cells in column P.

You are now ready to start entering the new pay details for month 2. This will require at least two files: one file will contain the main details of employees, and formulae for calculating wages and tax, and the other will contain the details of the previous month's pay and tax.

The main file containing employee details has already been saved as LESSON8, but you have altered the layout slightly so it is necessary to **save** this again to ensure that you have the most up-to-date copy saved copy. To save the file enter the following:

/	to call up commands
S	to select **Save**
LESSON8	to specify the file name (don't forget the A: or B: prefix)
O	to **overwrite** the file existing file of that name
A	to save all of the file

	J	K	L	M	N	O	P	Q
1								
2	1							
3	PAY TO	FREE	TAXABLE	TAX	TAX	TAX	NET	
4	DATE	PAY	PAY	DUE	TO DATE	DEDUCTED	PAY	
5	----------	----------	----------	----------	----------	----------	----------	----------
6	400	201.6667	198.3333	49.58333	49.58333	0	400	
7	803.75	262.5	541.25	135.3125	135.3125	0	803.75	
8	484	201.6667	282.3333	70.58333	70.58333	0	484	
9	400	150	250	62.5	62.5	0	400	
10	790	343.3333	446.6667	111.6667	111.6667	0	790	
11	486	201.6667	284.3333	71.08333	71.08333	0	486	
12	534	295.8333	238.1667	59.54167	59.54167	0	534	
13	1300	201.6667	1098.333	274.5833	274.5833	0	1300	
14	437.5	295.8333	141.6667	35.41667	35.41667	0	437.5	
15	418.25	162.5	255.75	63.9375	63.9375	0	418.25	
16	1300	201.6667	1098.333	274.5833	274.5833	0	1300	
17	538	322.5	215.5	53.875	53.875	0	538	
18	480	295.8333	184.1667	46.04167	46.04167	0	480	
19	545.5	341.6667	203.8333	50.95833	50.95833	0	545.5	
20	419.625	140.8333	278.7917	69.69792	69.69792	0	419.625	

```
LESSON8!P6                  Form=J6-O6
All  Values  Part  Duplicate  Level  Mode  Single
 19>/Save,LESSON8.cal,
MENU  Save entire spreadsheet with formats, options, titles, windows
```

Fig 9.2

The next step is to save the details of pay (column J) and tax (column O). You should have noticed that the **Save** command gives you the option of saving **Part** of a file – this is what is required in this instance as the only data we want in the new file are the details of **pay** and **tax**.

Unfortunately, you cannot save all of this information in one go as you have 2 *blocks*, and **Save** will only let you save one block at a time. Furthermore, if you try to save this information by saving the pay details first and then the tax details, the tax details will overwrite the pay details.

The solution is to create two files, one containing pay details and the other containing tax details. To do this type:

/	to select commands
S	to select **Save**
PAY1	to give the file a name (don't forget the A: or B: prefix)
P	to specify **Part** only
V	to select **Values** only
J6.J22	to specify range to save

The screen should show the following; if it does you can press **ENTER** to accept the command:

```
   |    J    ||    K    ||    L    ||    M    ||    N    ||    O    ||    P    ||    Q    |
1
2          1
3    PAY TO      FREE   TAXABLE      TAX        TAX       TAX       NET
4     DATE        PAY       PAY      DUE    TO DATE  DEDUCTED       PAY
5  ----------------------------------------------------------------------------------
6        400 201.6667 198.3333 49.58333 49.58333         0       400
7     803.75    262.5   541.25 135.3125 135.3125         0    803.75
8        484 201.6667 282.3333 70.58333 70.58333         0       484
9        400      150      250     62.5     62.5         0       400
10       790 343.3333 446.6667 111.6667 111.6667         0       790
11       486 201.6667 284.3333 71.08333 71.08333         0       486
12       534 295.8333 238.1667 59.54167 59.54167         0       534
13      1300 201.6667 1098.333 274.5833 274.5833         0      1300
14     437.5 295.8333 141.6667 35.41667 35.41667         0     437.5
15    418.25    162.5   255.75  63.9375  63.9375         0    418.25
16      1300 201.6667 1098.333 274.5833 274.5833         0      1300
17       538    322.5    215.5   53.875   53.875         0       538
18       480 295.8333 184.1667 46.04167 46.04167         0       480
19     545.5 341.6667 203.8333 50.95833 50.95833         0     545.5
20   419.625 140.8333 278.7917 69.69792 69.69792         0   419.625
LESSON8!P6                  Form=J6-O6
From? (Enter Range)
 30>/Save,PAY1,Part,Values,J6.J22
EDIT  F1:Help  F3:Names  Ctrl-Backspace:Undo  Ctrl-Break:Cancel  CAPS
```

Fig 9.3

Your next task will be to create another file to store details of the tax deducted to date. This is a similar process, but the block range and file name will be different. As this file will store details of the tax deducted in month 1 a suitable name would be **TAX1**. Save this by entering the following:

/	to select commands
S	to select **Save**
TAX1	to give the file a name (don't forget the A: or B: prefix)
P	to specify **Part** only
V	to select **Values** only
N6.N22	to specify range to save

9.3 Consolidating files

So far you have succeeded in saving the details of pay and tax from month 1. This data will be required again at the end of month 2. You can now assume that a month has passed and the payroll needs to be devised for month 2.

You should still have LESSON8 on the screen; this is the basic file that contains all of your formulae and will be the basis for each month's calculations.

To update this spreadsheet to month 2, move the cursor to the top of the screen and amend the **DATE** to **30th May 1990**; this will have to be entered as:

DATE(05,30,90)

or

EDAT(30,05,90) if preferred.

The display will show the date as 30-May-90 whichever method is used as the user-defined date format will still apply.

You can assume that the employees have done different amounts of overtime this month, so amend the figures in the OVERTIME HOURS column to whatever figures you consider suitable.

If you move the cursor to column O it should be apparent that these figures are now incorrect. This is because the FREE PAY column has altered to month 2, but you have not included the **pay** and **tax** from month 1.

It is now necessary to reload the pay and tax details from month 1, and to **add** them to the new figures. This process is achieved by using the **Consolidate** option in the **Load** command.

To consolidate last month's pay figures enter the following:

/	to select commands
L	to select **Load**
PAY1	to give the file a name (don't forget the A: or B: prefix)
C	to specify that figures need to be added

This should load last month's pay figures and add them to this month's details. Check this by comparing the figures in column J.

Note that the option to load **Part** of the file has a similar function to the **Consolidate** option, but after the ranges have been selected additional options can be selected by pressing the **,** key. These options are: **+**, **-**, ***** and **/** which are used to add, subtract, multiply or divide the values in the source cell and those in the destination cell.

The next step is to reload last month's tax details; these will not need to be consolidated as they have a separate column for **tax deducted to date**, but they will need to be copied into column N instead of column O. The entries to do this are:

/	to select commands
L	to select **Load**
TAX1	to give the file a name (don't forget the A: or B: prefix)
P	to specify **Part** only
N6.N22	to select the range required
N6	to specify cell to load to

The spreadsheet should now show:

	I	J	K	L	M	N	O	P
3	TAX	PAY TO	FREE	TAXABLE	TAX	TAX	TAX	NET
4	CODE	DATE	PAY	PAY	DUE	TO DATE	DEDUCTED	PAY
5								
6	242	804	403.3333	400.6667	100.1667	49.58333	50.58333	753.4167
7	315	1589.75	525	1064.75	266.1875	135.3125	130.875	1458.875
8	242	974	403.3333	570.6667	142.6667	70.58333	72.08333	901.9167
9	180	800	300	500	125	62.5	62.5	737.5
10	412	1570	686.6667	883.3333	220.8333	111.6667	109.1667	1460.833
11	242	989.75	403.3333	586.4167	146.6042	71.08333	75.52083	914.2292
12	355	1070	591.6667	478.3333	119.5833	59.54167	60.04167	1009.958
13	242	2606	403.3333	2202.667	550.6667	274.5833	276.0833	2329.917
14	355	850.25	591.6667	258.5833	64.64583	35.41667	29.22917	821.0208
15	195	836.5	325	511.5	127.875	63.9375	63.9375	772.5625
16	242	2600	403.3333	2196.667	549.1667	274.5833	274.5833	2325.417
17	387	1072	645	427	106.75	53.875	52.875	1019.125
18	355	989.25	591.6667	397.5833	99.39583	46.04167	53.35417	935.8958
19	410	1083.5	683.3333	400.1667	100.0417	50.95833	49.08333	1034.417
20	169	832.375	281.6667	550.7083	137.6771	69.69792	67.97917	764.3958
21	242	1591.75	403.3333	1188.417	297.1042	150.5208	146.5833	1445.167
22	324	998.25	540	458.25	114.5625	54.75	59.8125	938.4375

```
LESSON8!P22                         Form=J22-022
Width:  9  Memory:  177  Last Col/Row:P32
 1>
READY F1:Help  F3:Names  Ctrl-Backspace:Undo  Ctrl-Break:Cancel  CAPS
```

Fig 9.4

You could now proceed to enter details of each months pay by creating files to contain details of the current month's pay and tax, and then reloading and consolidating them at the beginning of each month.

However, it is clearly not going to be easy to remember all of the commands used in this lesson, especially as they will only have to be performed once a month. An easier way of dealing with this sort of problem, and of enabling completely inexperienced users to operate your spreadsheet, is to create a **macro** file. Lesson 7 you were shown a simple example of a macro; in this lesson we will go a stage further.

9.4 Macro files

A **macro** file is a spreadsheet that is used for performing certain SuperCalc commands that will *run* another spreadsheet for you. The benefits are two-fold: firstly it saves the user from having to remember infrequently used commands, and secondly it can enable someone who has only a very basic knowledge of SuperCalc to operate fairly complex programs.

You will now create a macro file which will be used to perform the operations described so far in this exercise. These files can be created by a word-processing program as well as by SuperCalc.

Your macro file will perform the following tasks:

a) **load** all of the file LESSON8
b) **remove** the border as the inexperienced user may find this off-putting.
c) allow the user to **amend** the overtime hours
d) **load** and **consolidate** last month's pay from the file PAY1
e) **load** the tax details from the file TAX1

The macro can be entered in one of two ways. The first way is to plan what the macro will contain and then enter the macro commands in the same way as explained in Lesson 7 section 6. An alternative way is to make use of the **//macro** commands.

To demonstrate the **//Macro** commands it may be advisable to start with a copy of the existing spreadsheet. This is a useful tip as most macros will involve merging or consolidating files, so if a mistake is made it is often difficult to revert to the original position.

You should currently have the updated spreadsheet on screen. **Load** LESSON8 again and select **Replace** to delete the existing data. Then **save** the file as a new spreadsheet called **BACKUP**. Then, if your spreadsheet LESSON8 does become a disaster area, you can simply delete it and replace it with the **backup** spreadsheet.

It is usual to create the macro somewhere to the right of the data in the spreadsheet, but actual position does not matter too much. If you were creating the macro in the style described in Lesson 7 it would possibly appear as follows:

/LA:LESSON8~	loads spreadsheet **LESSON8**
RY	selects **Replace** and **Yes**
/GB	removes the screen border

{SUSPEND}	suspends operation of macro to await new data
/LA:PAY1~	loads spreadsheet **PAY1**
C	selects **Consolidate**
/LA:TAX1~	loads spreadsheet **TAX1**
V	selects **Values**

Make sure that you understand what each of these steps is doing before you continue.

When designing your own macros you may prefer this method, although the alternative is easier. If so, remember that the suffix " must be entered at the beginning of each line and the symbol ~ must be used wherever the **ENTER** key should be pressed. Any items that relate to the performance of a specific keyboard or programming macro command (eg: **Suspend**) are entered in brackets { }.

There should be an additional line in this macro to **save** the updated file, but this has been left out at the moment as it will limit the amount of practising that can be done.

To use the proper **Macro** command you will have to select **//m** – do this now and the following menu will appear:

```
   |  I  ||  J  ||  K  ||  L  ||  M  ||  N  ||  O  ||  P  |
3     TAX   PAY TO   FREE  TAXABLE    TAX      TAX      TAX     NET
4    CODE    DATE    PAY     PAY      DUE   TO DATE DEDUCTED   PAY
5  ------------------------------------------------------------------
6     242     804 403.3333 400.6667 100.1667 49.58333 50.58333 753.4167
7     315 1589.75      525  1064.75 266.1875 135.3125  130.875 1458.875
8     242     974 403.3333 570.6667 142.6667 70.58333 72.08333 901.9167
9     180     800      300      500      125     62.5     62.5    737.5
10    412    1570 686.6667 883.3333 220.8333 111.6667 109.1667 1460.833
11    242  989.75 403.3333 586.4167 146.6042 71.08333 75.52083 914.2292
12    355    1070 591.6667 478.3333 119.5833 59.54167 60.04167 1009.958
13    242    2606 403.3333 2202.667 550.6667 274.5833 276.0833 2329.917
14    355  850.25 591.6667 258.5833 64.64583 35.41667 29.22917 821.0208
15    195   836.5      325    511.5  127.875  63.9375  63.9375 772.5625
16    242    2600 403.3333 2196.667 549.1667 274.5833 274.5833 2325.417
17    387    1072      645      427   106.75   53.875   52.875 1019.125
18    355  989.25 591.6667 397.5833 99.39583 46.04167 53.35417 935.8958
19    410  1083.5 683.3333 400.1667 100.0417 50.95833 49.08333 1034.417
20    169 832.375 281.6667 550.7083 137.6771 69.69792 67.97917 764.3958
21    242 1591.75 403.3333 1188.417 297.1042 150.5208 146.5833 1445.167
22    324  998.25      540   458.25 114.5625    54.75  59.8125 938.4375
LESSON8!P22               Form=J22-O22
Learn  Read  Write  eXecute  Analyze  Breakpoint  Convert  Trace
  9>//Macro,
MENU  Define Learn range to store your keystrokes (Alt-F4 starts Learn)
```

Fig 9.5

These are the options available with the **//Macro** command; very briefly, their functions are:

Learn	defines the range for storing the macro
Read	reads (loads) an existing macro from disk
Write	writes (saves) a macro onto disk
eXecute	executes (starts) a macro file from disk
Analyse	analyses a macro for checking on errors
Breakpoint	places *breakpoints* in a macro to aid checking
Convert	converts SuperCalc macros to or from Lotus macros
Trace	traces the execution of the macro, line by line

The last four options are useful in very complicated macros as they assist in identifying errors. Basically they allow the user to execute the macro a line at a time so that any errors can be spotted and the offending macro line identified. These options will be considered in the next chapter.

9.4.1 Macro options

SuperCalc makes use of the *function keys* (ie: keys marked **F1** to **F10**) in devising and checking macros. As there are a wide variety of options with macros there are a number of HELP screens devoted to macros. It may be useful to examine some of these HELP screens now – if you press **F1** the main **macro help screen** should appear:

```
Macros                                                   SuperCalc AnswerScreen

//Macro  Lets you build, run, save, debug, and analyze macros.

Learn      Sets up the target range for LEARN mode (ALT-F4).       See Learn.

Read       Puts the macro on disk into the specified range.         See Read.

Write      Saves a spreadsheet macro to an .XQT file.              See Write.

eXecute    Runs macros in an .XQT file directly from disk. Single letter
           execute files can be run directly from the spreadsheet using the
           ALT key. Example:  ALT-C runs file C.XQT.

Analyze    Analyzes the structure of a macro.                  See Analysis.

Breakpoint Places breakpoints within macros for debugging.  See Breakpoints.

Convert    Converts Lotus macro to SuperCalc and back again. See Conversions.

Trace    Controls STEP or AUTOSTEP tracing. Aids in debugging. See Tracing.

RELATED TOPICS: Macro Modes    Keyboard Macro {} Commands    Macro Function Keys
                Filenames      Programming Macro {} Commands
ESC=Return to SuperCalc     F2 = How to use Help     F3 = Help Index
```

Fig 9.6

It is recommended that you spend a few minutes examining some of the different HELP screens for macros. A lot of the contents may not make much sense as yet, but it will provide you with a general idea of the scope offered by the **Macro** command, and the sort of help offered, for when you try to create your own macro.

The method that you are now going to use may appear more complicated to begin with, but will prove easier if you use macros regularly.

Before you start it is be best to clear any existing data, so **zap** the screen first.

9.4.2 Macro learn (devising macros)

The first step is to specify the range that will be used to store the macro. The macro range is defined by the **Macro, Learn** option. Select the following:

/	to call up the commands
/	to select the second rank of commands
M	to select **Macro**
L	to select **Learn**
T2.T20	to select the learn range

This will not appear to do anything, but it has designated the range T2 to T20 as the area where the macro will be stored. Unlike the previous exercise involving macros this macro will be entered into the range automatically.

The macro that you will shortly be devising will not require 18 lines, but it is always useful to allow extra room to in case of amendments.

You will enter the macro commands by using the macro function keys of **Alt** and **F4**, and **Alt** and **F6**. The first of these commands will **learn** (or capture) any commands entered, and store them in the **Macro, Learn** range. The second option is similar, but will allow you to enter macro **keyboard** or **programming** commands that you do not want entered on the screen.

If you press the **Alt** key and **F4** together, you should notice that the word **Learn** appears at the bottom right of the screen. Any commands that you enter now will be *learned* and stored in the macro, and be carried out at the same time. The logic is that any error in the macro can be spotted immediately, as the command entered will not work properly if there is an error.

The first entry in our macro will be to load the spreadsheet file for LESSON8. This could be entered in the **Learn** mode, but does tend to cause problems, so it is better if it is included in the macro and that the file is not actually loaded just yet. This can be done by selecting **Alt** and **F6** which brings up the **Direct** mode. This will enable you to enter the commands that you require without them actually being carried out at the same time. Press **Alt** and **F6** now, and then type in:

/LA:LESSON8.CAL~RY

This is the same entry that would have been used in the last lesson except that you no longer have to remember to include the " at the start of the line. Press **ENTER** to finish this entry. The entry will be transferred to the first line in the **Macro, Learn** range – but don't look yet as any item or command selected at the moment will become part of your macro. NB: the ~ symbol is used to designate the **ENTER** key.

This command will load the file LESSON8 and replace any existing file.

You may as well remain in the **Direct** mode for the next few entries, as most of them involve programming commands.

The next line will remove the screen border – all that you have to do is type in the commands to do this followed by **ENTER**, so now type in **/GB**. Again, this will have been automatically captured by the macro.

The border is removed to make the spreadsheet less intimidating for inexperienced users. This screen can be further improved by removing the *entry line* prompt. The programming command that does this is **{ENTRYOFF}**, so type this in and then press **ENTER**. Make sure that you use the correct brackets.

When the spreadsheet has been loaded there will need to be an opportunity for the user to alter figures, particularly those for the overtime hours worked. The macro can pause to allow data entry by using the **{SUSPEND}** command; operation of the macro will only be resumed only when the key **F8** is pressed (a prompt to this effect will appear on the screen during operation of the macro). Type in **{SUSPEND}** and press **ENTER**.

The two remaining commands can be entered with the **Learn** option – to revert to this press **Alt** and **F4** again.

Any command entered now will be acted upon, but also stored in the macro. The first command is to load the file PAY1, and the sequence of commands to do this is **/LA:PAY1** followed by **ENTER** and then **C** for **Consolidate**. Enter these now and the relevant part of the PAY1 file will load (although it may be off the existing screen).

The final part of the macro will be to load the file TAX1 – the commands for this will be **/LA:TAX1** followed by **ENTER** and then **V** for **Values**. Enter this now.

It may not be apparent yet, but the above operations will have created the macro for you. Finally, press **Alt** and **F4** and make sure that the **Learn** prompt in the corner of the screen has disappeared.

If you now move the cursor back to the **Macro, Learn** range (T2 to T20) these commands should appear in the order in which they were entered.

```
 |  O  ||  P  ||  Q  ||  R  ||  S  ||  T  ||  U  ||  V  |
1
2                                     /LA:LESSON8.CAL~RY
3                                     /GB
4                                     {ENTRYOFF}
5                                     {SUSPEND}
6                                     /LA:PAY1~C/LA:TAX1~V
7
8
9
10
11
12
13
14
15
16
17
18
19
20
LESSON8!T1
Width:  9  Memory:  189  Last Col/Row:T22
  1>
READY F1:Help  F3:Names  Ctrl-Backspace:Undo  Ctrl-Break:Cancel  CAPS
```

Fig 9.7

If you make an error whilst creating the macro and use the BACKSPACE key to edit any entry, then this will appear as **{BS}** in the macro – this may not look very tidy and will slow the macro down slightly, but it shouldn't create any real problems.

9.4.3 Macro write (saving macros)

The Macro file is now complete and is almost ready to **save**, but unlike other spreadsheets macro files are not saved but are **written** to disk instead.

Before commencing this task it is worth noting that macro files are saved with an extension of **.PRN** or **.XQT**, instead of the usual **.CAL**. One problem created by this is that it is sometimes difficult to reload and edit a macro file once it has been saved. As this sort of file frequently contains errors you are *strongly recommended* to save your file using the normal **Save** command before you **write** it to disk, as this may assist you when making future alterations.

This macro also differs from the previous example in that it will be a **File Macro**, which means that it is run from its own spreadsheet file; the previous example was a **Spreadsheet Macro** as it was run from within another spreadsheet. The effect of this is that it is essential to **save** this, but it needs to be saved along with the **macro commands**, so before saving the file you can save the macro.

Before you save the macro you can enter a label (title). If you remember from the last lesson on macros, the labels are usually one word titles that can be used to invoke the macro. As the macro will be used with the **payroll program** it can simply be called **P**. Move the cursor to cell S2 and enter **\P**.

Writing the macro to disk instead of saving it simply appends the suffix **.XQT** instead of the usual **.CAL**. To save a macro in this way you need to select the following commands:

/	to call up the commands
/	to select the second rank of commands
M	to select **Macro**
W	to select **Write**
A:P	to enter filename and drive (P stands for payroll)
T2.T20	to select the macro range
A	to select **All** (macros, labels and comments)

```
    |  O  ||  P  ||  Q  ||  R  ||  S  ||  T              ||  U  ||  V  |
 1
 2                               \p    /LA:LESSON8.CAL~RY
 3                                     /GB
 4                                     {ENTRYOFF}
 5                                     {SUSPEND}
 6                                     /LA:PAY1~C/LA:TAX1~V
 7
 8
 9
10
11
12
13
14
15
16
17
18
19
20
LESSON8!S3
All  Macros-only  Labels-macros  Comments-macros
26>//Macro,Write,a:p,t2.t20,
MENU  Include all 3 columns: macros, labels, and comments
```

Fig 9.8

The macro has now been written to disk – the next step is to save the file in the normal way. The spreadsheet file can also be called **P** as it will be easier to remember the macro name if both files have the same name. The sequence of commands for saving the file are as follows:

/	to call up the commands
S	to select **Save**
A:P	to specify file name and drive
A	to select **All**

9.4.4 Executing macros (running macros)

You should now be ready to run your macro file. **Zap** the existing screen first. To run a macro file you need to use the **Macro, eXecute** command. Enter the following:

/	to select commands
/	to select the second row of options
M	to select **Macro**
X	to select **eXecute** (NB: **X** not **E**)
A:P	to select the macro

The screen will eventually clear and the **Macro** command will start to run; it will pause to allow you to enter the new **overtime** hours, but will continue when you press **F8**.

The difference between this and spreadsheet macros is that spreadsheet macros are invoked by pressing **Alt** and the file name only. However, file macros do have one advantage in that the macro can be started direct from the operating prompt.

To demonstrate, select **Quit** and return to the **C:** prompt (**Yes** option on most machines). To start the macro automatically on loading type in:

SC5 A:P

This will load SuperCalc and automatically run the macro. This method is advantageous as it reduces the amount of knowledge that an operator needs – only a single command has to be typed in.

Further exercises

The macro file could be further improved by **formatting** the columns containing decimal places to **$** format. See if you can insert a couple of extra rows into your file to do this for you.

Also, inexperienced users will find operation far simpler if they do not have to use the cursor movement keys. It is possible to achieve this by using the **Global, Tab** command, because the only entry that should need altering is the OVERTIME HOURS worked. See if you can create a new macro that incorporates the **Global, Tab** command by using the **Protect** command to safeguard entries (NB: you will probably need to **unprotect** these cells after the user has finished making alterations as your pay and tax files cannot be loaded on to **protected** cells).

You could also include a message providing basic instructions to the user on what is happening – this is probably best created somewhere else in the spreadsheet to save having to alter the cells onto which files are loaded.

Do not worry if you find this rather difficult – a similar macro will be demonstrated in Lesson 11.

Lesson 10 *Databases*

In this lesson we will examine how SuperCalc can be used as a database by using the // Data command. At the end of this lesson you will be able to:

a) define a block of data as a database using the **Input** option
b) select various records by using the **Criterion** option
c) find records that meet set criteria using the **Find** option
d) define a block for transferring various records to using the **Output** option
e) extract records from the main list to the output block
f) select those records that you require for extraction
g) delete records that are no longer required

In order to make sense of this lesson you first need to understand what a database is. Most of the work covered so far has involved the use of numerical data, and that is what spreadsheets were originally designed for. However, many firms will have records that are a mixture of numbers and text (eg: payroll) and the database functions have been incorporated into SuperCalc to allow users to use all of their data in a meaningful way.

A database is a list of information that consists of three component parts:

Files: A complete list is known as a file.

Records: Each file is made up of records, for example a telephone directory is a file, and the records contained within it are the names and addresses of subscribers.

Fields: Each record can be subdivided into fields. A field is a section containing some details which go to make up the full record. The fields for each record in a telephone directory would be the name, the address and the telephone number (ie: three fields).

There are many database programs available which are only suitable for maintaining such lists, but SuperCalc versions 3 onwards also have a database facility for examining and retrieving information stored in lists.

10.1 Designing a database

To save having to key in new details for a database we can use some of the data from the payroll example in Lesson 8. This file contains employee details and is therefore ideal as a database.

However, not all of the file will be required, so we want to load part of Lesson 8, to include the range A6:D22, into cell A2 as follows:-

/	to call up commands
L	to select **Load**
Lesson8	to specify file LESSON8 (remember the A: or B: prefix)
P	to select **Part** only
A6.D22	to specify the range required
A2	to designate position to load to

The blank line at the top can be used to load the headings from the file LESSON8. To do this, type in:

/	to call up commands
L	to select **Load**
Lesson8	to specify file LESSON8
P	to select **Part** only
A3.D3	to specify the range required
A1	to designate position to load to

Unfortunately, your cell width will need to be reformatted so that the headings can be seen clearly, so amend the headings to the following widths:

	A	B	C	D
Widths	5	15	15	5

You can also format column A to have numbers **left-justified.**

```
   | A ||      B       ||      C       || D ||  E  ||  F  ||  G  |
1   No:  FIRST NAME     SURNAME          GRADE
2    165 Tony           Adams              1
3    290 Viv            Anderson           4
4    319 John           Barnes             2
5    208 Peter          Beardsley          1
6    107 George         Best               4
7    170 Bobby          Charlton           2
8    104 Jack           Charlton           3
9    135 Brian          Clough             5
10   101 Nigel          Clough             1
11   133 Glenn          Hoddle             1
12   181 Kevin          Keegan             5
13   109 Bobby          Moore              3
14   180 Bobby          Robson             2
15   113 Bryan          Robson             3
16   210 Kenny          Sansom             1
17   148 Peter          Shilton            4
18   130 Nobby          Stiles             2
19
20
 TEMP1!A1                      Text="No:
Width:  5  Memory:  183  Last Col/Row:D18
  1>
READY F1:Help  F3:Names  Ctrl-Backspace:Undo  Ctrl-Break:Cancel
```

Fig 10.1

Now that the file looks tidy you can start using database commands.

The file that you now have contains a record for each employee (ie: each **row**); each record is subdivided into fields as follows:

NO: FIRST NAME SURNAME GRADE

The first step is to define the area of the Spreadsheet that contains the items that will be used in the database – this is known as the **Input range**. For this example we want to use the entire file, so the range will be the whole block displayed on screen. To specify this range press:

/	to call up commands
/	to call up **Data** commands
D	to select **Data**
I	to specify the **Input** range
A1.D18	to designate the **Input** range (or use the cursor keys)
ENTER	

Note that the **input range** must include the **field names** (from cells A1 to D1) as these are used as a reference point for making enquiries about the file.

```
   | A ||      B       ||      C       ||D || E || F || G |
1   No:  FIRST NAME      SURNAME         GRADE
2    165 Tony            Adams               1
3    290 Viv             Anderson            4
4    319 John            Barnes              2
5    208 Peter           Beardsley           1
6    107 George          Best                4
7    170 Bobby           Charlton            2
8    104 Jack            Charlton            3
9    135 Brian           Clough              5
10   101 Nigel           Clough              1
11   133 Glenn           Hoddle              1
12   181 Kevin           Keegan              5
13   109 Bobby           Moore               3
14   180 Bobby           Robson              2
15   113 Bryan           Robson              3
16   210 Kenny           Sansom              1
17   148 Peter           Shilton             4
18   130 Nobby           Stiles              2
19
20
 TEMP1!A1                      Text="No:
Enter range  (currently undefined)
 20>//Data,Input,a1.d18
EDIT  F1:Help  F3:Names  Ctrl-Backspace:Undo  Ctrl-Break:Cancel
```

Fig 10.2

Also note that, when the command has been entered, the command prompt remains on screen as SuperCalc assumes that you will require further enquiries in the **Data** options. If you want to leave this option now you can escape by pressing **ENTER.**

It is necessary to designate the range that will be used for searching the database, known as the **criterion block**. In order to analyse the contents of the database it will be necessary to *ask* various questions; the **criterion range** is simply the part of the spreadsheet used for entering these questions. This block is configured by selecting the **C** option on the **Data** list. We will use the block **F1:I2** – the **Data** commands should still be on the screen, so you only need to type the following:

C	to select **Criterion**
F1.I2	to designate the criterion range

Nothing will happen yet as you have not *asked* any questions. The top row of each criterion block must be reserved for field names; the **input range** already has the field names at the top, but these will need to be copied to the block that has just been designated as the **criterion range**. Use the **Copy** command to copy the field names from A1 to D1 to a new block starting at F1, then you can also format column G to 15 spaces (you will have to exit the **Data** command first).

Note that the field names must be an exact copy of the matching field names in the **input block** and, therefore, it is recommended that the **Copy** command is always used to enter the new field name.

10.2 Searching a database

Before you can search the database you will have to define what exactly it is that you are searching for. Move the cursor to cell G2 so that you can enter the question in the criterion block.

The record that we are looking for is that for John Barnes. Although you should be able to see this record on the screen in row 4, you can pretend that you do not know either his number or grade. Enter **John** in cell G2 and **Barnes** in H2.

This has entered the search criteria so that the record looked for will be that for John Barnes. In order to activate the search you need to select the **Data** command again:

/	to call up commands
/	to call up the second row of commands
D	to select **Data**
F	to select **Find**

When you have done this the cursor will move to the block **a4:d4**, which is the entry for John Barnes. The *prompt line* informs you of the keys to select to continue the search. If you select any of these keys a message should appear to the effect that there are no more matching records. Press **ENTER** to return to the normal screen prompts.

You can now change your **criterion** by blanking out the current entries in cells G2 and H2 (you will have to exit the **Data** command first). You will now be able to ask a different question using the criterion range. This time you can search the database for all records of employees on Grade 2 salaries.

Firstly, you will have to enter the criteria in the block F2 to I2. This time the only relevant field will be the **grade**, so the only entry required would be in cell I2. Enter **2** in cell I2 and then select the **//Data, Find** option again.

to press the down arrow key until the message appears **No more matching records**.

Note that the cursor will flash in the first cell in the **input block** and entries can be altered by using the right and left arrow keys and over-typing the entries.

```
    | A ||      B      ||      C       || D ||  E  ||  F  ||      G      |
 1   No:  FIRST NAME    SURNAME         GRADE        No:    FIRST NAME
 2   165 Tony           Adams             1
 3   290 Viv            Anderson          4
 4   319 John           Barnes            2
 5   208 Peter          Beardsley         1
 6   107 George         Best              4
 7   170 Bobby          Charlton          2
 8   104 Jack           Charlton          3
 9   135 Brian          Clough            5
10   101 Nigel          Clough            1
11   133 Glenn          Hoddle            1
12   181 Kevin          Keegan            5
13   109 Bobby          Moore             3
14   180 Bobby          Robson            2
15   113 Bryan          Robson            3
16   210 Kenny          Sansom            1
17   148 Peter          Shilton           4
18   130 Nobby          Stiles            2
19
20
 TEMP1!A18                       Form=130              No more matching records
 , Next field or   , Cancel <RETURN>
 12>//Data,Find
MENU  Find all records in the input range that meet the criteria
```

Fig 10.3

You can also use the **Data, Find** option with formulae as search criteria. Exit the **Data** command and then move the cursor back to cell I2 and enter the following as the new search criteria:

D2>3

This will appear as 0 in the criteria block, but if you now select the **//Data, Find** option, all records where the employee is on a grade higher than Grade 3 will be highlighted.

You can also search for characters by using wildcards:

- ***** will match any text with the same beginning, eg C* will match all records beginning with C.
- **?** will match all records containing other characters that are the same, eg J?ne will match Jane and June – remember the " marks must be used before this wildcard.

To demonstrate this, exit the **Data** command, then move the cursor to cell H2 and enter the search criteria as **C*** (note that using c would not result in any matching records as all the names in the surname field begin with a capital letter).

To demonstrate this, exit the **Data** command, then move the cursor to cell H2 and enter the search criteria as **C*** (note that using c would not result in any matching records as all the names in the surname field begin with a capital letter).

If you now select the **//Data, Find** option the first record identified will be that for Brian Clough, the other two records for the Charltons have been ignored because although they begin with the letter C, they do not match the other criteria of having a grade higher than 3 – remember that the **grade field** in the **criterion range** is still included the request for employees on a grade higher than Grade 3 – this demonstrates that the **Data** command will allow you to make some fairly complex analyses.

```
     | A ||      B       ||      C       || D || E  ||  F  ||     G      |
 1   No:  FIRST NAME      SURNAME          GRADE          No:       FIRST NAME
 2    165 Tony            Adams                1
 3    290 Viv             Anderson             4
 4    319 John            Barnes               2
 5    208 Peter           Beardsley            1
 6    107 George          Best                 4
 7    170 Bobby           Charlton             2
 8    104 Jack            Charlton             3
 9    135 Brian           Clough               5
 10   101 Nigel           Clough               1
 11   133 Glenn           Hoddle               1
 12   181 Kevin           Keegan               5
 13   109 Bobby           Moore                3
 14   180 Bobby           Robson               2
 15   113 Bryan           Robson               3
 16   210 Kenny           Sansom               1
 17   148 Peter           Shilton              4
 18   130 Nobby           Stiles               2
 19
 20
TEMP1!A9                       Form=135
 , Next field or  , Cancel <RETURN>
 12>//Data,Find
MENU  Find all records in the input range that meet the criteria
```

Fig 10.4

One other type of function that has not been considered yet is the **AND** function. This is similar to the **IF** statements, except that it enables you to carry out two formulae at a time instead of selecting one out of two formulae.

Blank out all of the existing criteria in the rows F2 to I2 and then enter the following formula in cell F2:

AND(A2<200,D2>1)

This formula is in two parts and the search will consist of all records that have a *No: (cell A2) below 200* **AND** *a grade higher than 1 (cell D2)*. NB: The AND function is a normal SuperCalc command and can be used in any type of spreadsheet, not just in **Data**.

The search can be further improved by selecting only those employees whose surname begins with S. Move the cursor to cell H2 and enter:

S*

```
    |      C       ||D||  E  ||  F  ||    G     ||  H  ||  I  |
1   SURNAME        GRADE     No:     FIRST NAME   SURNAME  GRADE
2   Adams            1        0                   S*
3   Anderson         4
4   Barnes           2
5   Beardsley        1
6   Best             4
7   Charlton         2
8   Charlton         3
9   Clough           5
10  Clough           1
11  Hoddle           1
12  Keegan           5
13  Moore            3
14  Robson           2
15  Robson           3
16  Sansom           1
17  Shilton          4
18  Stiles           2
19
20
 LESSON9!I2                                                 TEXT
Width:  9  Memory:  182  Last Col/Row:I18
  1>
READY F1:Help  F3:Names  Ctrl-Backspace:Undo  Ctrl-Break:Cancel
```

Fig 10.5

If you now select the **// Data, Find** option the cursor should move to the record for Peter Shilton, as this is the first record that satisfies all of your search criteria. The only other record with these criteria is the last record.

10.3 Extracting data

So far the **Data Management** option has only been used for simple searches; in larger databases it may be more appropriate to physically extract the required data from the existing database and copy it to another part of the spreadsheet.

Leave the **Data** command, move the cursor to cell G10 and enter **SURNAME**, then move to cell H10 and enter **FIRST NAME**. This has established the headings for the new database that we want to create and specified the order in which we want the data to appear. The next step is to specify the range of this block. To do this enter the following:

/	to call up commands
/	to call up **Data** commands
D	to select **Data**
O	to select **Output**
G10.H28	to specify the range for the output block

```
     | D || E  || F ||    G    ||  H  ||  I  ||  J  ||  K  |
 9      5
10      1             SURNAME     FIRST NAME
11      1
12      5
13      3
14      2
15      3
16      1
17      4
18      2
19
20
21
22
23
24
25
26
27
28
 TEMP1!H28
Enter range  (currently undefined)
 22>//Data,Output,G10:H28
POINT F1:Help F2:Edit F3:Names Home:1st End-Arrow:last Ctrl-Break:Cancel
```

Fig 10.6

This has stipulated where the new database will be copied to. The columns used are determined by the fields we require, but the length will normally be dictated by the size of the original database. As our database is 18 rows long, the **output block** needs to be the same length.

You can now alter the search criteria to identify only those employees with a number below 100 – move the cursor to cell F2 and enter **a2<200**. Make sure that you blank out the current entries in all of the other cells first. Check that your search works by selecting **//Data, Find.**

To copy these records to the **output block** select the following:

/	to call up commands
/	to call up **Data** commands
D	to select **Data**
E	to select **Extract**

The records selected will now be copied to the output block and the sequence of the fields should have altered to the new sequence requested.

```
     |    C     ||D||  E  ||  F  ||     G     ||  H  ||  I  |
  5  Beardsley    1
  6  Best         4
  7  Charlton     2
  8  Charlton     3
  9  Clough       5
 10  Clough       1                 SURNAME      FIRST NAME
 11  Hoddle       1                 Adams        Tony
 12  Keegan       5                 Best         George
 13  Moore        3                 Charlton     Bobby
 14  Robson       2                 Charlton     Jack
 15  Robson       3                 Clough       Brian
 16  Sansom       1                 Clough       Nigel
 17  Shilton      4                 Hoddle       Glenn
 18  Stiles       2                 Keegan       Kevin
 19                                 Moore        Bobby
 20                                 Robson       Bobby
 21                                 Robson       Bryan
 22                                 Shilton      Peter
 23                                 Stiles       Nobby
 24
  TEMP1!H24
 Width:  9  Memory:  181  Last Col/Row:I23
   1>
 READY F1:Help  F3:Names  Ctrl-Backspace:Undo  Ctrl-Break:Cancel  CAPS
```

Fig 10.7

10.4 Selecting data for extract

In some cases, especially with very large databases, it will not be possible to devise search criteria which will accurately identify all records that you want extracted. An option is included in the **Data Management** commands that will enable you to decide whether or not you want each record transferred to your output block.

First, blank out the records currently in the block G11 to H23. This should clear the **output block** and enable you to use the **Select** option in conjunction with the **Extract** command.

Type in the following:

/	to call up commands
/	to call up **Data** commands
D	to select **Data**
E	to select **Extract**

At this point the records will be copied to the output block, but the **Data** options still remain on screen.

Now press **S** for **Select**. The output block should clear and the cursor should move back into the **input block** and position itself over the first record identified by the search criteria of A2<200.

The prompt line should ask you if you want to **extract** this record; press **Y** and the record will be copied to the output block, and the cursor move to the next record identified.

```
   | A ||      B      ||     C      ||D ||  E  ||  F  ||    G    |
1  No:  FIRST NAME     SURNAME        GRADE       No:     FIRST NAME
2    165 Tony          Adams             1                1
3    290 Viv           Anderson          4
4    319 John          Barnes            2
5    208 Peter         Beardsley         1
6    107 George        Best              4
7    170 Bobby         Charlton          2
8    104 Jack          Charlton          3
9    135 Brian         Clough            5
10   101 Nigel         Clough            1                SURNAME
11   133 Glenn         Hoddle            1                Adams
12   181 Kevin         Keegan            5
13   109 Bobby         Moore             3
14   180 Bobby         Robson            2
15   113 Bryan         Robson            3
16   210 Kenny         Sansom            1
17   148 Peter         Shilton           4
18   130 Nobby         Stiles            2
19
20
 TEMP1!A6                       Form=107
Extract?  Y(es) or N(o), Next field or  , Cancel <RETURN>
 14>//Data,Select
MENU  Extract; confirm output of each qualified record        CAPS
```

Fig 10.8

Let us assume that you do not want this next record **extracted**, so press **N**. The cursor should simply move to the next record without extracting the previous record.

Continue through the file and extract or ignore the remaining records highlighted.

10.5 Deleting data

The **Data** command will also allow you to delete data that satisfies the criteria in the **criterion range**. **Blank** the entries in the criterion range and the output range. Then enter new criteria to select all records for employees whose Christian names begin with **B**. Try and do this yourself.

(If you get stuck, the solution is to enter **B*** in cell G2.) Now call up the **Data, Find** option, and the cursor should move to the entry for Bobby Charlton. If you examine the other records it should highlight all those with Christian names beginning with B.

You can now assume that some of these records will no longer be required. You could delete them with the **Blank** or **Delete** commands, but either of these commands will affect your **criterion** or **output ranges**. The **Data** command has an option for deleting records that will ensure that the other **Data** options are not affected.

Press **ENTER** to exit the **Data, Find** option and then select **Delete**. The cursor should move to the first entry in the range **First name = B***, which is Bobby Charlton again.

```
      | A ||     B     ||      C      || D ||  E  ||  F  ||     G      |
 1    No:  FIRST NAME   SURNAME        GRADE       No:     FIRST NAME
 2     165 Tony         Adams              1                B*
 3     290 Viv          Anderson           4
 4     319 John         Barnes             2
 5     208 Peter        Beardsley          1
 6     107 George       Best               4
 7     170 Bobby        Charlton           2
 8     104 Jack         Charlton           3
 9     135 Brian        Clough             5
10     101 Nigel        Clough             1               SURNAME
11     133 Glenn        Hoddle             1
12     181 Kevin        Keegan             5
13     109 Bobby        Moore              3
14     180 Bobby        Robson             2
15     113 Bryan        Robson             3
16     210 Kenny        Sansom             1
17     148 Peter        Shilton            4
18     130 Nobby        Stiles             2
19
20
 TEMP1!A7                       Form=170
 , Cancel <RETURN>
 14>//Data,Delete
MENU  Delete records that meet the criteria
```

Fig 10.9

This command will select the various records in the **criterion range** and then give you the option of deleting them. This record is not required, so you can select **Y(es)** by pressing **Y**. The record will now be removed and the remaining records moved up to replace it. Note that the **output range** will also be adjusted automatically.

The cursor will now move to the next record in the range (Brian Clough); this record will be required in future so select **N(o)** to retain it.

The cursor will continue to move through the remaining records in the criteria range and will allow you to decide whether the records should be deleted or not. You can assume that none of the remaining records are required so select **R(emaining)** to delete all other records in the range. These will be deleted one at a time until all matching records have been examined.

This last **Delete** option should be used with care as once records have been deleted they cannot be recalled in subsequent work sessions. However, if you select **Undo** (**Ctrl** and **BACKSPACE**) all of the records should be reinstated. Note that this will not happen if you have used any other commands in between.

The only other command in the **Data** list is the **Remain** command. This command is used to keep the cursor in its current location when the **Data** commands have finished, instead of returning to its original position. Choosing this option will also remove the **Data** options from the *entry line*. To demonstrate this, change the **criterion** in cell G2 to **Kenny** and then select **Data, Find**. The cursor should move to cell **A16**, the entry for Kenny Sansom. If you press **ENTER** to exit the **Data** command the cursor will return to the **Criterion** block. This is not a major problem in your database as it is very small, but if you had a large database and needed to amend the record for Kenny Sansom you would now have to use the **GoTo** command to return to cell A16. The **Data, Remain** command can be used to ensure that the cursor stays in the cell or record required. Select **Data, Find** again, and when the cursor moves to cell A16 press **ENTER** once. Now select **Remain** and the command line will clear leaving the cursor in cell A16 ready for you to make your alterations.

This lesson has demonstrated the main uses for the **Data** command. You will have noticed that not all of the options have been examined. The other options in this command tend to involve statistical and mathematical functions and will be examined in the next lesson.

Further exercises

Zap the existing screen and **load** part of LESSON8 again to practice additional **Data** options. You will need the same columns as in this example, but you will also require the BASIC PAY column which is column E. Unfortunately, this column used a LOOKUP table to calculate basic pay, and the only way of loading these figures without the table is to **Load values only**. The range required will be A6 to E22 and the cell to load to will be A2, when you have selected these ranges you will then have to select the further options in order to specify **values**.

Next, load the headings as described in the exercise, but remember to include the heading for BASIC.

You can now proceed to designate a criteria block as described previously.

When you have done this see if you can enter the **Search** criteria to find the following data:

1) All employees earning over £700.
2) All employees earning over £700 and with a number over 130.
3) All employees filling the conditions in (2) and with a surname beginning with A.
4) All employees with a Christian name of Bobby.
5) Specify an output block and extract all of the records fulfilling the conditions in (4).

Lesson 11 *Statistics and advanced graphics*

The previous lesson examined the use of the **Data** command in relation to the criteria and analysis of databases. Some of the **Data** options relate specifically to statistical uses and have not been examined yet. In this lesson you will see how SuperCalc can be used for statistical analysis and you will examine the charts and graphs available that have not yet been considered. At the end of this lesson you should be able to:

a) apply various statistical formulae
b) use the statistical options on the **Data** command
c) prepare graphs for representing statistical data
d) use the **Data** command for multiplying tables of data
e) customise **User-Defined** formats
f) create data with the **RANDOM** statement

11.1 Averages

In order to examine the various statistical formulae available it will first be necessary to have some data to work on. To save typing in new data you can use the data from Lesson 8, as in the last lesson. This time you can include the columns for **GRADE** and **BASIC** pay. To load the file type in the following:

/	to call up commands
L	to select **Load**
LESSON8	to specify Lesson 8 (remember to include the A: or B: prefix)
P	to select **Part**
A3.E22	to specify range from
A1	to specify range to (don't press **ENTER**), to select options
V	to request **Values**

As in the previous lesson, the **Load, Part** command will not copy the **Format** commands from the original file, so you will have to adjust the width of the cells and alter the justification in column A using the **Format** command. Your screen should now appear as in Fig 11.1.

```
      |  A  ||     B      ||   C   ||   D   ||   E   ||  F  ||  G  ||  H  |
1   No:       FIRST NAME  SURNAME  GRADE    BASIC
2
3   ---------------------------------------------------------------------------
4    165      Tony        Adams          1     400
5    290      Viv         Anderson       4     780
6    319      John        Barnes         2     480
7    208      Peter       Beardsley      1     400
8    107      George      Best           4     780
9    170      Bobby       Charlton       2     480
10   104      Jack        Charlton       3     530
11   135      Brian       Clough         5    1300
12   101      Nigel       Clough         1     400
13   133      Glenn       Hoddle         1     400
14   181      Kevin       Keegan         5    1300
15   109      Bobby       Moore          3     530
16   180      Bobby       Robson         2     480
17   113      Bryan       Robson          3     530
18   210      Kenny       Sansom         1     400
19   148      Peter       Shilton        4     780
20   130      Nobby       Stiles         2     480
 TEMP1!B1                     Text="FIRST NAME
Width: 12  Memory:  182  Last Col/Row:E20
  1>
READY F1:Help  F3:Names  Ctrl-Backspace:Undo  Ctrl-Break:Cancel
```

Fig 11.1

The first set of formulae is fairly straightforward and some were examined in the very first lesson. Move the cursor to cell G4 and type in:

COUNT(A4.A22)

This formula will count how many records or items there are in the range requested – the screen should show the answer as 17. Now move the cursor to cell G5 and type in:

AVERAGE(E4.E22)

This formula will calculate the average wage as being £614.7059. The AVERAGE formula can also be entered as **AVG(E4.E22)**. This formula actually calculates the arithmetic **Mean**, but there are also **Median** and **Mode** averages. if you examine the data in column E you should be able to see that the weakness of the **Mean** is that there is no *real* value of £614.7059. The arithmetic **Mode** is the value that occurs most frequently in a range of data, ie the *most common*. The **Median** can also be useful as it provides you with details of the *mid-point* value in a series of data.

Both of these values can be arrived at by simple observation or counting: if you examine the data you should be able to see that the **Mode** is £400 and, as the **Median** is the value that occurs in the middle of a range, the data will first have to be sorted into numerical order. The **Arrange** command could be used to sort the values for you, but the **//Data** commands will provide a slightly easier way of calculating both the **Mode** and the **Median**.

The **//Data** command has an option which has been included specifically to assist in statistical analysis – the **Analysis** option. This command can be used to devise *frequency distributions*, which will categorise data into groups depending upon how *frequently* they arise. Before you use this command you need to set up a **bin range** to identify the groups that you want. This example is straightforward as the categories will be the different pay rates.

Move the cursor to cell G13 and enter the different pay rates as shown:

	A	B	C	D	E	F	G	H
1	No:	FIRST NAME	SURNAME	GRADE	BASIC			
2								
3	----------	----------	----------	----------	----------	----------	----------	----------
4	165	Tony	Adams	1	400		17	
5	290	Viv	Anderson	4	780		614.7059	
6	319	John	Barnes	2	480			
7	208	Peter	Beardsley	1	400			
8	107	George	Best	4	780			
9	170	Bobby	Charlton	2	480			
10	104	Jack	Charlton	3	530			
11	135	Brian	Clough	5	1300			
12	101	Nigel	Clough	1	400			
13	133	Glenn	Hoddle	1	400		400	
14	181	Kevin	Keegan	5	1300		480	
15	109	Bobby	Moore	3	530		530	
16	180	Bobby	Robson	2	480		780	
17	113	Bryan	Robson	3	530		1300	
18	210	Kenny	Sansom	1	400			
19	148	Peter	Shilton	4	780			
20	130	Nobby	Stiles	2	480			

```
TEMP1!G18
Width:  9  Memory:  182  Last Col/Row:G20
  1>
READY F1:Help  F3:Names  Ctrl-Backspace:Undo  Ctrl-Break:Cancel
```

Fig 11.2

Now select the following to set up a frequency distribution:

/	to call up commands
/	to call up the second batch of commands
Data	to select the **Data** command
Analysis	to select the **Analysis** option
Distribution	to select the **Frequency distribution** option
E4.E20	to select the input range (use cursor keys if required)
ENTER	
G13.G17	to select the bin range
ENTER	

This will now produce a list of the frequencies in each **bin range**; your screen should show the values in Fig 11.3. Note that there are 5 values of £400, 4 values of £480, 3 values of £530, and so on. As the **Mode** is the most commonly occurring value then the **Mode** in this case must be £400.

```
   |  A  ||    B    ||    C    ||   D   ||   E   ||   F   ||    G    ||   H   |
1   No:     FIRST NAME SURNAME   GRADE     BASIC
2
3  ----------------------------------------------------------------------------
4    165    Tony       Adams          1      400                  17
5    290    Viv        Anderson       4      780            614.7059
6    319    John       Barnes         2      480
7    208    Peter      Beardsley      1      400
8    107    George     Best           4      780
9    170    Bobby      Charlton       2      480
10   104    Jack       Charlton       3      530
11   135    Brian      Clough         5     1300
12   101    Nigel      Clough         1      400
13   133    Glenn      Hoddle         1      400                 400        5
14   181    Kevin      Keegan         5     1300                 480        4
15   109    Bobby      Moore          3      530                 530        3
16   180    Bobby      Robson         2      480                 780        3
17   113    Bryan      Robson         3      530                1300        2
18   210    Kenny      Sansom         1      400                            0
19   148    Peter      Shilton        4      780
20   130    Nobby      Stiles         2      480
 TEMP1!G18
Width:  9  Memory:  182  Last Col/Row:H20
  1>
READY F1:Help  F3:Names  Ctrl-Backspace:Undo  Ctrl-Break:Cancel
```

Fig 11.3

As stated earlier, the **Median** can be found by **arranging** the data and then selecting the value which falls in the middle of the values. An alternative way, which will not involve disturbing the data, is to make use of the **frequency distribution** currently displayed on the screen. The **Median** will be found halfway along the list of data if it is sorted into order. The frequency distribution has sorted the data into block order – if you add another column to this distribution to show cumulative frequency you can then calculate the **Median**.

Clear the **Data** command from the entry line and move to cell I13. This column will be used for the cumulative frequency. The first cell can simply show the value from cell H13, so type in either H13 or 5. Now enter the formula **I13+H14** in cell I14 and **copy** it to all other cells in the range I15.I17.

The screen now shows the **cumulative** totals reached at each **bin**. As there are **17** values in total, the **Median** will be found half way through these values (ie: at the 9th value). If you have difficulty grasping this concept, just imagine that the data is sorted into order and that you are asked to select the middle value. The following example may make things a little clearer:

1,2,2,2,3,3,3,4,4,4,5,5,6

The list contains 13 values and the Median will be the value found at the mid-point, ie the 7th position, which is 3.

	B	C	D	E	F	G	H	I
1	FIRST NAME	SURNAME	GRADE	BASIC				
2								
3	----------	----------	----------	----------	----------	----------	----------	----------
4	Tony	Adams	1	400		17		
5	Viv	Anderson	4	780		614.7059		
6	John	Barnes	2	480				
7	Peter	Beardsley	1	400				
8	George	Best	4	780				
9	Bobby	Charlton	2	480				
10	Jack	Charlton	3	530				
11	Brian	Clough	5	1300				
12	Nigel	Clough	1	400				
13	Glenn	Hoddle	1	400		400	5	5
14	Kevin	Keegan	5	1300		480	4	9
15	Bobby	Moore	3	530		530	3	12
16	Bobby	Robson	2	480		780	3	15
17	Bryan	Robson	3	530		1300	2	17
18	Kenny	Sansom	1	400			0	
19	Peter	Shilton	4	780				
20	Nobby	Stiles	2	480				

```
>TEMP1!I14                    Form=I13+H14
Width:  9  Memory:  182  Last Col/Row:I20
  1>
READY F1:Help  F3:Names  Ctrl-Backspace:Undo  Ctrl-Break:Cancel
```

Fig 11.4

11.2 Advanced statistical techniques

SuperCalc can also be used to determine other statistical figures than simple averages . Move the cursor to cell G6 and type in:

STD(E4.E22,614.7059)

This formula uses the **average** from a range of data, and calculates how much deviation there is in the range from the average. The answer should be £273.4373, which means that approximately 70% of all values are either £273.4373 above or below the average. Any figures outside this range (either below or above the average) are outside the **Normal distribution**. The object of this formula is to give the user some idea of what sort of values to expect in the data range – in our example it means that the majority of wages will be between £341.26 and £888.14. There will invariably be some values that fall outside this range (ie: the two people are paid £1,300), but these are considered **exceptions**. Most **standard deviation** formulae will assume that 70% of values will fall within the normal range.

This formula is probably more useful in other areas such as determining the standard deviation for scrap in the manufacture of an product – the standard deviation figure will give the firm some idea of how much scrap can reasonably expect to be produced.

The contents of the standard deviation formula must always follow the format **range** required (eg: E4.E22) and **average** (eg: 614.7059). It is not necessary to type the average in the formula itself – try typing either of the following into cell G7 and you should still get the same standard deviation figure.

STD(E4.E22,G6)

or

STD(E4.E22,AVG(E4.E22))

The **VARIANCE** formula will calculate the population variance in a list. This formula needs to be entered in a similar form to that for standard deviation, in that both the **range** and the **average** need to be included. Type in the following:

VAR(E4.E22,G6)

This value is normally used in manual calculations of the **standard deviation**, and forms part of the formula for obtaining that figure. Its value is actually meaningless as it is the square of the averages. Your answer is therefore not £74,767.97 but £74,767.97^2. As it is impossible to have the square of a £, the answer has no value on its own but is useful as part of more complicated statistical formulae which will require the variance as part of the formula.

A more commonly used statistical calculation is **regression analysis**. This enables you to see how, and whether, one set of values is dependent upon another set of values. A practical illustration of **regression** would be trying to determine the relationship between rainfall and the rate at which grass grows – there is obviously some relationship, and regression analysis will use sets of data on rainfall and growth rates of grass to determine the exact relationship. This example demonstrates the problem with regression analysis, which is that there are often other factors that need to be considered (eg: hours of sunshine).

You can calculate the regression between the two columns shown on the spreadsheet (ie: grade and basic pay). To perform the **regression analysis** you can use the **Data** command again. Before doing so you should first **blank** cells G13.I18 so that you have a clear area on the screen to show the **regression analysis**.

Now type in the following commands:

/	to call up commands
/	to call up the second batch of commands
Data	to select the **Data** command
Analysis	to select the **Analysis** option
Regression	to select the **Regression analysis** option
X-range	to specify the first set of data (Grade)
D4.D20	to select the X-range (use cursor keys if required)
ENTER	

Y-range	to specify the second set of data (Basic pay)
E4.E20)	to select the Y-range
ENTER	
Output	to specify cells for results of analysis
G13	
ENTER	
Go	to perform analysis

The screen will now show the results shown in Fig 11.5. To understand most of these figures you need to understand something more about statistics, but the most important figure is that for **R Squared**, which shows the correlation between the two sets of data. A figure of 1 is a perfect correlation and –1 a perfect negative correlation; a figure of 0 shows that there is no relationship between the two sets of data.

```
  |  C  ||  D  ||  E  ||  F  ||  G  ||  H  ||  I  ||  J  |
1   SURNAME  GRADE   BASIC
2
3   ---------------------------------------------------------------------
4   Adams        1      400          17
5   Anderson     4      780    614.7059
6   Barnes       2      480    273.4373
7   Beardsley    1      400    273.4373
8   Best         4      780    74767.97
9   Charlton     2      480
10  Charlton     3      530
11  Clough       5     1300
12  Clough       1      400
13  Hoddle       1      400                Regression Output:
14  Keegan       5     1300    Constant                       137.3993
15  Moore        3      530    Std Err of Y Est               130.0130
16  Robson       2      480    R Squared(Adj,Raw) .7990419 .8116018
17  Robson       3      530    No. of Observations                  17
18  Sansom       1      400    Degrees of Freedom                   15
19  Shilton      4      780
20  Stiles       2      480    Coefficient(s)       184.4139
 TEMP1!J8
Width:  9  Memory:  181  Last Col/Row:J21
  1>
READY F1:Help  F3:Names  Ctrl-Backspace:Undo  Ctrl-Break:Cancel
```

Fig 11.5

The **R Squared** shows that there is some relationship between the two sets and that the **grade** does have some bearing on **pay**. The relationship is not 1 as there is not a perfect correlation because pay does not increase in direct relation to grade. You can alter the date for **basic pay** to show a perfect correlation.

Move the cursor to cell E4 and enter a new formula to calculate **basic pay**:

D4*400

Now **copy** this formula to all other cells in the range E5.E20. If you repeat the command to calculate regression the correlation should be **1**, as the two sets of data are perfectly matched. To repeat the command you will not have to set the **X** and **Y** ranges or the **output** range as these will remain the same. Simply call up **//Data** and then select:

Analysis
Regression
Go

This will recalculate the **regression** and should show **R Squared** as **1**.

```
   |  C  ||  D  ||  E  ||  F  ||  G  ||  H  ||  I  ||  J  |
1   SURNAME  GRADE    BASIC
2
3   -----------------------------------------------------------------
4   Adams         1     400              17
5   Anderson      4    1600        1035.294
6   Barnes        2     800        542.9288
7   Beardsley     1     400        534.3128
8   Best          4    1600        285490.2
9   Charlton      2     800
10  Charlton      3    1200
11  Clough        5    2000
12  Clough        1     400
13  Hoddle        1     400                 Regression Output:
14  Keegan        5    2000       Constant                      -4.5e-13
15  Moore         3    1200       Std Err of Y Est                     0
16  Robson        2     800       R Squared(Adj,Raw)          1        1
17  Robson        3    1200       No. of Observations                 17
18  Sansom        1     400       Degrees of Freedom                  15
19  Shilton       4    1600
20  Stiles        2     800       Coefficient(s)            400
 TEMP1!J4
Width:  9  Memory:  180  Last Col/Row:J21
  1>
READY F1:Help  F3:Names  Ctrl-Backspace:Undo  Ctrl-Break:Cancel
```

Fig 11.6

11.3 Altering user-defined options

This lesson is principally concerned with statistical uses of spreadsheets. One of the most frequently used methods of interpreting statistical data is by preparing graphs. Lessons 3 and 4 have already demonstrated the more commonly used graphs, but this lesson will introduce some additional types of graph. However, before you proceed you need to enter some new data.

You can begin this section by **zapping** the existing spreadsheet.

The new data to be used in this exercise will be a table showing sales of different products over a six month period.

Enter the heading in A1 as **SALES FOR FIRST 6 MONTHS - 1991**, and then enter the months in cells B2 to G2. Do not type these in, but use the **Data** command to enter them for you. This was covered in Lesson 6, but just to remind you, the sequence is:

/	to call up commands
/	to select the second bank of commands
D	to select **Data**
B	to select the **Block option**
B2.G2	to specify the range
D	to select **Date**
M	to use **Monthly** increments
date(01,31,91)	to enter start value
1	to set step value at one month intervals
ENTER	to accept default end value

The screen should now show the following:

```
   |  A  ||  B  ||  C  ||  D  ||  E  ||  F  ||  G  ||  H  |
 1 SALES FOR FIRST 6 MONTHS - 1991
 2          1/31/91  2/28/91  3/31/91  4/30/91  5/31/91  6/30/91
 3
 4
 5
 6
 7
 8
 9
10
11
12
13
14
15
16
17
18
19
20
 TEMP1!A2
Width:  9  Memory:  184  Last Col/Row:G2
  1>
READY F1:Help  F3:Names  Ctrl-Backspace:Undo  Ctrl-Break:Cancel
```

Fig 11.7

This display would if it showed the month as text rather than numbers, so you can now convert the display to show the month as text. This has also been demonstrated earlier, and involves the **Format** command and the **User-Define** options for the **Date**.

If you call up the **Format, User-Define, Date** options, you will be presented with the existing formats for displaying dates. The ideal display will be one that shows the *month* only and ignores the day and year.

Unfortunately, there is no format for this at present. The closest option is option **4**, which shows the month as text but also includes the year. If you press **4** to select this option it will appear on the *entry line*.

Notice that the *prompt line* states that pressing **F2** will edit the entry. If you press **F2** a cursor will appear which will allow you to **add** or **delete** items from the current display. Use the BACKSPACE key to delete the reference to the year so that the display shows **months** only.

```
USER-DEFINE DATE FORMAT MENU

     Format                Example (using March 8, 1980  7:09:10 AM)
  1.  _BM/BD/YYYY                 3/ 8/1980
  2.  DD-MMM-YY                  08-Mar-80
  3.  DD-MMM                     08-Mar
  4.  MMM-YY                     Mar-80
  5.  MM/DD/YY                   03/08/80
  6.  MM/DD                      03/08
  7.  YY-MM-DD                   80-03-08
  8.  DD.MM.YY                   08.03.80
  T.  BH:TT:SS_AM/PM              7:09:10 AM

      Use M, BM, MM, MMM, MMMM or R  for month
      Use D, BD, DD,                 for day
      Use Y, YY, YYYY                for year
      Use WWW, WWWW                  for weekday
      Use BH, HH                     for hour
      Use BT, TT                     for minute
      Use BS, SS                     for second
      Use A/P, a/p, AM/PM, am/pm     for clock
 TEMP1!A2
Use arrow keys to edit, <RETURN> when finished.
 28>/Format,User-define,Date,4,MMM
EDIT  Edit date string
```

Fig 11.8

When you have done this press **ENTER** and then select **Quit**. You will now have to use the **Format** command to alter the display by specifying that you want to alter **row 2** to **User-Define, Date number 4**.

You can now enter the other data as shown below. Note that the figures do not need to be entered manually as they have been devised with the use of the **RANDOM** statement which can be used to select random numbers between 0 and 1.

Unfortunately, on most occasions where random numbers are required, it will be desirable to have a number larger than 1. This is easily achieved by building the RANDOM statement into another formula.

You will have to type in the text entries in column **A**, but when you have done this move to cell B3 and enter the command **(RAN)*100**. This will produce a random number between 0 and 1 and then multiply it by 100.

You can now use the **Copy** command to copy the formula to all other cells in the block B3.G5. *Note that you are copying a cell to itself (B3) – this should not be done under normal circumstances but is OK here as the numbers are only being invented.*

The display could be improved by formatting numbers to 2 decimal places, use the **FORMAT** command to do this now and your display will then be similar to that in Fig 11.4 (NB: it will not contain the same numbers as your the numbers have been selected at random).

```
   |   A    ||   B    ||   C    ||   D    ||   E    ||   F    ||   G    ||   H   |
1  SALES FOR FIRST 6 MONTHS - 1991
2              Jan       Feb       Mar       Apr       May       Jun
3  Computers  95.33     15.64     54.52     14.57     20.87      8.32
4  Printers   39.79     73.69     10.83     53.73     16.08      9.53
5  Monitors   91.08     84.93     16.79     98.75     43.48     34.96
6
7
8
9
10
11
12
13
14
15
16
17
18
19
20
 TEMP1!A6                                                                  TEXT
Width:  9  Memory:  183  Last Col/Row:G5
  1>
READY F1:Help  F3:Names  Ctrl-Backspace:Undo  Ctrl-Break:Cancel
```

Fig 11.9

11.4 Additional types of graphs

One other use of the **Graphics** command not yet considered is for displaying statistical data. Arguably all graphs are used for displaying statistical data, but some graphs have more use in this area than others. One type of graph not yet examined is the **Hi-Lo** graph.

The **Hi-Lo** graph shows the spread of data in a set of data by drawing a line from the *lowest* value to the *highest* value. The graph can then be used to track a series of measurements over a period of time.

To devise a **Hi-Lo** graph you must first sort the data into highest and lowest values. In order to do this it will be best to **copy** the data into a new block before starting to sort the figures. The one problem with using the **RAN** formula is that the figures will alter every time you use a new command.

To demonstrate this try pressing the function key **F9** – this key is used to force a recalculation. All of your figures should change, as SuperCalc will produce some revised random numbers. The same thing would occur if you tried to copy the figures.

It is possible to prevent SuperCalc from automatically recalculating figures by using the **Global** command. Type in the following:

/	to select commands
G	to select **Global**
E	to select **Evaluation**
W	to select **When**
M	to select **Manual**

This now means that all figures will only be recalculated if the function key **F9** is pressed. This command is more useful when using very large spreadsheets as the constant recalculation when you are entering new figures will slow down operation quite noticeably. The **Manual** option will allow you to enter all data and then reset to **Auto** when the spreadsheet has been set up.

The next step is to sort the values into order. The appearance of the graph would be improved if the figures went down the page rather than across the row. You can alter the layout of **rows** by using **Copy** and selecting the **Transpose** option. Do this now by typing the following

/	to call up commands
C	to select **Copy**
B3.G5	to specify the range to copy from
B8	to specify range to copy to
,	to select **Options**
T	to select **Transpose**

The screen should then show the following:

	A	B	C	D	E	F	G	H
1	SALES FOR FIRST 6 MONTHS - 1991							
2		Jan	Feb	Mar	Apr	May	Jun	
3	Computers	95.33	15.64	54.52	14.57	20.87	8.32	
4	Printers	39.79	73.69	10.83	53.73	16.08	9.53	
5	Monitors	91.08	84.93	16.79	98.75	43.48	34.96	
6								
7								
8		95.33	39.79	91.08				
9		15.64	73.69	84.93				
10		54.52	10.83	16.79				
11		14.57	53.73	98.75				
12		20.87	16.08	43.48				
13		8.32	9.53	34.96				
14								
15								
16								
17								
18								
19								
20								

```
 TEMP1!A6
Width:  9  Memory:  183  Last Col/Row:G13
  1>
READY F1:Help  F3:Names  Ctrl-Backspace:Undo  Ctrl-Break:Cancel          CALC
```

Fig 11.10

This option will only transpose a row into a column and not vice-versa, but most data entered as a column can be transposed by copying it as a block.

The months have not been copied, as the **Hi-Lo** graph would not function properly – this will be explained later. The next step is to sort the data into ascending order. This will be achieved by using the **Arrange** command. You should know how to do this by now so try it yourself. If you are really stuck the sequence of commands is:

/	to call up commands
A	to select **Arrange**
B	to select **Block**
B9.B14	to specify the range
G	to start sort

The data will need to be sorted into order a block at a time; you should repeat the command for the blocks **C9.C14** and **D9.D14**. The data should be sorted into order as follows:

```
     |   A    ||   B    ||   C    ||   D    ||   E    ||   F    ||   G    ||   H    |
  1  SALES FOR FIRST 6 MONTHS - 1991
  2                  Jan       Feb       Mar       Apr       May       Jun
  3  Computers     95.33     15.64     54.52     14.57     20.87      8.32
  4  Printers      39.79     73.69     10.83     53.73     16.08      9.53
  5  Monitors      91.08     84.93     16.79     98.75     43.48     34.96
  6
  7
  8
  9                 8.32      9.53     16.79
 10                14.57     10.83     34.96
 11                15.64     16.08     43.48
 12                20.87     39.79     84.93
 13                54.52     53.73     91.08
 14                95.33     73.69     98.75
 15
 16
 17
 18
 19
 20
TEMP1!C9                          Form=(RAN)*100
Width:  9  Memory:  182  Last Col/Row:G14
  1>
READY F1:Help  F3:Names  Ctrl-Backspace:Undo  Ctrl-Break:Cancel          CALC
```

Fig 11.11

Now that the data has been sorted it will be possible to produce a **Hi-Lo** graph. Call up the **Graphics** command and select **Data**.

The sequence in which data is entered is important in **Hi-Lo** graphs, as SuperCalc will expect the *high* values to be in **Data Series range 1** and the *low* values in **Data Series range 2**. Therefore, you will have to enter the data slightly out of sequence. Your highest values should now be in the range **B14.D14**, so you can enter this as the range for **Series 1**; the lowest values will be in the range **B9.D9** so you can enter this for **Series 2**.

The remaining values will be recorded in sequence, so you can enter the following:

Series 3 B10.D10

Series 4 B11.D11

Series 5 B12.D12

Series 6 B13.D13

Press **Esc** to return to the main **Graphics** command line and select **Type**, then choose **Hi-Lo** from the options displayed.

Before viewing the graph it may be helpful to include an axis label to aid understanding. Select **Labels** and then choose the option for **Axis-labels**. The **X-Axis** should show the titles of each item, and these titles appear in the range **B8.D8** (ie; Computers, Printers, Monitors) if you want to be sure about this use the **F4** key to select the range.

If you now select **View** the screen should show:

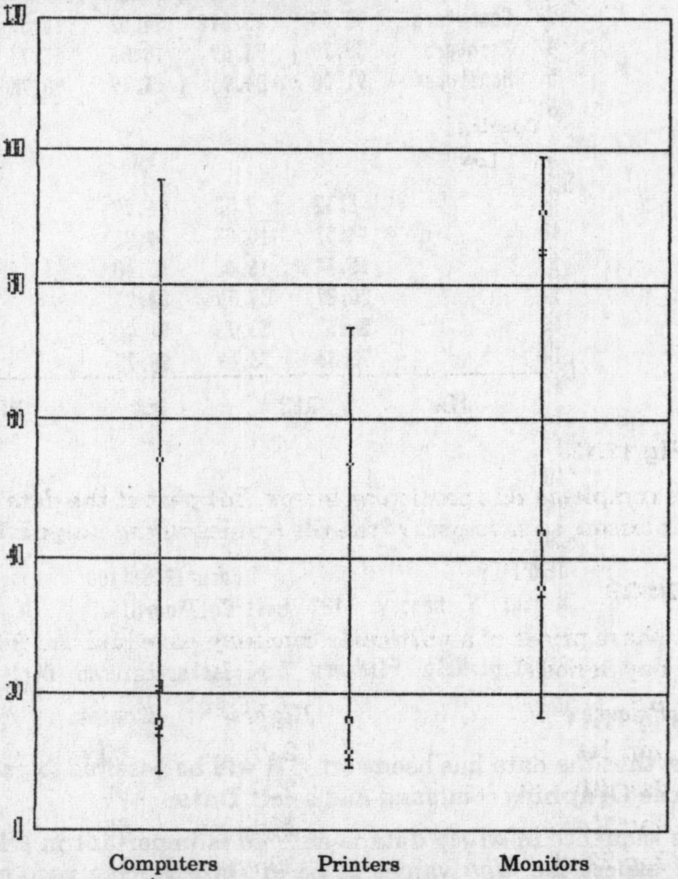

Fig 11.12

The graph shows the various values recorded for sales of each item, sorted into order.

This is not really a suitable application for **Hi-Lo** graphs as they are usually used to measure changes in stock exchange prices over a period of days. Consequently, each line would relate to the same share but a new line would be used to record the changes in prices during different days.

The following graph records price changes for a particular share over a period of five days.

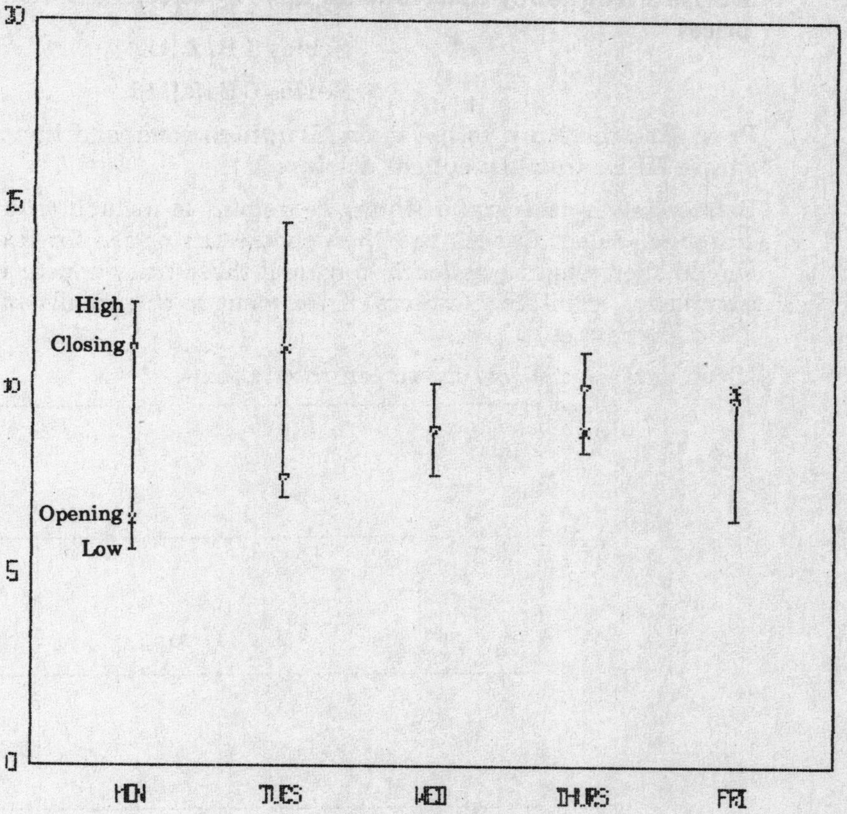

Fig 11.13

This completes this particular lesson, but part of the data used will be required in a later lesson, so save part of the file (values in the range **L2.R5** only) as **LESSON11**.

Further exercises

The share prices of a particular company have had the following movements over a five day period.

Prices:	*Highest*	*Lowest*	*Opening*	*Closing*
Jan 1st	210	90	135	167
Jan 8th	220	102	167	190
Jan 15th	190	55	190	154
Jan 22nd	195	150	154	180
Jan 31st	234	130	180	220

You are required to create a table showing the data and then produce a Hi-Lo chart to demonstrate the changes in value. Use formula and statements to enter the data wherever possible.

Also use various statistical formulae to calculate the arithmetic mean price and the median per day and over the month.

Devise a frequency distribution table by selecting suitable intervals for grouping prices.

Lesson 12 *Financial applications*

In this lesson you will see how some of the additional SuperCalc formulae, especially those associated with financial applications, are used. You will also be shown how to improve presentation for producing reports or for exporting files to another package for further editing.

At the end of this lesson you should be able to:

a) use **Investment appraisal** formulae
b) use **Annuity** formulae
c) calculate returns on investment
d) calculate **Depreciation**
e) improve presentation with the use of graphic characters
f) improve presentation of text with **Justify**
g) produce word charts to improve output
h) import and export files to other programs

12.1 Investment appraisal

Investment appraisal is essentially an accounting technique used to determine whether various long-term projects will be *profitable*. The problem with evaluating long-term projects is that the *value* of money changes over a period of time. The clearest evidence of this is in the effect of inflation: £1 receivable in one year's time is highly unlikely to buy as much as £1 today!

Investment appraisal recognises this problem, and a number of tables have been produced with which it is possible to forecast the value of money to be received in future years and indicate the current or present value of these amounts.

SuperCalc has two formulae which can be used to perform these calculations, using the two most common investment appraisal techniques: **Net Present Value** and **Internal Rate of Return**.

12.1.1 Net present values

You can assume that your firm has just budgeted income and expenditure for two new projects, and now wants to evaluate which of the two is likely to produce the best income and *present* values.

All projects to be assessed using investment appraisal techniques will have an **outflow** of funds – the initial investment in the project (eg: cost of a new factory/machinery), and a number of **Inflows** of funds – the budgeted or forecast income over the expected life of the project.

A straightforward calculation would be to simply deduct the outflow from the inflows and select the project with the highest profit.

However, as implied above, money does have a *time-value*, and a project that is not going to make much profit for ten years is unlikely to be as beneficial as one that will make a smaller profit but within three years.

The estimated details of the two projects to be used in this exercise are shown in Fig 12.1. Enter these onto your spreadsheet as shown (column A has been **formatted** to 20 characters wide to accommodate the text):

```
    |          A          ||    B    ||  C  ||    D    ||  E  ||  F  ||  G  |
1                             Project A       Project B
2    Investment                 -100000         -100000
3    Year 1                       12000           35000
4    Year 2                       20000           50000
5    Year 3                       28000           30000
6    Year 4                       50000           20000
7    Year 5                       40000           15000
8
9
10
11
12
13
14
15
16
17
18
19
20
TEMP1!A9
Width: 20  Memory:  184  Last Col/Row:D7
  1>
READY F1:Help  F3:Names  Ctrl-Backspace:Undo  Ctrl-Break:Cancel
```

Fig 12.1

If you add the total returns for each of the proposed projects together, you will notice that both will produce expected inflows of funds of £120,000.

The **Net Present Value** formula will determine which of the two projects produces the most money at *present day prices*. The style of the formula is:

NPV(Discount rate, row/column range)

The **Discount rate** is selected by the user and should indicate the expected *cost* of money over the period of the projects; this will often be interpreted as the expected *bank interest rates* or the rate of *inflation* over the project period.

The discount rate expected for the period of our projects is 10%, so move the cursor to cell A9 and enter **Net Present Value:** .

Now move to cell B9 and enter the formula for Project A as follows (the .1 represents the discount rate of 10%):

NPV(.1,b3.b7)

This should show that the **Net Present Value** of **Project A** is **£107,462.40**, which means that although the project will produce an income of £120,000 over five years, this income will only be worth £107,462.40 at current prices.

```
   |          A        ||    B    ||   C   ||    D    ||   E   ||   F   ||   G   |
1                        Project A           Project B
2  Investment              -100000             -100000
3  Year 1                    12000               35000
4  Year 2                    20000               50000
5  Year 3                    28000               30000
6  Year 4                    50000               20000
7  Year 5                    40000               15000
8
9  Net Present Value      107462.4
10
11
12
13
14
15
16
17
18
19
20
 TEMP1!C9
Width:  9  Memory:  184  Last Col/Row:D9
  1>
READY F1:Help  F3:Names  Ctrl-Backspace:Undo  Ctrl-Break:Cancel
```

Fig 12.2

See if you can enter the formula to calculate the **NPV** of Project B yourself, using cell D9. The answer should be £118,654, which means that **Project B** is the better project as its income at *present day values* is higher.

It is also possible to amend the formula so that it shows the NPV of the surplus (ie profit). As both projects require an investment of £100,000 and will produce income of £120,000, the profit on both is £20,000. If the investment is deducted from the Net Present Value it will be possible to identify the **NPV** of the **profits**.

Move the cursor back to cell B9 and select **Edit** with **/ E**, then press **ENTER** and the formula should appear on the *entry line*. Amend the formula by typing **+B2** at the end of the current entry as shown:

NPV(.1,B3.B7)+B2

The answer should now be £7,462.357, as this is the NPV of the profit from Project A.

```
 |         A        ||   B   ||  C  ||   D   ||  E  ||  F  ||  G  |
1                      Project A      Project B
2  Investment            -100000        -100000
3  Year 1                  12000          35000
4  Year 2                  20000          50000
5  Year 3                  28000          30000
6  Year 4                  50000          20000
7  Year 5                  40000          15000
8
9  Net Present Value    7462.357       118654.0
10
11
12
13
14
15
16
17
18
19
20
TEMP1!B9                     Form=NPV(.1,B3:B7)+B2
Width:  9 Memory:  184  Last Col/Row:D9
  1>
READY F1:Help  F3:Names  Ctrl-Backspace:Undo  Ctrl-Break:Cancel
```

Fig 12.3

See if you can **edit** the formula for Project B in the same way; the answer should be £18,654.03.

12.1.2 Internal rates of return

An alternative investment appraisal technique is **Internal Rate of Return** (or IRR). This method recognises that it is difficult to accurately predict discount rates for the future, and instead of trying to predict cash values at various discount rates it simply determines the lowest discount rate which will be acceptable before projects start to make a *loss* at *present values.*

The contents of the formula will be as follows:

IRR(Guess, row/column range)

The entry for **Guess** will be an estimate of what discount rate would be likely to produce a negative value for NPV, although when using SuperCalc you can insert any value and the program will do the hard work for you.

We already know from the NPV formula that a discount rate of 10% will result in positive NPVs; therefore, in order to for the future returns to reduce in value, the discount rates will have to be higher than 10% – use 20% as your guess. Enter the heading **IRR** in cell A10 and then enter the following formula in cell B10:

IRR(.2,B2.B7)

Note that you have to include the investment in the **column range** when using this formula. The answer is .1234910, which means that Project A will produce positive net present values providing that future discount rates are less than 12.34%.

```
   |          A         ||    B     ||  C  ||    D     ||  E  ||  F  ||  G  |
1                         Project A          Project B
2   Investment             -100000            -100000
3   Year 1                   12000              35000
4   Year 2                   20000              50000
5   Year 3                   28000              30000
6   Year 4                   50000              20000
7   Year 5                   40000              15000
8
9   Net Present Value     7462.357           18654.03
10  IRR                   .1234910
11
12
13
14
15
16
17
18
19
20
 TEMP1!C10
Width:  9  Memory:  184  Last Col/Row:D10
  1>
READY F1:Help  F3:Names  Ctrl-Backspace:Undo  Ctrl-Break:Cancel
```

Fig 12.4

See if you can enter the appropriate formula to calculate the **IRR** for **Project B**. The answer should show that the discount rate can go as high as 18.36% before Project B becomes unacceptable.

```
      |        A          ||    B    ||  C  ||    D    ||  E  ||  F  ||  G  |
 1                          Project A      Project B
 2  Investment               -100000        -100000
 3  Year 1                     12000          35000
 4  Year 2                     20000          50000
 5  Year 3                     28000          30000
 6  Year 4                     50000          20000
 7  Year 5                     40000          15000
 8
 9  Net Present Value       7462.357       18654.03
10  IRR                     .1234910       .1836161
11
12
13
14
15
16
17
18
19
20
 TEMP1!E10
Width:  9  Memory:  184  Last Col/Row:D10
  1>
READY F1:Help  F3:Names  Ctrl-Backspace:Undo  Ctrl-Break:Cancel
```

Fig 12.5

12.2 Improving display

The last two figures displayed are supposed to be percentages of 12% and 18%; this is not immediately apparent from the current display.

This could be remedied by multiplying the figures by 100. Move the cursor to cell B10 and select / **Edit**. This will transfer the formula to the *entry line* to await alterations.

As the cursor should be flashing at the end of the line you can simply add ***100** to the end of the formula. The display should now show the answer as **12.34910**.

Whilst this is an improvement as it does now show the answer as 12%, it still contains too many unnecessary decimal places. You should be able to alter this with the **Format** command, but there is another way of altering the number of decimal places with, the **ROUND** statement which has already been mentioned in Lesson 1.

The ROUND statement can be used before any formula and will round off an answer to the desired number of places.

You should still be in B10, so type in the following as the new formula, or use the **Edit** command:

ROUND(IRR(.2,B2.B7)*100)

Make sure that all brackets are closed, otherwise the formula will be interpreted as text.

```
      |        A         ||   B    ||  C  ||   D    ||  E  ||  F  ||  G  |
1                          Project A          Project B
2     Investment             -100000            -100000
3     Year 1                   12000              35000
4     Year 2                   20000              50000
5     Year 3                   28000              30000
6     Year 4                   50000              20000
7     Year 5                   40000              15000
8
9     Net Present Value     7462.357           18654.03
10    IRR                         12           .1836161
11
12
13
14
15
16
17
18
19
20
TEMP1!B10                     Form=ROUND(IRR(.2,B2:B7)*100)
Width:  9  Memory:  184  Last Col/Row:D10
  1>
READY F1:Help  F3:Names  Ctrl-Backspace:Undo  Ctrl-Break:Cancel
```

Fig 12.6

This should show the answer as **12**. the ROUND statement can be used to provide any number of decimal places – in our example it would be acceptable to give the answer to one decimal place. The formula for this will need to be amended to include a **1** as shown:

ROUND(IRR(.2,B2.B7)*100,1)

See if you can enter the appropriate formula for the other project, and use the ROUND statement to round off the NPV values to two decimal places; the formula for **NPV** in **Project A** will be:

ROUND(NPV(.1,B3.B7)+B2,2)

```
        |         A         ||    B    ||    C    ||    D    ||    E    ||    F    ||    G    |
   1                          Project A            Project B
   2  Investment               -100000              -100000
   3  Year 1                     12000                35000
   4  Year 2                     20000                50000
   5  Year 3                     28000                30000
   6  Year 4                     50000                20000
   7  Year 5                     40000                15000
   8
   9  Net Present Value       7462.357             18654.03
  10  IRR                         12.3                 18.4
  11
  12
  13
  14
  15
  16
  17
  18
  19
  20
TEMP1!B10                    Form=ROUND(IRR(.2,B2:B7)*100,1)
Width:  9  Memory:  184  Last Col/Row:D10
  1>
READY F1:Help  F3:Names  Ctrl-Backspace:Undo  Ctrl-Break:Cancel
```

Fig 12.7

12.3 Drawing boxes

Versions 3 onwards of SuperCalc have a graphic facility which will enable the user to draw boxes and various other characters. This facility is useful for improving the final appearance of a spreadsheet before printing.

To examine the various alternatives available you need to call up the SuperCalc HELP screen; press **F1** to load the main **HELP INDEX**.

The item that you require is under the **Keys** section, and is headed **Entering ASCII chars**. Move the cursor to this item and press **ENTER**. The screen should now show the following:

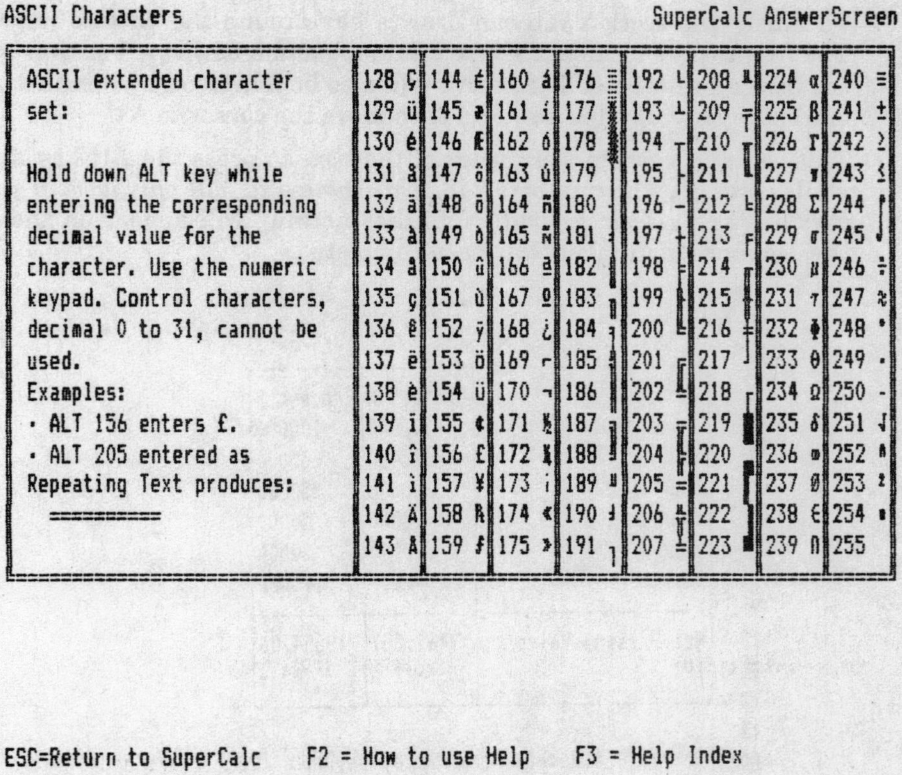

ASCII Characters
SuperCalc AnswerScreen
ASCII extended character set:
Hold down ALT key while entering the corresponding decimal value for the character. Use the numeric keypad. Control characters, decimal 0 to 31, cannot be used.
Examples:
• ALT 156 enters £.
• ALT 205 entered as Repeating Text produces:
══════════
128 Ç 144 É 160 á 176 ░ 192 └ 208 ╨ 224 α 240 ≡
129 ü 145 æ 161 í 177 ▒ 193 ┴ 209 ╤ 225 ß 241 ±
130 é 146 Æ 162 ó 178 ▓ 194 ┬ 210 ╥ 226 Γ 242 ≥
131 â 147 ô 163 ú 179 │ 195 ├ 211 ╙ 227 π 243 ≤
132 ä 148 ö 164 ñ 180 ┤ 196 ─ 212 ╘ 228 Σ 244 ⌠
133 à 149 ò 165 Ñ 181 ╡ 197 ┼ 213 ╒ 229 σ 245 ⌡
134 å 150 û 166 ª 182 ╢ 198 ╞ 214 ╓ 230 µ 246 ÷
135 ç 151 ù 167 º 183 ╖ 199 ╟ 215 ╫ 231 τ 247 ≈
136 ê 152 ÿ 168 ¿ 184 ╕ 200 ╚ 216 ╪ 232 Φ 248 °
137 ë 153 Ö 169 ⌐ 185 ╣ 201 ╔ 217 ┘ 233 Θ 249 ∙
138 è 154 Ü 170 ¬ 186 ║ 202 ╩ 218 ┌ 234 Ω 250 ·
139 ï 155 ¢ 171 ½ 187 ╗ 203 ╦ 219 █ 235 δ 251 √
140 î 156 £ 172 ¼ 188 ╝ 204 ╠ 220 ▄ 236 ∞ 252 ⁿ
141 ì 157 ¥ 173 ¡ 189 ╜ 205 ═ 221 ▌ 237 Ø 253 ²
142 Ä 158 ₧ 174 « 190 ╛ 206 ╬ 222 ▐ 238 ε 254 ■
143 Å 159 ƒ 175 » 191 ┐ 207 ╧ 223 ▀ 239 ∩ 255
ESC=Return to SuperCalc
F2 = How to use Help
F3 = Help Index

Fig 12.8

This screen shows all of the extended characters and the keys used to select them. All of these keys are selected by using the **Alt** key and a combination of numbers from the **numeric keypad**. The **Alt** key must be held down for the whole sequence of numbers selected.

The extended character set will allow you to use a variety of different characters, but is most useful for drawing boxes. It is possible to draw boxes with single, double or thick lines. Examine the screen carefully and see if you can identify the appropriate characters.

The most commonly used characters for single line boxes are:

Alt 196 ─

Alt 218 ┌ ┐ Alt 191

Alt 179 │ │

Alt 192 └ ┘ Alt 217

If you want to sub-divide boxes then the following Alt keys will also be useful:

Alt 194	Alt 193	Alt 195	Alt 180	Alt 197
┬	┴	├	┤	┼

To finish this section you can draw a box around the data to improve the layout. The first task is to **insert** a new column **A** and a new row **1** so that there is room for the box to be entered. The layout will also be improved by **formatting** column **A** to one space only. Do this now and then move the cursor to A1.

This cell will contain the corner of the box. so press the **Alt** key and hold it down whilst pressing the numbers 218. *This command will only work if you use the numbers on the numeric keypad.* Note that nothing will appear on the *entry line* until the sequence of numbers has been completed.

```
     |          B          || D  || F  || G || H || I |
 1
 2   ┌──────────────────┬─────────┬─────────┐
 3   │Investment        │Project A│Project B│
 4   │Year 1            │  -100000│  -100000│
 5   │Year 2            │    12000│    35000│
 6   │Year 3            │    20000│    50000│
 7   │Year 4            │    28000│    30000│
 8   │Year 5            │    50000│    20000│
 9   │                  │    40000│    15000│
10   ├──────────────────┼─────────┼─────────┤
11   │Net Present Value │ 7462.357│ 18654.03│
12   │IRR               │     12.3│     18.4│
     └──────────────────┴─────────┴─────────┘
13
14
15
16
17
18
19
20
TEMP1!E10                    Text="|
Width:  1  Memory:  183  Last Col/Row:G12
  1>
READY F1:Help  F3:Names  Ctrl-Backspace:Undo  Ctrl-Break:Cancel
```

Fig 12.9

The character will appear in the corner of the cell A1. You can the move the cursor to cell B2 and enter ' followed by **Alt 196**. This will enable you to use the **Repeating Text** key to save having to continually press the **Alt** key.

Notice that the box does not join up in column A; this is because these characters are text characters and are therefore automatically **left-justified**. The box can be joined up by using the **Format** command to either shorten the column to one character-width, or to make it right-justified for text.

Now move the cursor to cell A2 and type **Alt 179** followed by **ENTER**. Unfortunately you cannot use the **Repeating Text** therefore to repeat this command down the screen, but you can use the **copy** command to replicate it down to cell A11.

See if you can finish off the box as shown. You will need to **insert** another column C and format both this column and the new column E to one space only.

12.4 Importing/exporting data

SuperCalc now has options for transferring spreadsheet data to and from other programs. This facility will enable the user to use SuperCalc's commands for calculating or ordering data, and then transfer it to a different program to make use of other commands specific to that program.

As there is such a large range of software available it is clearly impossible for SuperCalc to accommodate every single software program. This means that the writers of SuperCalc have attempted to make it virtually compatible with as much software as possible – as it is only virtually compatible there will invariably be some slight problems with the transfer of data; therefore it is always worth saving your SuperCalc file first, so that if there are any major problems you can always start again. As this lesson will be used in the further exercises you should **save** it now as **LESSON12.**

In order to transfer a spreadsheet to another program you will need to use the **Export** command. You can transfer the existing spreadsheet to demonstrate how **Export** works.

Export is in the second bank of commands, so press / twice and then select the **Export** option. You will then see that **Export** has four options; the function of each of these options is as follows:

XDIF	saves data in the **extended Data Interchange Format**
DIF	saves data in the standard **Data Interchange Format**
CSV	saves data as **Comma Separated Values** (for use in BASIC files)
dBase	saves data for use in **dBase 3** files

Data Interchange Format is a standard means of translating data so that it can be transferred between a variety of other programs. The XDIF differs from DIF in that XDIF will copy values and formulae, whereas DIF will only copy values. The XDIF files will have the suffix of SDI.

If you are intending to load the data into a different program but are unsure which option to use it is suggested that you try **DIF** first.

To export the current spreadsheet select **DIF** and then enter the filename as **LESSON12**. Prefix this with **A:** if A: is not the default drive. The next prompt will ask if you want the data transferred column by column or row by row – this will depend upon the nature of the data and whether it is in column order or row order, but for this example the difference is not really relevant. If the data was a budget (as in lesson 5) it would be necessary to select column order so that each month was saved as a distinct column. Select **Colwise** and then select **All** for the range required.

This should export the spreadsheet to a new file called **LESSON12.DIF**; you can check this by using a new command the **File** command. Press / twice and then select **File**.

This command is used to set the default directory, which will enable you to specify where your spreadsheets will be stored, and means that you won't have to type in the A: prefix as all files will automatically go to the correct disk. It will also allow you to display a list of the current files stored on the default drive.

Select **List**, and your screen should now show:

```
  |        B          ||   D     ||    F    ||  G  ||  H  ||  I  |
1
2                        Project A  Project B
3  Investment              -100000    -100000
4  Year 1                    12000      35000
5  Year 2                    20000      50000
6  Year 3                    28000      30000
7  Year 4                    50000      20000
8  Year 5                    40000      15000
9
10 Net Present Value      7462.357   18654.03
11 IRR                        12.3       18.4
12
13
14
15
16
17
18
19
20
LESSON12!E10              Text="
SuperCalc  1-2-3  Print  Macro  Config  All
 13>//File,List,
MENU  List .CAL files
```

Fig 12.10

These options will enable you to identify which files you want displayed. The options will display the following file types:

SuperCalc	displays all **SuperCalc** files (ie: suffix .CAL)
1-2-3	displays all **Lotus** files (ie: suffix .WKS or .WK1)
Print	displays all files saved using the **Output** command (ie: suffix .PRN)
Macro	displays all **Macro** files (ie: suffix .XQT)
Config	displays all **Config** files (ie: suffix .CFG)
All	displays all files regardless of suffix

As the file just exported has a suffix **.DIF** it will only be displayed if you select the **All** option. Press this now and the screen should display a list of all files currently on your disk.

Press **Esc** to continue. This file can be loaded by a variety of other programs by typing the filename **LESSON12.DIF**. You can quit SuperCalc now and try it. You should note that there is no guarantee that the file will be saved in a usable form, and also that it may be necessary to translate the file first by using the new program's equivalent of SuperCalc's **Import** command. To demonstrate this it is usually necessary to re-translate the data. You can now **zap** the existing screen and try to re-load **LESSON12.DIF**.

You should find that you get an error message stating that the **file is not loadable**. This is because the data needs to be **imported** rather than loaded, so that SuperCalc can convert it back into a form which it can read. In order to do this press / twice and then select **Import**. This command has three additional options to those in **Export**, which are:

Numbers	used to load numbers and text from ASCII files
Text	used to load ASCII files as text, one line per cell
VisiCalc	used to load spreadsheets devised in VisiCalc

ASCII is the American Standard Code for Information Interchange and is similar to the Data Interchange Format as it converts data into standard characters.

The option that you require is **DIF**, so select this and enter the filename as **LESSON12**. The next prompt will ask if you want the data imported **Colwise** or **Rowwise**; as it was exported in column order it will be appropriate to import it in the same fashion, so select **Colwise**. You can then select **Replace**.

The screen will now show the following:

```
      |  A  ||  B  ||  C  ||  D  ||  E  ||  F  ||  G  ||  H  |
  1
  2             Project A         Project B
  3   Investmen       -100000           -100000
  4   Year 1            12000             35000
  5   Year 2            20000             50000
  6   Year 3            28000             30000
  7   Year 4            50000             20000
  8   Year 5            40000             15000
  9
 10   Net Prese      7462.357          18654.03
 11   IRR                12.3              18.4
 12
 13
 14
 15
 16
 17
 18
 19
 20
 LESSON12!A1              Text="
 Width:  9  Memory:  183  Last Col/Row:G12
  1>
 READY F1:Help  F3:Names  Ctrl-Backspace:Undo  Ctrl-Break:Cancel
```

Fig 12.11

This demonstrates that there will frequently be a need to modify any files **imported** or **exported**, as there will inevitably be some minor differences between programs. In this instance the file has reloaded everything except the **format** of columns A, C, and E.

12.4.1 Exporting with output

If you check to see whether you can load your **DIF** file onto a word-processor you are unlikely to get very good results, unless your word-processor has a command for importing/translating files. However, if you want to transfer part of a spreadsheet to a word-processing package this can be achieved, for most packages, by using the **Output** command.

Let us suppose that the current spreadsheet will form part of a larger report which is going to be word-processed. This file can be **output** to disk as a file of the type **.PRN** which will enable it to be read (ie; loaded) by most other programs.

Before you use the **Output** command for this sort of purpose it is always worth turning the border display **off** – this will save having to delete it with your word-processor.

.PRN files are similar to **.XQT** files in that they cannot be edited in SuperCalc, so you should always **save** your file before you **output** it. Remove the border and save the file as **LESSON12**.

To create a file of type **.PRN** enter the following:

/	to select commands
Output	to select **Output**
File	to select **File**
LESSON12	to specify filename
Range	to select **Range**
All	to designate range
Go	to select **Go**

This will automatically create a file with a suffix of **.PRN**, so this file will be different from the file previously saved which will have a suffix **.CAL**.

If you want to load this file onto another program remember to type the full name of **LESSON12.PRN**.

12.4.2 Exporting graphs

Comprehensive though SuperCalc may be, there is still one area that the makers have overlooked. This is that there is no way of exporting graphs to load into word-processing programs. One of the main reasons for this is that most word-processors cannot handle graphic data; however, it is possible to produce files that contain the graphs only that can be loaded onto other programs.

The principle use of such files will be for the production of colour slides or overhead projector transparencies. It is also possible to export graphs as Lotus PIC files which can be loaded by Lotus or other software.

To export graphs in this fashion you will need to use the **Graphics, Global, Device** command. To demonstrate this, **load** the file **LESSON5** which contains a simple break-even graph (if you no longer have this file any file with a graph will suffice).

Once this file has loaded, select **Graphics** and press **View** to ensure that the graph is still on file. If it is you can then select **Global, Drivers** from the **Graphics** options. This will produce a list of three additional options:

Normal	this will send charts to the normal device (ie: a printer)
PIC-file	this will send graphs to a PIC file (a Lotus graphics file)
CGI	this will send graphs to *computer graphics interface* devices which are used for taking slides, photographs or specialist output devices

	A	B	C	D	E	F	G	H
1	Break-Even Analysis							
2	----------	----------	----------	----------	----------	----------	----------	----------
3	Units	Fixed	Variable	Total	Revenue	Profit/		
4	Produced	Costs	Costs	Costs		Loss		
5	----------	----------	----------	----------	----------	----------	----------	----------
6	0	20,000	0	20,000	0	(20,000)		
7	1,000	20,000	3,000	23,000	5,000	(18,000)		
8	2,000	20,000	6,000	26,000	10,000	(16,000)		
9	3,000	20,000	9,000	29,000	15,000	(14,000)		
10	4,000	20,000	12,000	32,000	20,000	(12,000)		
11	5,000	20,000	15,000	35,000	25,000	(10,000)		
12	6,000	20,000	18,000	38,000	30,000	(8,000)		
13	7,000	20,000	21,000	41,000	35,000	(6,000)		
14	8,000	20,000	24,000	44,000	40,000	(4,000)		
15	9,000	20,000	27,000	47,000	45,000	(2,000)		
16	10,000	20,000	30,000	50,000	50,000	0		
17	11,000	20,000	33,000	53,000	55,000	2,000		
18	12,000	20,000	36,000	56,000	60,000	4,000		
19	13,000	20,000	39,000	59,000	65,000	6,000		
20	14,000	20,000	42,000	62,000	70,000	8,000		

```
LESSON5!C6          U1      Form=A6#3
Quit  Normal  PIC-file  CGI
 27>//Graphics,Global,Drivers,
MENU  Global device quit
```

Fig 12.12

Select the option for **PIC-file** and then enter the filename as **graph**. Nothing will appear to happen, but the program has now been set up so that when you select **Plot** from the **Graphics** menu the graph will be sent to a file called **graph.pic** instead of to the printer.

You can test this now by selecting the **Plot** option from the **Graphics** menu or pressing **Alt** and **F10**. The file should now be saved on your disk.

This file can be loaded by Lotus, or you can try and load it into a *desk top publishing* or word-processing program (be warned that most word-processors will not be able to load it properly).

12.5 Other financial functions

There are still a number of financial functions not yet considered. Although these are described by SuperCalc as financial functions, they differ from Net Present Value and Internal Rate of Return, as the majority are concerned with payments rather than income and also relate more to an individual's finance than to an organisation's.

12.5.1 Calculating interest payments

In order to demonstrate these functions you can first **zap** the existing spreadsheet. SuperCalc now has quite a range of formulae for computing returns or payments on investments/loans. Most of the formulae can be used to determine income from investments or payments on loans; the only difference is whether you are viewing the answer from the position of a borrower or lender. The first formula will calculate the monthly repayment due on a mortgage. The formula follows the sequence:

PMT(amount, rate, term)

so these three items need to be entered on the screen. Type in the following details:

```
     |   A    ||   B    ||   C    ||   D    ||   E    ||   F    ||   G    ||   H    |
 1   Mortgage     75000
 2   Rate           .12
 3   Period         240
 4
 5   Payment
 6
 7
 8
 9
10
11
12
13
14
15
16
17
18
19
20
 LESS12A!A6
Width:  9  Memory:  184  Last Col/Row:B5
   1>
READY F1:Help  F3:Names  Ctrl-Backspace:Undo  Ctrl-Break:Cancel
```

Fig 12.13

This shows that the amount to be borrowed is £75,000 at an annual rate of interest of 12%, and the mortgage is to be spread over 20 years (20 years × 12 months = 240 months). Note that the **term** needs to be expressed monthly. Also, if you enter the rate as **12%** it will be interpreted as *text*, therefore all % figures must be entered as decimals (ie: .12).

Most of the financial functions will assume that the **period** and **interest rate** is expressed *monthly* – if you use these formulae and get an answer which is obviously incorrect then it will usually be because you have entered one of these items as an annual amount. The interest rate in this example has been shown as an annual amount as this makes more sense, but the formula will divide it into a monthly rate.

Move the cursor to cell A5 and enter the heading **Payment**, then move to cell B5 and enter the formula as:

PMT(B1,B2/12,B3).

This should show that the monthly repayment on this mortgage is £825.8146.

It is also possible to compute the outstanding balance owing on the mortgage if the number of payments (periods passed) is known. In this case you can assume that the number of periods is 24 (ie: two years). The sequence for this formula is **Balance(present value, rate, term, periods)**.

Move the cursor to cell A6 and enter the heading **Balance**, then move to cell and enter the formula as:

BALANCE(B1,B2/12,B3,24)

This should show that the current amount outstanding is £72,955.02.

The first two sections of this lesson considered the Net Present Values of future income; the **FV** or **Future Value** formula works the opposite way around and will determine the future value of amounts paid now. This formula can be used to determine the future value of the total payments made on the mortgage. The sequence is **FV(payment, rate, term)**. Enter the heading **FV** in cell A7 and then enter the formula in cell B7 – see if you can determine the formula for yourself (the correct formula is shown after the screen display).

```
     | A       || B      || C || D || E || F || G || H |
1     Mortgage    75000
2     Rate          .12
3     Period        240
4
5     Payment  825.8146
6     Balance  72955.02
7     FV       816941.5
8
9
10
11
12
13
14
15
16
17
18
19
20
 TEMP1!B7                          Form=FV(B5,B2/12,B3)
Width:  9  Memory:  220  Last Col/Row:B7
  1>
READY F1:Help  F3:Names  Ctrl-Backspace:Undo  Ctrl-Break:Cancel
```

Fig 12.14

The correct formula is:

FV(b5,b2/12,b3)

There may be occasions when the rate of interest is not known. The interest rate can be determined in two ways: the **Anrate** formula calculates the annual rate of interest (as opposed to the APR), and the **Rate** formula calculates the periodic interest rate required for the *present value* to grow to the *future value* in term periods (NB: this inevitably means that both will be slightly different from the declared rate).

The **Anrate** formula follows the sequence **ANRATE(payment, present value, term)** and the **Rate** formula follows the sequence **RATE(future value, present value, term)**.

Enter the headings **Annual** and **Rate** in cells A8 and A9, and then enter the following formula in cells B8 and B9:

B8 **ANRATE(B5,B1,B3)**

B9 **RATE(B7,B1,B3)**

Note that neither of these produce the same rate as that in B2, and that they both appear to show the same rate. They do not show the same rate as that in B2 because they are calculated in a slightly different way and they are in fact slightly different, but the difference is limited to a few decimal places.

It is also possible to calculate how much interest has been paid so far on a mortgage. This uses the formula **PAIDINT** which should contain the following **PAIDINT (present value, rate, term, periods)**. Enter the heading **Paid int** in cell A10 and the formula in cell B10 (the number of periods paid is 24 as before).

PAIDINT(B1,B2/12,B3,24)

The financial formulae not yet considered are mostly variations on the formulae examined so far, and will calculate items such as interest paid per period, amount of principal repaid in period, etc. There are also others that calculate missing figures. One example of this type is the **Term** formula. This assumes that the monthly payment, rate of interest and future value are known, but not the number of periods. This follows the sequence **TERM(payment, rate, future value)**, you can enter the heading **Term** in cell A11 and the following formula in cell B11:

TERM(b5,b2/12,b7)

```
    |   A    ||   B    ||   C    ||   D    ||   E    ||   F    ||   G    ||   H    |
 1   Mortgage     75000
 2   Rate           .12
 3   Period         240
 4
 5   Payment   825.8146
 6   Balance   72955.02
 7   FV        816941.5
 8   Annual         .01
 9   Rate           .01
10   Paid int  17774.57
11   Term           240
12
13
14
15
16
17
18
19
20
 LESS12A!D6
Width:  9  Memory:  184  Last Col/Row:B11
  1>
READY F1:Help  F3:Names  Ctrl-Backspace:Undo  Ctrl-Break:Cancel
```

Fig 12.15

Most of the other financial formulae are devised in a similar way and you should now be capable of entering them yourself.

12.5.2 Calculating depreciation

However, there are three additional formulae included under the heading of *financial formulae* that relate to accounting functions. These are the formulae for determining depreciation.

You do not need the existing data anymore so you can **zap** the current screen.

SuperCalc has formulae for calculating depreciation in three different ways, but all three formulae require the same basic data which is: the **cost** of the asset, its **disposal** or salvage value at the end of its useful life and the estimated **life** of the asset.

You can now devise a short spreadsheet to calculate the depreciation on an asset using each of the three methods. Enter the following as the basic data:

```
    |  A  ||  B  ||  C  ||  D  ||  E  ||  F  ||  G  ||  H  |
 1  Cost Price          20000
 2  Disposal value       2000
 3  Life (years)            5
 4
 5
 6
 7
 8
 9
10
11
12
13
14
15
16
17
18
19
20
LESS12B!A5
Width:  9  Memory:  184  Last Col/Row:C3
  1>
READY F1:Help  F3:Names  Ctrl-Backspace:Undo  Ctrl-Break:Cancel
```

Fig 12.16

This shows that you have just acquired an asset for £20,000 and that you will keep it for five years; at the end of the five years the estimated scrap/disposal value of the asset is £2,000.

The next step is to create some columns to show the depreciation per year. Enter the heading **Year** in cell A5 and use the **Data** command to create a **block** of numbers in the range **A6.A10** as follows:

/	to call up commands
/	to call up the second level of commands
D	to select **Data**
B	to select **Block**
A6.A10	to select the range
N	to select **Number**
1	to select start number
ENTER	
1	to select step
ENTER	

99999 to accept default stop value
ENTER

This should show years 1 to 5 in the cells A6 to A10. You can also **format** row **5** to show **text centre** so that all headings, when entered, will be centred.

Now move to cell B5 and enter the heading as **DDB**, short for *Double-Declining Balance* method of depreciation, which is very similar to what is known in the UK and most other countries as the *Reducing Balance* method of depreciation and provides for most depreciation in the first few years of the life of the asset. The formula follows the sequence **DDB (cost, salvage, life, period)** and will automatically adjust itself to ensure that the total depreciation is equal to the cost minus the disposal value.

Move the cursor to cell A6 and enter the formula as follows:

DDB(C1,C2,C3,A6)

The cell reference for A6 is necessary to show that this is period 1. The screen should show that depreciation in year 1 is £8000.

This formula can now be **copied** to all other cells in the range **A7.A10** so that depreciation can be calculated for each year. You should be able to do this for yourself.

```
    |  A  ||  B  ||  C  ||  D  ||  E  ||  F  ||  G  ||  H  |
 1  Cost Price          20000
 2  Disposal value       2000
 3  Life (years)            5
 4
 5     Year     DDB
 6      1        8000
 7      2       ERROR
 8      3       ERROR
 9      4       ERROR
10      5       ERROR
11
12
13
14
15
16
17
18
19
20
 LESS12B!B6               Form=DDB(C1,C2,C3,A6)
Width:  9  Memory:  184  Last Col/Row:C10
  1>
READY F1:Help  F3:Names  Ctrl-Backspace:Undo  Ctrl-Break:Cancel
```

Fig 12.17

Unfortunately, the new cells are marked as **ERROR** – if you check the formula for each cell you should be able to see why.

The **Copy** command has upgraded each of the cell references as it has copied the formula, and consequently the cell references are now all wrong. It would be possible to correct this by selecting **Ask** for adjustment when copying, but there is another way around this problem. SuperCalc will allow you to make cells **absolute reference cells** – these cells will not be altered. This is a very useful function as it means that cell ranges can be fixed permanently.

To make a cell reference **absolute**, all that is needed is the **$** symbol immediately before the cell reference. This can be used in a variety of ways, for example:

$C1	will ensure that the column remains as C, but the row can be altered
C$1	will ensure that the row number remains constant, but the column can be altered
C1	will ensure that both the column and row number remain constant

Therefore, in the formula just entered you wanted the first three cell references to be **absolute**, as it was only cell A6 that would alter. The formula should have been:

DDB(C1,C2,C3,A6)

You could retype this, but it is probably quicker to use the **Edit** command and the **F4** key. Move the cursor back onto cell A6 and select **Edit**. When the formula appears on the *entry line* move along and enter the **$** symbol before each column letter and each row number by pressing the **F4** key. When the formula matches that shown above press **ENTER** and then **copy** the new formula to the range **A7.A10**. The screen should now show:

```
    |  A  ||  B  ||  C  ||  D  ||  E  ||  F  ||  G  ||  H  |
1   Cost Price         20000
2   Disposal value      2000
3   Life (years)           5
4
5      Year     DDB
6       1        8000
7       2        4800
8       3        2880
9       4        1728
10      5         592
11
12
13
14
15
16
17
18
19
20
 LESS12B!B6                  Form=DDB($C$1,$C$2,$C$3,A6)
Width:  9  Memory:  184  Last Col/Row:C10
  1>
READY F1:Help  F3:Names  Ctrl-Backspace:Undo  Ctrl-Break:Cancel
```

Fig 12.18

The second formula for calculating depreciation calculates the *straight line* method of depreciation, and uses the sequence **SLN(cost, salvage, life)**. It is not necessary to include the period with this method as it uses the same amount of depreciation for each year.

Move the cursor to cell C5 and enter the heading as **SLN**, then enter the following formula in cell C6:

SLN(C1,C2,C3)

*NB: You can enter the $ symbol by typing in the formula and then selecting **Edit**, you can then select $ by pressing **F4**.*

You can now copy this formula to the other cells in the range. Note that this method calculates depreciation as £3600 for each year.

The third method of depreciation is known as *Sum-of-the-Years Digits* depreciation, and is probably better known to most users as the **Reducing Balance** method (this is very similar to the DDB method). The formula for this method requires **SYD(cost, salvage, life, period)**. You should be able to enter and copy this formula yourself now; remember that all the cell references except the period will have to be **absolute cell references**. Once you have entered this formula the screen should show:

```
     |  A  ||  B  ||  C  ||  D  ||  E  ||  F  ||  G  ||  H  |
 1   Cost Price            20000
 2   Disposal value         2000
 3   Life (years)              5
 4
 5      Year      DDB       SLN       SYD
 6       1         8000      3600      6000
 7       2         4800      3600      4800
 8       3         2880      3600      3600
 9       4         1728      3600      2400
10       5          592      3600      1200
11
12
13
14
15
16
17
18
19
20
LESS12B!A11
Width:  9  Memory:  183  Last Col/Row:D10
  1>
READY F1:Help  F3:Names  Ctrl-Backspace:Undo  Ctrl-Break:Cancel
```

Fig 12.19

The one thing still missing from this spreadsheet is the total depreciation for each method. All three methods should have a total amount of depreciation of £18,000, but you should put in a total entry just to be sure.

Move the cursor to cell A11 and enter the heading as **Total**. Now move to cell B11 to enter the **SUM** formula. You do not need to work out which cells are needed as you can **point** to them in the same way that you do with other commands.

Type in **SUM(** and then press **F4**; the current cell should appear on the *entry line*. Move the cursor up to cell B6 by using the cursor movement keys and then press **.** , then move back to the bottom cell in the range (B10). **Do not** press ENTER but press **)** instead, then **ENTER**. The command should now be entered as **SUM(B6.B10)** and you can copy this to the other two columns.

```
   |    A    ||    B    ||    C    ||    D    ||    E    ||    F    ||    G    ||    H    |
 1  Cost Price             20000
 2  Disposal value          2000
 3  Life (years)               5
 4
 5     Year      DDB       SLN       SYD
 6       1       8000      3600      6000
 7       2       4800      3600      4800
 8       3       2880      3600      3600
 9       4       1728      3600      2400
10       5        592      3600      1200
11  Total       18000     18000     18000
12
13
14
15
16
17
18
19
20
LESS12B!A11                 Text="Total
Width:  9  Memory:  183  Last Col/Row:D11
  1>
READY F1:Help  F3:Names  Ctrl-Backspace:Undo  Ctrl-Break:Cancel
```

Fig 12.20

12.6 Improving display of text

Many SuperCalc applications will include some text, it may simply be a heading or it could involve some detailed explanation of the figures shown in the spreadsheet. Headings do not normally create a problem as they will generally be brief and are unlikely to take up more than one line. Explanations, however, can be a problem as they will frequently scroll off the screen.

Text display can be improved by the use of the **Justify** command. Clear the existing spreadsheet with **Zap** and then type the following text entries in the appropriate cell (do not worry about the display at this point):

A1 FINANCIAL FUNCTIONS

A3 SuperCalc contains the following Financial Functions for the following areas:

A5 INVESTMENT APPRAISAL TECHNIQUES: including NPV and IRR

A7 MORTGAGE REPAYMENT AND LOANS: including payments, rate of interest and periods

Not all of this text will fit on to the screen; you could try and guess where the entry should be broken-off and try and reform the text yourself, but it is easier to allow SuperCalc to do it for you.

Press / and then select **Justify**. This will give you three options: **Single** will justify text over a range until a non-text cell is encountered, **Multiple** will justify text over a range and will continue until two consecutive non-text cells are encountered, and **Word-wrap** will let you type continuously without having to press **ENTER**.

You will now examine each of these options in turn, starting with **Justify, Single**. Select this option, and when asked for the **range**, enter **A1.D14** (you can use the cursor movement keys). The next prompt will ask whether you want the text to be **Left, Right or Centre** justified – select **Left**.

Nothing will happen on this occasion because the first text item in this range (A1) was already within the range specified, and **Justify, Single** stops at the first non-text cell (ie: A2).

Try **Justify, Single** again, but this time select the range as **A3.D14**, still **Left** justified. The screen should now show the following:

```
     |  A   ||  B   ||  C   ||  D   ||  E   ||  F   ||  G   ||  H   |
  1   FINANCIAL FUNCTIONS
  2
  3   SuperCalc contains the following
  4   Financial Functions for the
  5   following areas:
  6
  7   INVESTMENT APPRAISAL TECHNIQUES: including NPV and IRR
  8
  9   MORTGAGE REPAYMENT AND LOANS: including payments, rate of interest and p
 10
 11
 12
 13
 14
 15
 16
 17
 18
 19
 20
LESS12B!A8
Width:  9  Memory:  184  Last Col/Row:A9
  1>
READY F1:Help  F3:Names  Ctrl-Backspace:Undo  Ctrl-Break:Cancel
```

Fig 12.21

The second line of text has been justified within the new range and a new row 5 has automatically been inserted. Once again the command stopped at this point as it encountered a non-text cell (A5).

This example is possibly more unusual than most as it is composed entirely of text entries, so the **Justify, Single** command has limited use. To reform all text in one go you will have to use the **Justify, Multiple** command. Type in the following:

/	to call up commands
J	to select **Justify**
M	to select **Multiple**
A1.E14	to specify the range
L	to select **Left** justify

This should reform all of the text in one go; note that this will only be the case where there is no more than one blank line between text entries. Also, the range has increased by one column so that the entries cannot run into one another.

The final **Justify** command is for **Word-wrap**. This allows you to justify text as you enter it rather than tidy it up later. Your screen has ignored the depreciation functions so you can use the **Word-wrap** facility to enter another line of text.

Type in the following commands:

/	to call up commands
J	to select **Justify**
W	to select **Word-wrap**, then **Range**
A12.E15	to specify the range
G	to select **Go**

Now type in the following (you should find that the entry line will clear part way through when **Word-wrap** reaches the end of column E):

DEPRECIATION: including Double-Declining, Straight-Line, Reducing Balance methods

```
   |  A  ||  B  ||  C  ||  D  ||  E  ||  F  ||  G  ||  H  |
1  FINANCIAL FUNCTIONS
2
3  SuperCalc contains the following Financial
4  Functions for the following areas:
5
6  INVESTMENT APPRAISAL TECHNIQUES: including
7  NPV and IRR
8
9  MORTGAGE REPAYMENT AND LOANS: including
10 payments, rate of interest and periods
11
12 DEPRECIATION: including Double-declining, Straight-line,
13 Reducing Balance methods
14
15
16
17
18
19
20
 LESS12B!A14
Width:  9  Memory:  184  Last Col/Row:A13
 1>
WRAP  F1:Help  F3:Names  Ctrl-Backspace:Undo  Ctrl-Break:Cancel
```

Fig 12.22

12.7 Word charts

The example currently on the screen is not a particularly good use of a spreadsheet from the point of view of commands used, but does provide a good basis for the final topic in this chapter, which is the production of **Word Charts**. SuperCalc has one advantage over many word-processing programs in that it can make very basic printers produce high quality printing through graphics characters. This means that whilst your word-processing program may only be capable of producing a very limited number of fonts, most printers will be capable of producing a very large range of fonts from SuperCalc's **Graphics** commands.

The **Word Chart** option is especially designed for the production of simple but informative charts (such as those used on overhead projector transparencies).

To produce a word chart of the current screen you will first have to select the **//Graphics** command. When this appears select **Type** and then select the last option on this list which should be **Word**.

You will now need to specify the **Data**, so select this option. Word charts can be arranged in 1, 2 or 3 columns. This spreadsheet will only require one column for the data, so if you move into the box for **Data series 1** you can enter the range as **A6.A13** (if you select this range with **F4** you will notice that it only includes the first cell reference for each block of text – this is because each text entry is still only using one cell).

You can make some alterations to the appearance of the text and then alter some of the **Word** options on this same menu: change the **Paragraph Bullet** to **Unfilled box** (move the cursor to this item and then press **ENTER**, then select **Unfilled box** from the sub-menu); if you have a colour printer or screen then you can also change the colour.

```
                      WORD CHART APPEARANCE AND OPTIONS MENU       TYPE: WORD

                      COLUMN 1        | COLUMN 2       | COLUMN 3
WORD DATA RANGE       A6:A13          |                |

WORD OPTIONS
 Color                2Green          | Black          | Black
 Font                 Auto            | Auto           | Auto
 Size                 Auto            | Auto           | Auto
 Justify              Auto            | Auto           | Auto
 Indent               0               | 0              | 0
 Hang Indent          0               | 0              | 0
 Paragraph Bullet     UnfilledBulle   | FilledBullet   | FilledBullet
 Line Bullet          Dash            | Dash           | Dash



2Green
 17>//Graphics,Data,
MENU  F4:Point  F5:Row/Col  F6:Copy
```

Fig 12.23

This chart will also need some headings (the entries in cells A1 and A3). To enter headings return to the main **Graphics** command line and then select **Labels, Titles.**

The **Top Title** will be cell reference **A1**, so you can enter this by using the **F4** key; the **Subtitle** will be cell A3, so enter this in the same way.

You can alter the font and size of the headings from the **Titles options** menu which is called up by pressing **PgDn**. Alter the font for **Top Title** to **RomanBold** and the **Subtitle** to **Block** size **8**.

If you now press **F10** you should have the following word chart.

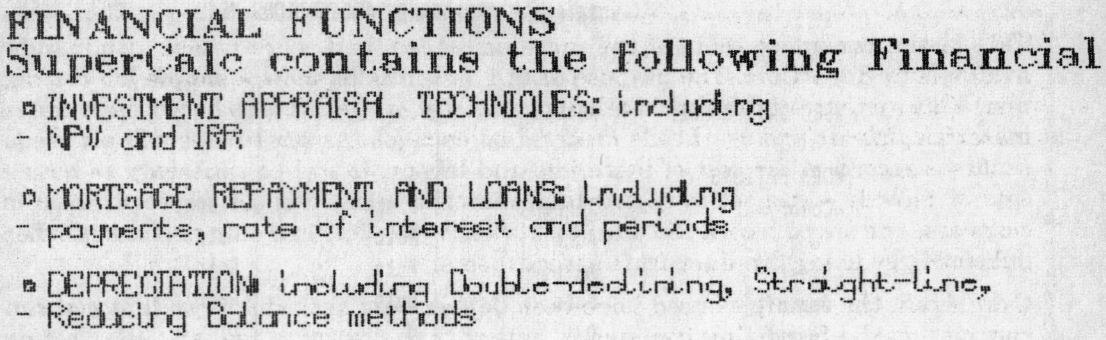

FINANCIAL FUNCTIONS
SuperCalc contains the following Financial
▫ INVESTMENT APPRAISAL TECHNIQUES: including
- NPV and IRR
▫ MORTGAGE REPAYMENT AND LOANS: including
- payments, rate of interest and periods
▫ DEPRECIATION: including Double-declining, Straight-line,
- Reducing Balance methods

Fig 12.24

The headings are still a little bit too cramped but this can be improved by reselecting **Labels, Titles** and entering the blank cells A2 as the **Top Title 2** and A5 as the **Sub Title 2.**

The word chart can be printed as any other graph by selecting **Plot** or **Alt** and **F10.**

Further exercises

Reload Lesson12 and see if you can add another project to the two already under appraisal. Assume that the investment is still £100,000, but make up your own figures for returns.

When you have added these details and copied the formula see if you can redesign the boxes to produce a double line instead of a single line surround.

The details of the keys to use are displayed on the **Help** screen.

Add some text to the screen and use the **Justify** command to **centre** the text.

Lesson 13 *Job costing*

This lesson considers some of the more advanced, and more recent, commands now available in SuperCalc. The purpose of this lesson is to show a simple job costing system. This system is intended to calculate the cost of specific jobs based upon the cost of materials, labour and overheads incurred on each job. As most firms will also require a separate record of the cost of materials and labour, it will be necessary to have three sets of records – one set to record total material costs, one set to record total labour costs and one set to record the total cost of each job. This can only be accomplished satisfactorily by using three separate spreadsheets.

Once again the examples used have been deliberately kept simple so that you can concentrate on the SuperCalc commands, rather than portray a realistic Job Costing system.

At the end of this lesson you should be able to:

a) devise your own **User-Define** formats
b) multiply tables of data using **Data, Matrix**
c) create multiple-page spreadsheets
d) create linked spreadsheets using **Spreadsheets**

13.1 Creating user-define formats

As previously explained, in order to maintain proper **job costing** records it will be necessary to create three sets of records. The first set will be the records for **materials** used in each job. A stock control program was devised in Lesson 7. The spreadsheet in this example need only record materials *issued* to the various jobs – a more detailed spreadsheet can be devised as a further exercise if required.

The jobs currently being produced by this firm are all given numbers, starting at number 123, and there are three types of materials that can be used in each of the jobs. The materials used are called Widgets, Sprockets and Dongles.

Load SuperCalc and create a spreadsheet with the following details:

```
    |  A  ||  B  ||  C  ||  D  ||  E  ||  F  ||  G  ||  H  |
1             STOCK RECORDS
2
3
4   Job No   Widgets  Dongles  Sprockets    Total
5       123       10       15         5       30
6       124        5        3         2       10
7       125        5        0         2        7
8       126        2       10         8       20
9
10
11
12
13
14
15
16
17
18
19
20
STOCK!B2
Width:  9  Memory:  184  Last Col/Row:E8
  1>
READY F1:Help  F3:Names  Ctrl-Backspace:Undo  Ctrl-Break:Cancel
```

Fig 13.1

The figures under the materials relate to the cost of materials used by each job. The figures in the Total column have been calculated by using a simple SUM statement – you should be able to enter this for yourself.

All of the figures relating to material issues are in monetary terms and, therefore, it may be more appropriate if they were prefixed by a £ sign. If you were to enter them with a £ sign as a prefix then SuperCalc would interpret the figures as text not figures.

It is possible to alter the appearance of the figures by using the User-Define format from the Format command. Call up the Format command and select User-Define, Number. When this appears select **Number 1**.

The current *default* **value for this item is to prefix all numbers with a $ sign. If you now select the item Before you will be presented with three options:**

Default	uses the $ symbol before all numeric entries
None	has no prefix before numeric entries
Enter	allows the user to specify the character to prefix numeric entries

Select Enter and then, when the cursor is flashing on the *entry line*, **type in £ as the new prefix.**

You can now select **Quit** to leave this menu and return to the main **Format** command. Select **Entry** and set the range as **B5.E8** and then choose **User-Define, Number, 1** as the **Format** option. Your screen should now show:

```
    | A || B || C || D || E || F || G || H |
1        STOCK RECORDS
2
3
4   Job No   Widgets  Dongles  Sprockets    Total
5       123   £10.00   £15.00     £5.00   £30.00
6       124    £5.00    £3.00     £2.00   £10.00
7       125    £5.00     £.00     £2.00    £7.00
8       126    £2.00   £10.00     £8.00   £20.00
9
10
11
12
13
14
15
16
17
18
19
20
STOCK!B2
Width:  9  Memory:  184  Last Col/Row:E8
  1>
READY F1:Help  F3:Names  Ctrl-Backspace:Undo  Ctrl-Break:Cancel
```

Fig 13.2

This file will be needed later to calculate the cost of each job, so you can **save** it now as **STOCK**.

13.2 Multiplying tables

The next spreadsheet required will be for labour costs. Each job is designated by a number between 123 and 126 and each employee has a works number beginning with KKK. As each employee will have some involvement with each job it is necessary to set up a table showing hours worked on each job. **Zap** the existing screen and then type in the following. The **Total** column is again created using a simple **SUM** statement and should ensure that all employees have worked a 40 hour week (enter the formula yourself).

The block underneath the **Hours worked** is used to state the hourly rate of pay of each employee. Unfortunately, each employee is paid at a different rate, which means that it is not going to be easy to calculate the total labour cost of each job. You should use the **Copy** command to copy the employee numbers down to the new block starting at cell A11.

```
   |  A  ||  B  ||  C  ||  D  ||  E  ||  F  ||  G  ||  H  |
1            LABOUR COSTS
2            Hours worked
3  Employee     Job No
4                  123       124       125       126  Total
5  KKK12             5        10        20         5     40
6  KKK13            13         6        11        10     40
7  KKK14             2         8        22         8     40
8  KKK15            10        10        10        10     40
9
10 Rate of pay
11 KKK12           2.5
12 KKK13          1.75
13 KKK14           3.5
14 KKK15             4
15
16
17
18
19
20
 LABOUR!A16
Width:  9  Memory:  184  Last Col/Row:F14
  1>
READY F1:Help  F3:Names  Ctrl-Backspace:Undo  Ctrl-Break:Cancel
```

Fig 13.3

The next step will be to calculate the total labour cost of each job. The first stage in this task will be to enter the **job numbers**. You should be able to **copy** these from the range **B4.E4** and then use the **Transpose** option to enter them in the range starting at A16.

The formula to calculate total cost will the hours worked by each employee multiplied by the rate of pay for each employee; for Job 123 this would involve a formula in the form of:

(B5*B11)+(B6*B12)+(B7*B13)+(B8*B14)

This is not only confusing to look at, but would also require all of the cells in the range **B11.B14** to be marked as **absolute reference cells** if it was intended to copy the formula to calculate the costs of the other three jobs. The proliferation of $ symbols would make this formula appear even more daunting!

A simpler way of calculating costs for this sort of table is to use the **Data, Matrix** command. This command will multiply tables of data such as that shown on the screen, but can only be used where the number of columns is equal to the number of rows.

As you need to multiply four columns (**B, C, D and E**) by four rows (**11, 12, 13 and 14**) it should work. Press / twice and select **Data**. When this appears select the option for **Matrix**.

This command will require three ranges, the first two are the ranges to multiply (in this instance **hours** times **rate of pay**) and the third range is the **output** range for the answers.

Enter **B5.E8** as **range 1** (hours worked) and **B11.B14** as **range 2** (rates of pay), then enter the **output** range as **B16.B19** (the labour cost of each job).

The screen should now show:

```
   |  A   ||  B   ||  C   ||  D   ||  E   ||  F   ||  G   ||  H   |
1               LABOUR COSTS
2               Hours worked
3   Employee       Job No
4                     123      124      125      126  Total
5   KKK12               5       10       20        5       40
6   KKK13              13        6       11       10       40
7   KKK14               2        8       22        8       40
8   KKK15              10       10       10       10       40
9
10  Rate of pay
11  KKK12             2.5
12  KKK13            1.75
13  KKK14             3.5
14  KKK15               4
15
16           123      120
17           124    121.5
18           125      128
19           126    117.5
20
 LABOUR!A16                  Form=123
Width:  9  Memory:  184  Last Col/Row:F19
  1>
READY F1:Help  F3:Names  Ctrl-Backspace:Undo  Ctrl-Break:Cancel
```

Fig 13.4

If you check these figures you should agree that the **Data, Matrix** command has multiplied out all of the figures correctly (and much more simply than the original formula proposed).

These figures will also be required later on, so **save** this file as **LABOUR** and then **zap** the screen again.

13.3 Using multiple spreadsheets

The final part of this project will be to create a record for each Job. The cost of any job will normally consist of three main elements: material costs, labour costs, and a proportion of overheads. The cost of **overheads** can be recovered in a variety of ways, but in this example it will be charged as **£2** per labour hour worked on the Job.

Unfortunately, this means that all of the main figures for the job cost will have to be extracted from another spreadsheet. Up until now you would probably have **quit** the existing spreadsheet and **loaded** the old files to ascertain the appropriate figures. SuperCalc has devised a command called **Spreadsheets** which will enable you to view and alter a maximum of 255 spreadsheets all at the same time (*this figure does depend upon available memory and is highly unlikely to be achieved by most computers – in fact you will almost certainly find that* **Undo** *will be* disenabled *during the next few sections as your computer runs short of memory*).

Enter the following:

/	to select commands
/	to select the second level of commands
S	to select **Spreadsheets**
N	to open a **New** spreadsheet

Nothing especially different will have happened yet, but SuperCalc has opened a new blank spreadsheet (NB: **Ctrl and ENTER** will perform the same function).

You can now enter the following headings on your new spreadsheet:

```
 1||  A  ||  B  ||  C  ||  D  ||  E  ||  F  ||  G  ||  H  |
 1          JOB COSTS
 2
 3          MATERIALS
 4          LABOUR
 5          OVERHEADS
 6
 7          MARK-UP
 8          PRICE
 9
10
11
12
13
14
15
16
17
18
19
20
 TEMP1!1!C3
Width:  9  Memory:  114  Last Col/Row:B8
  1>
READY F1:Help  F3:Names  Ctrl-Backspace:Undo  Ctrl-Break:Cancel
```

Fig 13.5

The first two figures to be included in this spreadsheet are on your previous files **STOCK** and **LABOUR**. You can now open some more spreadsheets so that you can refer to each one without having to close the existing spreadsheet. Before you do that though, it would be wise to **rename** the existing spreadsheet. To give this file a name type in the following:

/	to select commands
/	to select the second level of commands
S	to select **Spreadsheets**
R	to **Rename** the spreadsheet
JOB	to enter the new spreadsheet name

This name should appear in the bottom left-hand corner of the screen, just above the *prompt line*, and has replaced the word **TEMP1**.

You will now have to repeat the **Spreadsheet, New** command to create additional multiple spreadsheets for the files **STOCK** and **LABOUR**. To open a spreadsheet you will first have to create a **new** spreadsheet and then **load** the existing file into it. Follow the instructions below to create a new file for **STOCK**:

/	to select commands
/	to select the second level of commands
S	to select **Spreadsheets**
N	to open a **New** spreadsheet

This will create spreadsheet number 2; don't worry that **JOB** has temporarily disappeared. Now **load** the spreadsheet for **STOCK** in the normal fashion and it should appear on screen as spreadsheet number 2.

```
      |    A    ||    B    ||    C    ||    D    ||    E    ||    F    ||    G    ||    H    |
1              STOCK RECORDS
2
3
4      Job No    Widgets  Dongles  Sprockets     Total
5            123   £10.00   £15.00     £5.00    £30.00
6            124    £5.00    £3.00     £2.00    £10.00
7            125    £5.00     £.00     £2.00     £7.00
8            126    £2.00   £10.00     £8.00    £20.00
9
10
11
12
13
14
15
16
17
18
19
20
STOCK!B2
Width:  9  Memory:  144  Last Col/Row:E8
  1>
READY F1:Help  F3:Names  Ctrl-Backspace:Undo  Ctrl-Break:Cancel  CAPS
```

Fig 13.6

You still need one more spreadsheet for the **LABOUR** file. Press **Crtl** and **ENTER** and this should perform the **Spreadsheet, New** command for you (this is one of SuperCalc's own macros), then **load** the spreadsheet **LABOUR** as normal.

You will now have all three spreadsheets in memory. It is possible to move from one spreadsheet to another by using the **Spreadsheet, GoTo, Next** or **Spreadsheet, GoTo, Previous** commands. Try both of these yourself to see.

A quicker alternative for moving from one spreadsheet to another is to use the **Ctrl** and **+** keys to move to the **next** spreadsheet and the **Ctrl** and **–** keys to move to the **previous** spreadsheet. Try these now, and also see what happens if you continue to press **Ctrl** and **–**.

The main objective in creating these multiple spreadsheets is to copy data from one sheet to another without having to continue opening and closing files. You should now be able to extract the relevant figures from the **STOCK** and **LABOUR** files and transfer them to the **JOB** file.

However, even though this is a very simple example it is clearly not that easy to remember which cells to use. Consequently, the **Spreadsheets** command will allow you to show up to three spreadsheets on the screen at any time. This works in a very similar way to the **Window** command shown in Lesson 5.

As you conveniently only have three spreadsheets you can display all three together. To display multiple spreadsheets select the following.

/	to select commands
/	to select the second level of commands
S	to select **Spreadsheets**
D	to select **Display**
3	to display the maximum three screens

```
STOCK   A  ||  B  ||  C  ||  D  ||  E  ||  F  ||  G  |
1             STOCK RECORDS
2
3
4   Job No   Widgets  Dongles  Sprockets    Total
5         123   £10.00   £15.00      £5.00   £30.00
6         124    £5.00    £3.00      £2.00   £10.00
JOB |   A  ||  B  ||  C  ||  D  ||  E  ||  F  ||  G  ||  H  |
5            OVERHEADS
6
7            MARK-UP
8            PRICE
9
10
LABOUR  A   ||   B  ||   C  ||   D  ||   E  ||   F  ||   G  ||   H  |
4                 123       124       125      126Total
5   KKK12           5        10        20        5       40
6   KKK13          13         6        11       10       40
7   KKK14           2         8        22        8       40
8   KKK15          10        10        10       10       40
9
 LABOUR!B9
Width:  9  Memory:  142  Last Col/Row:F19
  1>
READY F1:Help  F3:Names  Ctrl-Backspace:Undo  Ctrl-Break:Cancel  CAPS
```

Fig 13.7

Notice that the **Spreadsheet, Display** command has an option similar to that used in **Window** which will allow you to move the screen display in **Synchronized** or **Unsynchronized** fashion. This is not relevant in this simple example but you may find it useful in your own work.

Although this command will only display a maximum of three spreadsheets at any one time it is possible to alter the display by using the **Ctrl +** or – keys to replace the files shown (as you only have three spreadsheets this will not work at present).

You can move the cursor from one spreadsheet to another by pressing **Ctrl** and **F6**. Try this now and then move the cursor to cell C3 in the **JOB** file.

This cell should display the cost of materials used in Job 123. If you glance at the other spreadsheets you should be able to identify the relevant figure as being in cell E5 of the **STOCK** spreadsheet.

If you merely entered E5 as the cell reference for **materials** in the **JOB** file it would look for that value in the file **JOB** (currently nil). In order to copy the correct value across it is necessary to specify not just the **cell reference** but also the **spreadsheet name** – this is known as *spreadsheet linking*. In order to copy this value you must follow the sequence **Spreadsheet NAME! CELL REFERENCE**. The value in cell C3 should show:

STOCK!E5

Type this in now and the value should be copied across from the other spreadsheet.

The value for **labour** costs in cell C4 will be similar as it requires the value from cell B16 in the **LABOUR** file (if you cannot see this value in the **LABOUR** file move back into that file and scroll the screen using the normal cursor keys). The entry for this formula will be:

LABOUR!B16

The next item is slightly more complicated. The **overheads** are based on the **labour hours worked** and are charged at **£2.00** per labour hour.

If you examine the screen for **LABOUR** you should be able to see that the hours worked are shown in the range **B5.B8** (you may have to scroll the screen again first).

Ideally, the formula to copy this should be **LABOUR!SUM(B5.B8)**, unfortunately SuperCalc will not allow the formula in this style and it will only allow you to create links that will yield a single value. For this reason SuperCalc's authors suggest that you use **named** ranges for commonly used data so that your formula will be simplified.

However, it is still possible to link the two spreadsheets by carefully planning the formula; the sequence **SUM(LABOUR!B5.B8)** is acceptable.

Alternatively you could return to the **LABOUR** file and create a **named** range called **HOURS1** for the range **B5.B8** in which case the formula would be **SUM(LABOUR!HOURS1)**. The corresponding figures for Job 124 would be **named** as **HOURS2** and so on.

As the total hours needs to be multiplied by £2.00 the final formula will have to be:

(SUM(LABOUR!B5.B8)*2)

The screen should now show:

```
STOCK   A  ||  B  ||  C  ||  D  ||  E  ||  F  ||  G  |
1                STOCK RECORDS
2
3
4    Job No   Widgets  Dongles  Sprockets    Total
5          123   £10.00   £15.00     £5.00  £30.00
6          124    £5.00    £3.00     £2.00  £10.00
JOB |   A  ||  B  ||  C  ||  D  ||  E  ||  F  ||  G  ||  H  |
2
3              MATERIALS      30
4              LABOUR        120
5              OVERHEADS      60
6
7              MARK-UP
LABOUR  A   ||  B  ||  C  ||  D  ||  E  ||  F  ||  G  ||  H  |
4               123     124     125     126Total
5   KKK12         5      10      20       5      40
6   KKK13        13       6      11      10      40
7   KKK14         2       8      22       8      40
8   KKK15        10      10      10      10      40
9
 JOB!C5                     Form=(SUM(LABOUR!B5:B8)*2)
Width:  9  Memory:  142  Last Col/Row:C8
  1>
READY F1:Help  F3:Names  Ctrl-Backspace:Undo  Ctrl-Break:Cancel  CAPS
```

Fig 13.8

The other two spreadsheets are no longer required and the screen can be returned to normal display. The other screens can be shut down in one of three ways:

//Spreadsheet, Display, 1	closes all windows except the current display window
//Spreadsheet, Display, Zoom, Yes	displays the current display window only
Ctrl and **F7**	same as **Zoom** above

The main difference between **Display, 1** and **Display, Zoom** is that **Zoom** is a *toggle* switch and will switch the display **on** and **off**. The **Ctrl** and **F7** keys are merely macros for this command. Try pressing **Ctrl** and **F7** a couple of times to see what happens.

Return to the display of **JOB** only and complete the entries for this job. The line below **OVERHEADS** is to show the sum of materials, labour and overheads.

The **MARK-UP** is to be 20% added to the value in C6, and the **PRICE** will be cell C6 plus the mark-up. Your answers should be as follows:

```
   |  A  ||  B  ||  C  ||  D  ||  E  ||  F  ||  G  ||  H  |
1           JOB COSTS
2
3           MATERIALS       30
4           LABOUR         120
5           OVERHEADS       60
6                          210
7           MARK-UP         42
8           PRICE          252
9
10
11
12
13
14
15
16
17
18
19
20
 JOB!C9
Width:  9  Memory:  142  Last Col/Row:C8
  1>
READY F1:Help  F3:Names  Ctrl-Backspace:Undo  Ctrl-Break:Cancel  CAPS
```

Fig 13.9

The **Spreadsheets** command also has an option for **Save.** If you select this item it will save **all** of your files now – you should note that it will ask you if you want the files to **Backup** or **Overwrite** – select **Overwrite** to save disk space.

This will ensure that all files are saved with their *links* intact. Note that if you intended to use these files again you will have to **load** each one separately. The reason for this is that it is not really necessary to have each file in memory as the spreadsheet links will ensure that any alterations are made to affected files.

13.4 Multiple pages

As well as having multiple spreadsheets it is possible to have single spreadsheets with multiple pages. These are sometimes preferable to multiple spreadsheets as it is normally possible to have them all in memory at one time, and they will all load as one spreadsheet.

The **JOB** file currently only contains details for the one job (number 123). There is clearly a need for additional records to show the costs of the other three jobs; however, it is not worth having duplicate spreadsheets, so you can create some additional pages in the **JOB** file.

Pages can be amended using a variety of normal commands, to which you may already have noticed some reference. To insert new pages into an existing file you simply use the **Insert** command. You want three new pages for jobs 124, 125 and 126. Type in the following:

/	to call up commands
I	to select **Insert**
P	to select **Page**
2.4	to specify new pages 2, 3 and 4

If you press the **Ctrl** and **+** keys you should find that you now have three additional pages to this file – each page is distinguished by its own page number in the top left-hand corner.

Unwanted pages can be removed with the **Delete** command, and single pages can be printed with the **Output** command.

You can also use the **Copy** command in multiple-page files. Each page will need to contain the same text and formulae as page 1. This can be copied one page at a time as follows:

/	to call up commands
C	to select **Copy**
B1.D8	to select the range to copy from
2!B1	to specify range to copy to as page 2 cell B1

```
      2|  A  ||  B  ||  C  ||  D  ||  E  ||  F  ||  G  ||  H  |
 1          JOB COSTS
 2
 3          MATERIALS        30
 4          LABOUR          120
 5          OVERHEADS        60
 6                          210
 7          MARK-UP          42
 8          PRICE           252
 9
10
11
12
13
14
15
16
17
18
19
20
  JOB!2!A1
Width:  9  Memory:   99  Last Col/Row:C8
  1>
READY F1:Help  F3:Names  Ctrl-Backspace:Undo  Ctrl-Break:Cancel  CAPS
```

Fig 13.10

You will need to repeat this procedure to **copy** the entries to the same range on pages 3 and 4. These will need to separate actions.

When you have copied the structure to pages 3 and 4 return to Page 2 to amend the formula. The formula on all of the pages at present refers to the cell references for **Job 123**. Page 2 is the costs for **Job 124** so you can enter **124** in cell E1 first.

Now move to cell C3; this should now show the cell reference from the **STOCK** file for the materials used in **Job 124**. If you press **Ctrl** and **F7** you should get the multiple screen display again. Notice that this time your pages are included in the screen display. If you press **Ctrl** and **+** or **–** you can alter the files shown, however, you will not be able to get **page 2** and **STOCK** on the screen together.

```
    2|  A   ||  B   ||  C   ||  D   ||  E   ||  F   ||  G  |
    1             JOB COSTS         Job 124
    2
    3             MATERIALS       30
    4             LABOUR         120
    5             OVERHEADS       60
    6                            210
  JOB |  A   ||  B   ||  C   ||  D   ||  E   ||  F   ||  G   ||  H  |
    1           JOB COSTS         Job 123
    2
    3           MATERIALS       30
    4           LABOUR         120
    5           OVERHEADS       60
    6                          210
LABOUR  A   ||  B   ||  C   ||  D   ||  E   ||  F   ||  G   ||  H  |
4                 123      124      125      126Total
5  KKK12            5       10       20        5       40
6  KKK13           13        6       11       10       40
7  KKK14            2        8       22        8       40
8  KKK15           10       10       10       10       40
9
JOB!1!C1
Width:  9  Memory:   97  Last Col/Row:D8
  1>
READY F1:Help  F3:Names  Ctrl-Backspace:Undo  Ctrl-Break:Cancel
```

Fig 13.11

This is one of the unfortunate problems of having more than three pages or spreadsheets, and means that you will need to make a note of any cells to be used for spreadsheet **linking**.

Return the cursor to page 2 and then press **Crtl** and **F7** to go back into **Zoom** mode. The cell reference containing the materials used for Job 124 is in fact **STOCK!E6** (which hopefully you noted). You can now use the **Edit** command to alter the formula in page 2 so that it gives the details of the costs for Job 124. The only items that need altering are MATERIALS, LABOUR and OVERHEADS, and the correct references/formulae are as follows:

MATERIALS	**STOCK!E6**
LABOUR	**LABOUR!B17**
OVERHEADS	**(SUM(LABOUR!C5.C8)*2)**

Enter these alterations now using Edit and the screen should show:

```
   2|  A   ||  B  ||  C  ||  D  ||  E  ||  F  ||  G  ||  H  |
1             JOB COSTS       Job 124
2
3             MATERIALS      10
4             LABOUR      121.5
5             OVERHEADS      68
6                         199.5
7             MARK-UP      39.9
8             PRICE       239.4
9
10
11
12
13
14
15
16
17
18
19
20
 JOB!2!C6                    Form=SUM(C3:C5)
Width:  9  Memory:   97  Last Col/Row:D8
  1>
READY F1:Help  F3:Names  Ctrl-Backspace:Undo  Ctrl-Break:Cancel
```

Fig 13.12

You should really alter the figures for pages 3 and 4 as well, but this will not really serve any great purpose so you can ignore it for the time being.

The only other aspect that has been overlooked is that there is no record of **total** job costs. This can be remedied quite easily by adding another page to the spreadsheet. To do this type in the following:

/	to call up commands
I	to select **Insert**
P	to select **Page**
1	to specify new page 1

You now need to copy the structure from page 2 to the new page 1 so that the total costs can be added to it. The simplest way will be to go back to Page 2 and **copy** the structure to Page 1; this has already been demonstrated so you should be able to do it yourself by now.

When you have copied the structure move back to the new page 1 using **Ctrl** and –. The existing figures refer to the calculations for the individual job costs. This page will show **total** costs for all jobs, so you can **blank** out the current entries in the block **C3.C8**.

The entry for MATERIALS should show the total of cell C3 from pages 2, 3, 4 and 5 (or would do if they had been amended properly). The advantage of using multiple pages is that this sort of addition is much easier, all that is required is the following **SUM** statement:

SUM(2.5!C3)

This will add the value in cell C3 on each of the pages between 2 and 5. This formula can also be **copied** to all of the other cells in the range **C4.C8** to calculate the total costs for each item.

```
   1|  A  ||  B  ||  C  ||  D  ||  E  ||  F  ||  G  ||  H  |
 1        JOB COSTS
 2
 3        MATERIALS      100
 4        LABOUR       481.5
 5        OVERHEADS      248
 6                     829.5
 7        MARK-UP      165.9
 8        PRICE        995.4
 9
10
11
12
13
14
15
16
17
18
19
20
 JOB!1!C9
Width:  9  Memory:   83  Last Col/Row:C8
  1>
READY F1:Help  F3:Names  Ctrl-Backspace:Undo  Ctrl-Break:Cancel
```

Fig 13.13

These spreadsheets will not be required again unless you are attempting the further exercises, so you can use the **Spreadsheet, Zap** command to delete all files (remember that you will still have the original files for **STOCK, JOB** and **LABOUR** on your disk).

Further exercises

A useful amendment to the existing files would be to amend the formulae in pages 4 and 5 so that they include the correct cell references. Do this first.

Now create a new spreadsheet to allocate **overheads** properly, rather than simply on the basis of labour hours. The figures to use are as follows:

	Dept A	*Dept B*	*Dept C*	*Dept D*
Job 123	10	20	15	5
Job 124	7	11	10	10
Job 125	16	21	20	14
Job 126	10	7	8	5

The above table shows the machine hours used in each department and the *overhead absorption rate* per machine hour for each department is as follows:

Dept A	£2.50
Dept B	£3.00
Dept C	£2.10
Dept D	£4.00

Use the **Data, Matrix** command to calculate the total overheads per job and then link these costs into the various spreadsheets.

Lesson 14 *Macros and audit commands*

This lesson attempts to cover the more advanced SuperCalc commands, macro commands in particular. These commands enable users to perform some very complex operations and are now one of the major attributes of the SuperCalc program.

The lesson will also examine the AUDIT function which allows the user to check the accuracy of spreadsheets and highlights any errors.

At the end of this lesson you should be able to:

a) use **screen control** macro commands
b) use **logic** macro commands
c) use **data input** macro commands
d) use **file control** macro commands
e) use **keyboard** macro commands
f) use the **AUDIT** function
g) test macros
h) restrict access to work areas

14.1 Screen control macro commands

The major part of this lesson will be concerned with creating a **macro**. The macros created in earlier lessons were fairly straightforward and concentrated on demonstrating the ability of macros to *capture* keyboard commands (such as automatically **loading** and **saving** files). This macro will be much more detailed and show how powerful macros can be.

The first stage in creating the macro will be to set up the opening screen. Remember the main aim of most macros will be to allow an inexperienced user to enter data into a spreadsheet without having to learn how to use SuperCalc; therefore, the more *surplus* information that can be removed from the screen the better.

Open a new spreadsheet and move the cursor to cell AA1 – this will allow you room to enter the actual spreadsheet details and instruction menu's in the block between columns **A** and **Z**.

The macro **label** can be entered in cell AA1: type in the **label** as **\s** for **Setup**. *Entering the label as a single letter means that the macro can be started by pressing* ***Alt*** *and* ***s*** *instead of typing in* ***Setup***.

The macro **statements** (the important bits) will be entered in column AB, and the macro **comments** (the optional explanations) will be entered in column AC. In order to ensure that as much information as possible can be seen you can alter the width of column **AB** to **25** spaces using the **Format** command.

When you have altered the width you can enter the macro as shown in Fig 14.1. All of these commands are **screen control macro commands** and effect the display shown. An explanation of each command is given in the **comments** column, and a further explanation is given on the next page.

```
   |  AA  ||        AB           ||  AC  ||  AD  ||  AE  ||  AF  |
1   \S     {WINDOWSOFF}            Suppresses display window updates
2          {INDICATOR "WELCOME"}   Alters Program mode indicator
3          {ENTRYOFF}              Removes Entry Line display
4          {PROMPT "MACRO LESSON"} Prints message on Prompt line
5          {STATUS "ABC Limited"}  Prints message on Status line
6          {MESSAGE "STAGE 1"}     Prints message in HELP area
7          {PANELOFF}              removes normal entry line
8          {SUSPEND}               Awaits Function key 8
9          {BEEP 1}                One beep
10         {PANELON}               Restores normal entry line
11         {MESSAGE "STAGE 2"}     Prints new message
12         {macroprompt "OK"}      Prints message at macro prompt
13         {MESSAGE "STAGE 3"}     Prints new message
14         {SUSPEND}               Awaits Function key 8
15         {BEEP 3}                Three beeps
16
17
18
19
20
MACRO!AA1                  Text="\S
Width:  9 Memory:  173 Last Col/Row:AC15
  1>
READY F1:Help  F3:Names  Ctrl-Backspace:Undo  Ctrl-Break:Cancel
```

Fig 14.1

These commands do not necessarily have to be in this order, nor is it necessary to enter them in UPPERCASE. However, they should all be enclosed by braces (brackets) and text used for *strings* has to be enclosed in double quotes "".

WINDOWSOFF/WINDOWSON is a toggle command which is used to suppress the window updates (ie: stop the screen from changing).

INDICATOR can be used to print a message at the **program mode indicator position** (ie: bottom left of the screen) – this will normally display the word **READY**. In this example the word displayed will be **WELCOME**. However, you will discover when you run this macro that this message can only contain a maximum of five characters. The command **{ INDICATOR "" }** will ensure that nothing appears in this position.

ENTRYOFF/ENTRYON is another toggle which can be used to remove or restrict access to the *entry line*, or restore normal operation of the *entry line*. Whilst **ENTRYOFF** is the mode no entries can be made on the *entry line*.

PROMPT can be used to display a message on the *prompt line*, the command **{ PROMPT "" }** will ensure that there is no display on the *prompt line*.

STATUS and **MESSAGE** are similar to **PROMPT** except that the text displays will appear on the *prompt line* (**PROMPT**) or in the space usually reserved for

HELP information (**MESSAGE**). Once again, typing in "" will suppress all display in these areas.

PANELOFF/PANELON is another toggle which *freezes/unlocks* the *status*, *prompt* and *entry lines*. This means that, in the macro shown, the lines in the *panel* will be *frozen* in the first section but will be unlocked when the **PANELON** command is read. This means that the **MESSAGE** STAGE 2 will not be seen as it will almost immediately be overwritten by the **MESSAGE** STAGE 3.

MACROPROMPT is another message which will appear in the bottom right hand corner of the screen and will overwrite the normal *prompt* display; again "" will eliminate all displays in this area.

SUSPEND has been used in previous macro files and will suspend all further processing of the macro until the key **F8** is selected (this will be shown in the prompt position unless overwritten by a **MACROPROMPT**.

BEEP, not surprisingly, produces a *beep* (providing that the volume is turned on!). The number accompanying it indicates the number of beeps.

Read through these descriptions carefully and then practice the simple macro below.

Your first task will be to **write** (ie: save) the macro, so press // and then select **Macro**. When the prompts appear select **Write** and enter the filename as **\s**.

The range for the macro will be **AB1.AB15** (remember the macro range includes the *Statements* only). Then select **ALL** to save **Labels, Statements** and **Comments**.

You can now test the macro by pressing **Alt** and **s**. The main part of the screen should remain fixed as there are no cursor movement keys involved in this macro, but the bottom part of the display should change. See if you can identify which line relates to each entry and don't forget to press **F8** to continue (the end of the macro will be signified by the three beeps).

```
        |  AA  ||          AB            ||  AC  ||  AD  ||  AE  ||  AF  |
   1    \S        {WINDOWSOFF}              Suppresses display window updates
   2              {INDICATOR "WELCOME"}     Alters Program mode indicator
   3              {ENTRYOFF}                Removes Entry Line display
   4              {PROMPT "MACRO LESSON"}   Prints message on Prompt line
   5              {STATUS "ABC Limited"}    Prints message on Status line
   6              {MESSAGE "STAGE 1"}       Prints message in HELP area
   7              {PANELOFF}                removes normal entry line
   8              {SUSPEND}                 Awaits Function key 8
   9              {BEEP 1}                  One beep
  10              {PANELON}                 Restores normal entry line
  11              {MESSAGE "STAGE 2"}       Prints new message
  12              {macroprompt "OK"}        Prints message at macro prompt
  13              {MESSAGE "STAGE 3"}       Prints new message
  14              {SUSPEND}                 Awaits Function key 8
  15              {BEEP 3}                  Three beeps
  16
  17
  18
  19
  20
ABC Limited
MACRO LESSON

WELCO STAGE 1                                OK
```

Fig 14.2

14.2 Keyboard macro commands

The next batch of macro commands are the **keyboard macro commands**. These are mainly used for cursor movement and will perform all of the functions of the normal cursor movement keys. These can be demonstrated with another macro.

Move the cursor to cell **AA17** and enter a new macro label as **\c** for cursor movement. Then enter the following **statements** and **comments**. Don't forget to include the braces .

```
   |  AA  ||          AB          ||  AC  ||  AD  ||  AE  ||  AF  |
17  \c        {HOME}                 Moves to A1
18            {DN}                   Moves DOWN one cell
19            {DELAY 1}              One second pause
20            {RT}                   RIGHT one cell
21            {DELAY 1}
22            {TAB}                  Sets TAB ON
23            {DN}                   Moves to Bottom cell in column
24            {DELAY 1}
25            {PGUP}                 Moves cursor up one page (20 cells)
26            {DELAY 1}
27            {PGRT}                 Moves cursor page right (6 columns)
28            {DELAY 1}
29            {PGRT 2}               Moves cursor 2 pages right
30            {UP 5}                 Moves up 5 rows
31            {DELAY 1}
32            {GOTO}A20~             Goto cell a21 ( ~ = Return )
33            {DELAY 1}
34            {UP}                   UP one cell
35            {DELAY 1}
36            {LT}                   LEFT one cell
 MACRO!AC17               Text="Moves to A1
Width:  9  Memory:  172  Last Col/Row:AC36
  1>
READY F1:Help  F3:Names  Ctrl-Backspace:Undo  Ctrl-Break:Cancel
```

Fig 14.3

The **comments** shown should make clear what each command will do; the **DELAY** statement is not a **keyboard** macro command, but is needed to slow down the changes in display so that you will have time to see what each change is doing. The **DELAY** command can be set for a pause of any interval between 1 and 99 seconds.

Select // **Macro** and **write** this macro to disk as filename **\c**; the range will be **AB17.AB36** and you can write **all** contents.

Once you have done this you can **eXecute** the macro by pressing **Alt** and **c**. The cursor should then move around the screen in the set sequence and should finish in cell **A19**.If the cursor movement was too fast for you then you can edit the macro to change the **DELAY** to 2 seconds.

Note that the **TAB** command doesn't do anything on its own, but when the **DN** command is operated it will move not just one cell, but to the bottom cell in the range. **TAB** will actually move to the next *occupied* cell – as there are no occupied cells in this column the cursor will move to the very end.

There are a number of other **keyboard** macro commands, but they all have one similarity in that they could normally be invoked by using one of the cursor keys or a function key, for example key **F10** is normally used to **view** graphs, and the **key-**

board macro command for this function is **{VIEW}**. A full list of these commands can be found on both the **HELP** menu and in the SuperCalc manual. Fig 14.4 shows the first page of the on-screen **HELP** but if you are creating a macro then it is worth remembering that all commands normally selected from the cursor and function keys will have a **keyboard** macro equivalent.

Keyboard Macro Commands Page 1 SuperCalc AnswerScreen

Keyboard Macro	Corresponding Key
~	Return
{ABS}	F4 (toggle absolute coordinates/graphics point)
{ADD1} - {ADD10}	Shift-F1 through Shift-F10 (invokes attached add-in)
{AUDIT}	ALT-F1 (turns AUDIT mode on)
{BACKSPACE} or {BS}	Backspace
{BTAB}	Back Tab (Shift-Tab)
{CALC}	F9 (calculate spreadsheet)
{DELETE} or {DEL}	Del
{DOWN} or {DN} or {D}	Down Arrow
{EDIT}	F7 (toggle data EDIT mode)
{END}	End
{ENDSCREEN} or {ENDSCR}	Ctrl-End
{ESCAPE} or {ESC}	Esc (Escape)
{GOTO} location	F5 (go to location/cell address)
{GOTOSHEET} sheetname	Ctrl-F5 (go to spreadsheet)

RELATED TOPICS: Page 2 - H to O Screen Control Commands Data Input Commands
Page 3 - P to Z Logic Commands File Control Commands
ESC=Return to SuperCalc F2 = How to use Help F3 = Help Index

Fig 14.4

14.3 Data input and logic macro commands

Most macros will require some data to be entered by the user. The **data input commands** are used to control the data that is being entered. Any macro doing this will be likely to use a selection of macro commands from each of the different command categories so that the whole spreadsheet is improved.

In order to demonstrate a more complete macro, **zap** the existing spreadsheet and start a new macro.

Once again you will want to reserve the first few columns for the data entry, so move to cell AK1 so that the macro can be stored out of the way. You can also **format** column AL to 25 spaces as before.

Enter the following as the new macro (the first two commands are normal SuperCalc commands and need to be prefixed by a " or SuperCalc will try to perform the commands immediately):

```
      |  AK  ||              AL                 ||  AM  ||  AN  ||  AO  |
  1   \D      /gb                                 Remove screen border
  2           /be31~                              Blank cell E31
  3           {HOME}                              Move to A1
  4           {WINDOWSOFF}                        Suppress window display
  5           {INDICATOR ""}                      Suppress indicator display
  6           {ENTRYOFF}                          Freeze Entry line
  7           {PROMPT ""}                         Suppress Prompt display
  8           {STATUS "ABC LIMITED"}              Print Company name
  9           {MESSAGE "LOGGING ON"}              Print procedure name
 10           {MACROPROMPT ""}                    Suppress prompt display
 11           {PANELOFF}                          Freeze Panel display
 12           {DELAY 2}                           Pauses until any key presse
 13           {PGDN}                              Page down
 14           {GOTO}E31~                          Move to cell E31
 15
 16
 17
 18
 19
 20
 MACRO1!AL15
Width: 32  Memory:  171  Last Col/Row:AM202
  1>
READY F1:Help  F3:Names  Ctrl-Backspace:Undo  Ctrl-Break:Cancel
```

Fig 14.5

Most of the macro commands used here have been described in the last two sections. Most of the *panel* lines do not have a message displayed this time, but the normal display will be suppressed by the "".

The first part of this macro is going to check whether a particular user is *authorised* to access the program. In order to do this the macro will have to perform three functions:

1) **get the users name**
2) **check that this name is an authorised users name**
3) **determine whether the user can proceed or should be *ejected***

The Data Input command GETTEXT can be used to elicit an entry of text. There are a number of similar Data Input commands that perform comparable functions: GETNUMBER will request a numeric entry, GETROWS a row number entry, GETCOLS a column number entry and GETKEY for any type of entry.

Move the cursor to cell AL15 and enter the following as the command and then enter the comments in cell AM15.

{GETTEXT "Enter User Name in Capitals", E31} Enter user name in E31

The part shown inside the "" will be printed as a prompt on the *entry line* to give the user some guidance.

Having obtained the text it is now necessary to check whether these users are authorised. This part of the operation will require a **logic macro** command. These commands control the flow of the macro program and are used to determine which sequence should be followed – in our example they will be used to determine whether the user can proceed or whether further access should be refused.

There are only two authorised users for this program, TOM and JACK (*NB: in real situations users should never use their own name , or any other word that can easily be guessed by other staff, for passwords*).

The **logic macro** command to be used to determine whether these users are valid is the **IF** command. The macro **IF** command performs a similar function to the normal **IF** command but is potentially much more powerful.

Move the cursor to AL16 and enter the command as follows:

{IF E31="TOM"} {BRANCH UPDATE}

The statement in the prompt in the previous line concerning the use of **capitals** is necessary as this command will only match exact text. If the text entered is TOM then the macro will divert to a new macro called **UPDATE**. The **branch** command is another **logic** command and is used to re-direct the program.

The other users name is JACK so the entry on the next line will be:

{IF E31="JACK} {BRANCH UPDATE}

Note that the closing " after JACK has been deliberately omitted.

If the correct user name is entered then the program should *branch* to the new macro called **UPDATE** (which will have to be created before the macro can be run).

However, the macro will also have to include some commands for those users who are not authorised to access the program. Many commercial programs will give users a second, or even third, chance to re-enter the user names. This is not really good practice as it tends to encourage *hackers*. If the user has entered the wrong name then they should be *ejected* immediately.

Type in the entries in Fig 14.6 to finish off this part of the macro. You can leave out the comments if you prefer. The last command is the **Zap** command and must be prefixed by a ".

```
      |  AK  ||                  AL                  ||  AM  ||  AN  ||  AO  |
4              {WINDOWSOFF}                          Suppress window display
5              {INDICATOR ""}                        Suppress indicator display
6              {ENTRYOFF}                            Freeze Entry line
7              {PROMPT ""}                           Suppress Prompt display
8              {STATUS "ABC LIMITED"}                Print Company name
9              {MESSAGE "LOGGING ON"}                Print procedure name
10             {MACROPROMPT ""}                      Suppress prompt display
11             {PANELOFF}                            Freeze Panel display
12             {DELAY 2}                             Pauses until any key presse
13             {PGDN}                                Page down
14             {GOTO}E31~                            Move to cell E31
15             {GETTEXT "Enter Name", e31}           Enter user name in E31
16             {IF E31="TOM"} {BRANCH UPDATE}
17             {IF E31="JACK} {BRANCH UPDATE}
18             {BEEP}                                One beep for invalid name
19             {MESSAGE "ILLEGAL ENTRY"}             Warning message
20             {DELAY 1}
21             {PROMPT "QUITTING PROGRAM"} {DELAY 5}
22             /zy                                   ZAP spreadsheet
23
 MACRO1!AL17               Text="{IF E31="JACK} {BRANCH UPDATE}
Width: 32  Memory:  170  Last Col/Row:AM202
  1>
READY F1:Help  F3:Names  Ctrl-Backspace:Undo  Ctrl-Break:Cancel
```

Fig 14.6

These last few lines will only operate if the user has entered an unauthorised name; the macro will first sound one warning beep, and then display a warning message for one second before issuing a further five-second warning and then **zapping** the spreadsheet. It is important to zap the spreadsheet as the data to be used will be included on the same spreadsheet, and if it is **not** zapped then the unauthorised user could still find the data by using the cursor movement keys.

You can now **write** this macro to disk using the **//Macro** command as filename **\d**. The range will be **AL1.AL22** and you can save **ALL**.

The next task will be to devise the **UPDATE** macro. This can be entered underneath the existing macro as this will make checking easier. The command **{BREAKOFF}** should really have been used at the beginning of the first macro as it disenables the use of the **Ctrl** and **Break** keys. It is normally possible to stop a macro at anytime by simply pressing these two keys together; if an unauthorised user knows this then the check on the passwords would be useless, so this command can be used to prevent the macro being halted. Move the cursor to cell AL23 and enter the details as in Fig 14.7.

```
   |  AK  ||              AL                 ||  AM  ||  AN  ||  AO  |
21        {PROMPT "QUITTING PROGRAM"} {DELAY 5}
22        /zy                                 ZAP spreadsheet
23 UPDATE {PGRT 2}                            Move 2 pages right
24        {BREAKOFF}                          Disenables Ctrl-Break key
25        //RJ4.J10~                          Restrict entry to block
26        {PROMPT "Press ENTER to insert new figures"}
27        {STATUS "PRESS F8 WHEN COMPLETE"}
28        {SUSPEND}
29
30
31
32
33
34
35
36
37
38
39
40
 MACRO2!AM28
Width:  9  Memory:  170  Last Col/Row:AM202
  1>
READY F1:Help  F3:Names  Ctrl-Backspace:Undo  Ctrl-Break:Cancel
```

Fig 14.7

The entry on line 25 is another SuperCalc / command and will need to be prefixed by the " symbol.

14.3.1 Restricting access

Most of this macro is devoted to preventing unauthorised access. Lesson 7 showed how the **Protect** and **Global, Tab** commands can be used to limit access to certain areas, but there is another command which will perform a similar function.

The **Restrict** command will limit data input to a specified range. This command is accessed from the second bank of commands and can be used in any type of spreadsheet program.

The range is specified in the usual manner (in this instance the data entry range is restricted to the range **J4:J10**). However, the **Restrict** function will only apply until the **RETURN** or **Esc** keys are pressed when the *entry line* is blank. This puts a limit on its effectiveness in normal spreadsheets, but is useful in macros as the macro will continue once the **RETURN** key has been pressed.

The final few entries in this macro will give the user instructions on how to enter data.

We haven't actually set up a spreadsheet for the data yet, but this doesn't matter at the moment. Once you have entered the macro commands as shown you can select

//Macro and **write** this macro as **UPDATE** and select range **AL23.AL28** – save **All**.

14.4 Testing macros

Now that both macros have been saved it should be possible to test them. The test needs to ensure that both user names will be allowed and that all other names will result in a **zapped** spreadsheet. As this final alternative will **zap** everything you should **save** the spreadsheet as filename **Macro** first.

In order to test the macro just press **Alt** and **d**. When the macro asks for user name enter **TOM**.

The macro should work through all of the commands down to cell AL16 and will then branch off to the new macro **UPDATE**, providing that all of the macros are stored on the default drive. You will not need to make any entries other than the user name (TOM) and can simply press **RETURN** then **F8** to complete the macro.

If the macro fails to work properly then move the cursor back to the macro range (**AL1.AL28**) and check that you have entered everything properly.

The next test will be to see if the macro accepts the other user name. Repeat the macro by pressing **Alt** and **d** but this time enter the user name as JACK (the second line of the macro is needed to **blank** the existing entry).

You should get the following result:

```
                                        JACK
                                        TOM






 MACRO2!E31                   Text="JACK         Error in macro at   53/  1
Width:  9  Memory:  170  Last Col/Row:AM203
  1>
READY F1:Help  F3:Names  Ctrl-Backspace:Undo  Ctrl-Break:Cancel  CAPS
```

Fig 14.8

The macro error message is telling you which row the error occurs in. Unfortunately this is not always clear, especially in large macros, as it may be a result of an earlier error.

The **//Macro** command can assist in error detection by use of the **Trace** option. This can be used to run through the macro whilst simultaneously displaying the macro command currently in operation. The error in this macro should be that there is a " missing at the end of the name **"JACK** in line 17. However, you can use the **//Macro, Trace** option to confirm this.

Call up **//Macro** and select the **Trace** option. This gives three other options – the macro *tracing* can be directed towards the screen (console), where it will print on the **HELP** line (unfortunately this will obscure any messages printed here), to the printer as a line by line summary, or to an ASCII file for future editing. The **Console** option is the default and is also the one required in this example, so select this option.

Nothing will happen immediately as you have to start running the macro first. Press **Alt** and **F2** and the word **STEP** should appear on the bottom corner of the screen.

Now start the macro by pressing **Alt** and **d**. As the macro performs each command the command will appear at the bottom of the screen.

```
                                                  JACK
                                                  TOM








Optimum Keep Graphics Spreadsheet Evaluation Values 1-2-3 + -
Formula " Labels Protection Border Next Tab Unprotected Zoom
  9>/Global,
(F8)STEP L:1  D.XQT          3        /gb
```

Fig 14.9

In order to execute each line you will have to press **F8** to carry out each successive statement – as the first command actually requires three key strokes you will have to press **F8** three times.

Once you have done this the next command will appear and you can press **F8** again to carry out each part of the command. This will enable you to check each part of the macro commands and determine exactly where the macro breaks down.

As pressing **F8** can get a bit tedious (especially when you think you know where the error is) you can press **Alt** and **F8** to invoke the **AUTOSTEP** mode. This is an automatic version of **STEP** and performs each part of the command in 1/4 second intervals. Try this now and see what happens.

You can revert to normal **STEP** mode at any time if you want to go slower, by pressing **Alt** and **F8** again.

When the prompt asks for the user name enter **JACK**, because this is clearly the line causing a problem as the preceding entry for **TOM** worked.

When you get to this entry the error message will appear but the command is displayed on the screen. This makes errors easier to spot as it highlights the part of the program at fault and reduces the amount of error-checking involved. It is fairly easy now to see that the problem is the *syntax* error caused by the missing **"**.

```
ABC LIMITED


(F8)STEP L:1  D.XQT          34        {IF E31="JACK } {BRANCH UPDATE}
```

Fig 14.10

You can now return to the macro and enter the missing " after **JACK** in line 17. You will also need to re-**write** the macro.

You can now check the third part of the macro by running it once more, only this time entering a different name; the macro should finish by **zapping** the spreadsheet.

14.5 Devising a complete macro

The last few sections of this lesson have been used to demonstrate the various macro commands without showing how they could be used in a proper example. The problem with devising a realistic demonstration of a **macro** is that it would take such a long time to set up the spreadsheet for the data before you could even start on writing the **macro**. However, this section will devise a simple **macro** for use on a very basic spreadsheet. The object of the spreadsheet is to record **sales** and calculate **VAT**.

Initially the first part of this spreadsheet will need to be set up. Do not **zap** the existing spreadsheet as the original macro can still be used to **load** the program and check for the correct user password.

Move the cursor to cell A42 and enter the headings for the new spreadsheet and some sample data as shown below (the columns for **VAT** and **TOTAL** are calculated by use of formula which you should be able to insert yourself):

```
   |           A            ||  B  ||  C  ||  D  ||  E  ||  F  |
41
42 NAME                      ACCOUNT   AMOUNT    VAT     TOTAL
43 ------------------------------------------------------------------
44 EVANS & CO                EV123      100.45   15.07   115.52
45 W. WILLIS LTD             WI100      230.90   34.64   265.54
46 SMITH & JONES             SM78       302.15   45.32   347.47
47
48
49
50
51
52
53
54
55
56
57
58
59
60
 MACRO2!A48
Width: 25  Memory:  170  Last Col/Row:AM201
  1>
READY F1:Help  F3:Names  Ctrl-Backspace:Undo  Ctrl-Break:Cancel  CAPS
```

Fig 14.11

It will make things a little easier when writing the macro if you can refer to ranges as **names** rather than cell references, so you can use the **Name** command to create the following four **named** ranges:

Name	**Range**
SALES	A44.E48
AMOUNT	C44.C48
VAT	D44.D48
TOTAL	E44.E48

The **named** range **SALES** will be used in the macro to refer to this part of the spreadsheet, and the other **named** ranges will be used as part of the calculations in the spreadsheet.

Move the cursor two lines below the last cell (ie: row 48) and enter a **SUM** formula to calculate the totals of the AMOUNT, VAT and TOTAL columns. This formula would normally be entered as a range, but you can enter the **name** instead. Type in the formula for the AMOUNT column as **SUM(AMOUNT)**.

This technique takes some getting used to, but is often easier in the long run as you no longer have to identify the cell ranges.

You can also **copy** this formula as the program should recognise that you require the formula upgraded to the new **named** ranges. Use the **Copy** command to copy the formula to the cells **D48.E48**. The screen should now show:

```
   |          A          || B || C || D || E || F |
41
42 NAME                 ACCOUNT   AMOUNT    VAT   TOTAL
43 ------------------------------------------------------------
44 EVANS & CO           EV123      100.45   15.07  115.52
45 W. WILLIS LTD        WI100      230.90   34.64  265.54
46 SMITH & JONES        SM78       302.15   45.32  347.47
47
48 TOTAL                           633.50   95.03  728.53
49
50
51
52
53
54
55
56
57
58
59
60
 MACRO2!D48                  Form=SUM(VAT)
Width:  9  Memory:  170  Last Col/Row:AM201
 1>
READY F1:Help  F3:Names  Ctrl-Backspace:Undo  Ctrl-Break:Cancel  CAPS
```

Fig 14.12

If you move the cursor to the cells D48 and E48 the formula should show **SUM(VAT)** and **SUM(TOTAL)**.

You are now ready to write the new macro, which will move the cursor to the **sales** range and allow the user to enter new sales details.

Move the cursor back to cell AK24 and **blank** the existing **UPDATE** macro. The new macro will also be called **UPDATE** (this will save having to alter the main macro) so you can enter this in cell AK24. now type in the following macro; no **comments** have been included as a full description of each line is given below:

```
      |  AK  ||             AL              ||  AM  ||  AN  ||  AO  |
22          /zy                              ZAP spreadsheet
23
24  UPDATE  {GOTO}SALES
25          ~ {UP 2}
26          {DN ROWS(SALES)+1}
27          /IR~
28          /th
29
30
31
32
33
34
35
36
37
38
39
40
41
 MACRO2!AL29
Width: 32  Memory:  171  Last Col/Row:AM202
  1>
READY F1:Help  F3:Names  Ctrl-Backspace:Undo  Ctrl-Break:Cancel  CAPS
```

Fig 14.13

Each line of the macro will perform the following function:

{GOTO}SALES	moves the cursor to the SALES range (A44.E48)
~{UP 2}	selects ENTER for the previous command and moves up two lines to include the headings on rows 42 and 43
{DN ROWS(SALES)+1}	moves the cursor to the end of SALES plus one extra row (ie: row 48 +1)
/IR~	inserts one extra row at row 4 (to allow for new data)
/th	sets **title** lock on **horizontal** to prevent headings from scrolling off the screen

The next stage of the macro will be to display suitable instructions for the user, and uses the **screen control commands** explained earlier. Type **{PANELOFF}** in cell AL29 and then enter the following in cell A30:

{STATUS" set Caps Lock ON"} {PROMPT "ENTER NEW DETAILS"} {MESSAGE "PRESS ENTER TO COMPLETE"}

This is to demonstrate that you can exceed the column width when entering macro commands and save space. This sort of command is unlikely to cause errors (providing all braces and quotes are included) and will usually be some of the easiest macro commands.

You can now type in the remaining lines as shown:

```
   |  AK  ||            AL              ||  AM  ||  AN  ||  AO  |
24 UPDATE  {GOTO}SALES
25         ~ {UP 2}
26         {DN ROWS(SALES)+1}
27         /IR~
28         /th
29         {PANELOFF}
30         {STATUS "set caps lock ON"} {PROMPT "ENTER NEW DETAILS"} {M
31         /CD47,[ENDCOL(VAT);CROW]~
32         /CE47,[ENDCOL(TOTAL);CROW]~
33         {ENTRYON}
34         //R.[ENDCOL(SALES)-2;CROW]~
35
36
37
38
39
40
41
42
43
 MACRO2!AL35
Width: 32  Memory:  170  Last Col/Row:AM202
  1>
READY F1:Help  F3:Names  Ctrl-Backspace:Undo  Ctrl-Break:Cancel  CAPS
```

Fig 14.14

These commands serve the following purposes:

The commands in cells A31 and A32 are used to **copy** the **SUM** formula from the last entry in both the VAT and TOTAL columns (ie: /CD47); this can then be used to calculate the amounts for any new entries.

Unfortunately, it is not possible to include a cell reference for this entry as the cell number will be different every time a new entry is made. The cell to **copy** to will always be the **last** cell in the VAT and TOTAL ranges.

As these have both been made **named** ranges the range will automatically be updated when the new row is **inserted** by the macro command in AL27. Therefore, the command **ENDCOL(VAT)** will find the end of the VAT column (ie Column D) and **CROW** will identify the current row (ie 48). This means that the **SUM** formula will be copied to Column **D** row **48** (**D48**).

The command in cell Al32 does the same thing, but for the TOTAL column. The **ENDCOL** (or **ENDROW**) and **CROW** (or **CCOL**) commands are especially useful for applications where the spreadsheet will be *growing*.

The **ENTRYON** command has been used before, and the next command is the **RESTRICT** command which is restricting data entry to the first three columns (ie: ENDCOL-2) and the current row only. *NB: This will make much more sense if you re-examine the entries in the SALES range so that you can compare the cell ranges with those on the screen.*

This will restrict the user to entering the NAME, ACCOUNT and AMOUNT only.

The section of the macro that you have just entered will insert a new row and allow the user to enter the new details for **one** invoice only. Clearly, on most occasions, the user will want to enter more than one invoice, therefore the next part of the macro will ask the user if there are any more entries to made; if the answer is **yes** then the macro routine will be restarted; if the answer is **no** then the macro will save the changes and **quit**.

Type in the following commands:

```
      |  AK  ||               AL              ||  AM  ||  AN  ||  AO  |
  24  UPDATE   {GOTO}SALES
  25           ~ {UP 2}
  26           {DN ROWS(SALES)+1}
  27           /IR~
  28           /th
  29           {PANELOFF}
  30           {STATUS "set caps lock ON"} {PROMPT "ENTER NEW DETAILS"} {M
  31           /CD47,[ENDCOL(VAT);CROW]~
  32           /CE47,[ENDCOL(TOTAL);CROW]~
  33           {ENTRYON}
  34           //R.[ENDCOL(SALES)-2;CROW]~
  35           /be29.e30~~
  36           {STATUS "ENTER MORE DETAILS Y/N?"}
  37           {GETKEY "PRESS Y OR N", E30}
  38           {IF E30="Y"} {STATUS "SETTING UP FOR NEW DATA"} {CALL UPDAT
  39           {STATUS ""} {PROMPT "SAVE ALTERATIONS?"}
  40           {GETKEY "PRESS Y OR N", E29}
  41           {DELAY 1} {IF E29="Y"}/SMACRO1~OA/QY
  42           {IF E29<>"Y"}/QY
  43
   MACRO2!AL35                    Text="/be29.e30~~
  Width: 32  Memory:  170  Last Col/Row:AM202
    1>
  READY F1:Help  F3:Names  Ctrl-Backspace:Undo  Ctrl-Break:Cancel  CAPS
```

Fig 14.15

The macro will be asking the user if he or she wants to continue entering more details The response will need to be stored somewhere, and cells E29 and E30 will be used for this purpose. The first line of this section of the macro is used to clear (**blank**) the existing entries in those cells.

The next two lines are used to alter the screen display and await the input of the users response (**GETKEY**). The first response will be stored in cell E30.

If the user does ask to enter more data then the macro will **call up** the appropriate macro file, in this case it simply involves running the macro again, so the file name is the name of this macro (**UPDATE**). Note that you can call up any macro with the **Call** command.

The next lines will only be used if the response to the prompt in cell **AL37** was **N**. The next few lines ask the user if the changes are to be **saved**, again, using the **GETKEY** command to obtain some input (this time into cell E29).

The last two lines are used to either **save** the alterations and then **quit**, or to **quit** without making changes. You should be able to make sense of these commands yourself by now.

When you have entered all of the macro as shown, try running it a few times to make sure that all parts work as they should do, and perhaps adding new data.

14.6 Auditing spreadsheets

The // **Macro** command includes a number of options for testing macro files, most of which have already been demonstrated in this manual. The most useful macro command for testing spreadsheets is almost certainly by using the **STEP** and **AUTOSTEP** functions which will allow you test the macro as it is being run.

SuperCalc 5 now includes a new command called **TEST**. This command does not do anything on its own, but loads a new set of commands in the **AUDIT** mode. These commands can be used to test and search for possible errors, not just in macros, but in all sorts of spreadsheet files.

Move the cursor back to A1, and then select // **Test**. Nothing obvious will happen except that the word **AUDIT** appears at the bottom left of the screen.

If you press the / now you will discover that there is a different range of commands on offer. These are the **AUDIT** mode commands and are designed specifically for error searching and testing. *The **AUDIT** mode can also be invoked by using the **Alt** and **F1** keys.*

The function of each of these commands is as follows:

Details	displays cells currently highlighted
Highlight	locates and highlights cells matching set criteria
Names	lists named ranges meeting set criteria
Replace	searches for selected strings and replaces with new strings
Squeeze	rearranges formulae to minimise amount of memory used
View	changes display so that more of highlighted cells can be viewed

14.6.1 Highlighting cells

The most significant of these options is the **Highlight** option which is used to specify which type of cells you want to examine. Select this option now and you should get the following screen:

```
   |          A          || B || C || D || E || F |
 1
 2
 3
 4
 5
 6
 7
 8
 9
10
11
12
13
14
15
16
17
18
19
20
Area  Block  Cells  Find  Links  Modified  Output-attr  Pre-zap
Relationships  Zap
 12>/Highlight,
AUD-A Limits AUDIT tests to specific range and cells             CAPS
```

Fig 14.16

The functions of each of these options is as follows:

Area — sets the **range** to be used for highlighting and selects *filters* to describe which cells should be included

Block — used to set **further** highlighting within the area specified

Cells — selects **types** of cells to be highlighted

Find — **searches** for the value contents of cells, used to find *matching* cells, identify relationships between cells, etc

Links Highlights — highlights all cells that contain links with other spreadsheets

Modified — determines whether cells should be highlighted during recalculation

Output-attr Highlights	highlights cells that contain **output** attributes such as borders, fonts, etc
Pre-zap	determines whether new cells should be highlighted after recalculation or not
Relationships	searches for relationships between cells
Zap	**clears** all highlighted cells

If the **Area** option is not selected then the default value is to **highlight** cells in the entire spreadsheet.

To test the **AUDIT** mode you will need to specify which sort of cells need **highlighting**; to do this you will need to select the option for **Cells**.

The screen will now show a new set of options which refer to the different types of cell which can be highlighted. If you press **F1** then the following **Help** screen will appear which should give some more explanation as to what the different types of cells are:

```
Cell Type Auditing                                    SuperCalc AnswerScreen

/Highlight,Cells highlights cells based on type of contents. Limit the test
area with /Highlight,Area, or use Alt-F1 to change the filter mode. View
details of highlighted cells on screen with Spacebar.
```

Attribute	Control text.	Lone	Cells not referenced by another cell.
Blank-ref	Formulas that reference blank cells.	Macro	First character is / or (.
Constant	Numeric constants.	NA	N/A (Not Available).
Date	Result in date.	fOrmat	Entry level formatting, empty or not.
Error	Contain or result in ERROR.	Protected	Protected cells.
Formula	Formulas that are not invariant.	Referenced	Cells referenced by another cell.
Hidden	Cells hidden at entry level.	String	Text or string values.
		Time	Times.
Invariant	Formulas or functions whose values never change (i.e. 8*7), but not constants.	Unprotected	Unprotected cells.
		emptY	Entry-level formatted cells that contain no data.

```
RELATED TOPICS: Auditing Spreadsheets     Highlighting Cells    Filters
ESC=Return to SuperCalc    F2 = How to use Help    F3 = Help Index
```

Fig 14.17

As the current spreadsheet contains a couple of macros it will be appropriate to **highlight** the **macro** cells. Press **Esc** to return to the spreadsheet and then select **Macro** as the cell-type.

The screen will now show a display line giving the total number of highlighted cells (this should be 40).If you move the cursor to AK1 you will be able to see that the macro cells have all been highlighted (NB: the **highlighting** is not always very good on poorer quality monitors).

If you now press / and then select **Details**, the bottom half of the screen will alter to show the cell references of all of the macro cells currently highlighted and the contents of the cell first in the list.

You can examine the details of each of the macro cells by simply moving the cursor along the list of cells. The contents of each cell will be displayed as the corresponding cell reference is highlighted.

```
     |  AI  ||  AJ  ||  AK  ||              AL                ||  AM  |
1                     \D      /gb                               Remove sc
2                             /be31~                            Blank cel
3                             {HOME}                            Move to A
4                             {WINDOWSOFF}                      Suppress
5                             {INDICATOR ""}                    Suppress
6                             {ENTRYOFF}                        Freeze En
7                             {PROMPT ""}                       Suppress
8                             {STATUS "ABC LIMITED"}            Print Com
9                             {MESSAGE "LOGGING ON"}            Print pro
10                            {MACROPROMPT ""}                  Suppress
11                            {PANELOFF}                        Freeze Pa
12                            {DELAY 2}                         Pauses un
   40 highlighted MACRO cells
AL1 AL2 AL3 AL4 AL5 AL6 AL7 AL8 AL9 AL10 AL11 AL12 AL13 AL14 AL15 AL16 AL17
===========================================================================
AL4:    "{WINDOWSOFF}



 MACRO2!AM1                     Text="Remove screen border
Width:  9  Memory:  170  Last Col/Row:AM202
  1>
AUDIT Display details                                             CAPS
```

Fig 14.18

Press **Esc** to leave the **Details** mode. The **Names** option will show the details of any **named** ranges that overlap. As this spreadsheet includes a number of **named** ranges it will be worthwhile examining this option now. Press / then **Names** to select this option.

Most of the commands offered here are used in ensuring that the named ranges are correct, for example the **Duplicate** option is intended to ensure that you haven't accidentally given the same range two names. The only option that will demonstrate anything on this spreadsheet is the **Overlap** option, as this is a very small spreadsheet.

Select the **Overlap** option and the screen should show:

```
NAMED RANGE DIRECTORY -- OVERLAP
AMOUNT        C44:C48                  SALES      A44:E48
SALES         A44:E48
TOTAL         E44:E48
VAT           D44:D48











 Press ESC key to exit
  16>/Names,Overlap,
 AUDIT List ranges that share one or more cells                CAPS
```

Fig 14.19

This shows two columns. The column on the left shows that some of the cells in the **AMOUNT** range overlap with some in the **SALES** range. If you move the cursor down the list of the **NAMED** ranges then the column on the left will also alter to show the other named ranges that overlap.

14.6.2 Viewing highlighted cells

One of the problems in finding errors is the limited amount of the spreadsheet which can be displayed on screen at any one time. The **View** option is designed to condense and *code* data so that more data can be displayed. Press **Esc** to quit the **Names** option and then press **/ View**. This gives three options: **Normal** is used to return to normal display after selecting one of the other options; **Formula** shows the formula used (this differs from the **Global, Formula** command as the **Highlight** option will automatically widen cells to show the full formula); and **Map** condenses the display by using *codes* to represent different types of data.

Select **Map** and then **Standard**; the screen will alter once again and each cell will be re-formatted to only two characters wide. The display shows all cell contents by a single character: all macro cells are marked as **m**, text cells as **"**, numbers and formulae as **f** and invariant formulae (eg: DATE) as **i**. If you move the cursor to cell A41 you will be able to see the display of formulae, text and numbers.

```
    A B C D E F G H I J K L M N O P Q R S T U V W X Y Z aAaBaCaDaEaFaGaHaIaJaK
41
42  " " " " " "
43  '                                                                     £
44  " " £ f f
45  " " £ f f
46  " " £ f f
47  " " £ f f
48
49  "   f f f
50
51
52
53
54
55
56
57
58
59
60
 MACRO2!A41
Width:  2  Memory:  170  Last Col/Row:aM202
  1>
AUDIT Represent each element with a unique character                CAPS
```

Fig 14.20

This command is useful on large spreadsheets to ensure that cells do contain formulae and not numbers. This spreadsheet is too small to really do justice to this command, so you can **quit** the **AUDIT** mode and **load LESSON8** instead. This is a much larger file and contains far more formulae.

When you have loaded this file, select the **AUDIT** mode again by pressing **Alt** and **F1**, then select the **View, Map, Standard** option again. This will give a similar display to that in the other file but with more characters.

The object of this display can be demonstrated by altering one of the figures. Move the cursor to cell H11. This currently contains the formula **E11+G11**, and the answer to this is 486. If you type in **486** the spreadsheet will still show the correct figures – but it will not amend/update as before, as the cell now contains a number instead of a formula.

Fortunately the display should draw your attention to this error as it is the only cell in this column with a character other than **f**.

The **View, Map, Pattern** option is similar, but also identifies links between formulae so that all cells are given similar codes – all related formulae will have the same code letter.

Select this option now and your screen should show:

```
    A B C D E F G H I J K L M N O P Q R S T U V W X Y Z aAaBaCaDaEaFaGaHaIaJaK
1   "   " i
2                 " f
3   " " " " " " " " " " " " " " " "
4             " " " " " " " " " " "
5   ,
6   £ " " £ A £ B C £ D f E F G E H
7   £ " " £ f £ B C £ D f E F G E H
8   £ " " £ f £ B C £ D f E F G E H
9   £ " " £ f £ B C £ D f E F G E H
10  £ " " £ f £ B C £ D f E F G E H
11  £ " " £ f £ B £ £ D f E F G E H
12  £ " " £ f £ B C £ D f E F G E H
13  £ " " £ f £ B C £ D f E F G E H
14  £ " " £ f £ B C £ D f E F G E H
15  £ " " £ f £ B C £ D f E F G E H
16  £ " " £ f £ B C £ D f E F G E H
17  £ " " £ f £ B C £ D f E F G E H
18  £ " " £ f £ B C £ D f E F G E H
19  £ " " £ f £ B C £ D f E F G E H
20  £ " " £ f £ B C £ D f E F G E H
 LESSON8!H12                 Form=E12+G12
Width:  2  Memory:  164  Last Col/Row:P32
  1>
AUDIT Display text, numbers, formulas coded for identification  CAPS
```

Fig 14.21

14.6.3 Finding relationships

The **Highlight** command can also show links between different formulae by highlighting cells satisfying certain criteria. Select the **Highlight** option now (it should work in all **View** modes). Then select the **Relationships** option.

This option can be used to highlight formula cells that **Support** other cells, are **Dependent** on other cells, contain **Circular** references to other cells, or **Group** relationships within cells.

The variety of different tests that can be carried out using this command are very numerous, but you can try just one. The **Group, None** command should highlight all formula cells that are unique and not dependent upon other formulae.

You should note that this highlights cells in columns **E** and **K,** if you examine the formulae in either of these columns you will note that these cells do contain formulae that are related, but one value is unique to each cell. The cells **highlighted** will be shown as underlined, in colour, or in a different intensity.

Now try the **Highlight, Relationships, Group, First** option. This will show the *parent* or first occurrence of each formula (this is usually the cell that the formula was **copied** from).

The screen should now show:

```
      A B C D E F G H I J K L M N O P Q R S T U V W X Y Z aAaBaCaDaEaFaGaHaIaJaK
   1  "   " i
   2                  " f
   3  " " " " " " " " " " " " " " " "
   4            " " " " " " " " " " "
   5  '
   6  £ " " £ A £ B C £ D f E F G E H
   7  £ " " £ f £ B C £ D f E F G E H
   8  £ " " £ f £ B C £ D f E F G E H
   9  £ " " £ f £ B C £ D f E F G E H
  10  £ " " £ f £ B C £ D f E F G E H
  11  £ " " £ f £ B £ £ D f E F G E H
  12  £ " " £ f £ B C £ D f E F G E H
  13  £ " " £ f £ B C £ D f E F G E H
  14  £ " " £ f £ B C £ D f E F G E H
  15  £ " " £ f £ B C £ D f E F G E H
  16  £ " " £ f £ B C £ D f E F G E H
  17  £ " " £ f £ B C £ D f E F G E H
  18  £ " " £ f £ B C £ D f E F G E H
  19  £ " " £ f £ B C £ D f E F G E H
  20  £ " " £ f £ B C £ D f E F G E H
   LESSON8!H12              Form The total number of highlighted cells is 8
  Width:  2  Memory:  164  Last Col/Row:P32
    1>
  AUDIT For debugging, searches; press / to display the AUDIT menu CAPS
```

Fig 14.22

The **Highlight** command can also be used to **find** selected numbers or text. Lesson 8 contained the payroll details of all employees, and each employee has a grade between 1 and 4. The **Find** option could be used to find all employees with any of the numbers in this range.

Select **Highlight** again and then **Find**, this gives two options; **Contents** or **Value**, the **Contents** option is used for finding specific formula or text entries in cells. You can select the **Value** option.

The next two options will ask whether you want to search for a **Text** value or a **Number** value. Select the **Numbers** option. This has four options: **Go** to start the search; **Relation** to specify the type of search; **Value** to specify the exact value required; and **Quit** to exit. You could enter the exact number required using **Value**, but the **Relation** option offers more scope. Select the **Relation** option now.

The **Relation** option allows you to specify the exact scope required within the search. You can set the search so that all grades below **3** are highlighted. To do this select **Below**. This will not do anything until you enter the search value so you then need to select **Value** and then enter the value as **3**. Then select **Go** to start the search.

The screen should now show the following:

```
     A B C D E F G H I J K L M N O P Q R S T U V W X Y Z aAaBaCaDaEaFaGaHaIaJaK
  1  "   " i
  2                    " f
  3  " " " " " " " " " " " " " " " " " " "
  4              " " " " " " " " " " " " "
  5  '
  6  £ " " £ A £ B C £ D f E F G E H
  7  £ " " £ f £ B C £ D f E F G E H
  8  £ " " £ f £ B C £ D f E F G E H
  9  £ " " £ f £ B C £ D f E F G E H
 10  £ " " £ f £ B C £ D f E F G E H
 11  £ " " £ f £ B £ £ D f E F G E H
 12  £ " " £ f £ B C £ D f E F G E H
 13  £ " " £ f £ B C £ D f E F G E H
 14  £ " " £ f £ B C £ D f E F G E H
 15  £ " " £ f £ B C £ D f E F G E H
 16  £ " " £ f £ B C £ D f E F G E H
 17  £ " " £ f £ B C £ D f E F G E H
 18  £ " " £ f £ B C £ D f E F G E H
 19  £ " " £ f £ B C £ D f E F G E H
 20  £ " " £ f £ B C £ D f E F G E H
 LESSON8!H12                 For The total number of highlighted cells is 41
Width:  2  Memory:  164  Last Col/Row:P32
  1>
AUDIT For debugging, searches; press / to display the AUDIT menu CAPS
```

Fig 14.23

This command has highlighted all cells within the spreadsheet which are below **3**, not just those in the GRADE column. To avoid this you will have to use the **Highlight, Block** command to limit the area being **audited** to the range **D6.D22**.

Most of the other **Highlight** commands will not be of any use in this lesson as it does not have any **links** with other spreadsheets or any **output** attributes.

14.6.4 Replacing entries

The **Squeeze** command is used to *compress* formulae so as to conserve memory. **Squeeze** notes the first occurrence of any formula (the original, or *parent*) and stores all subsequent occurrences of the identical formula as references to the original. The **Copy** command already does this, and as all of the formulae on this spreadsheet were copied using the **Copy** command, the **Squeeze** command will not make any difference.

The remaining **AUDIT** command is the **Replace** option. In order to demonstrate this command you should first revert the screen to **normal** display using the **View** command. Once you have done this move to A1.

The **Replace** command has some similarity with the **Highlight, Relationships** option as it can be used to search for specific entries, but with the added attribute of being able to replace the contents with a new entry.

Select **Replace** and then **Old-String**. This will ask you to enter the *string* that you want replacing – this could be a whole or part word. You can use the command to replace the names of some of the employees as a demonstration. Type in **bobby** and press **ENTER**, then select **New-String** and enter **Robert** as the replacement.

If you now select **Go** all occurrences of the word bobby should be replaced with the word Robert – unfortunately this will not happen as the screen will display a prompt stating **Old-String not found**. The reason for this is that there is no exact match for the old-string as all of the Bobbys begin with a capital B.

You should still have the **Replace** options on the screen, so select the **Case** option – this will allow you to replace **any** string that contains the characters, regardless of case. Select this and then select **Prompt** – this option can be used to *ask* whether each occurrence should be replaced or not. As you will want all occurrences replaced select **No**, then select **Go**.

The screen should now show:

```
     | A ||      B       ||      C       ||   D   || E || F || G ||   H   |
1    PAYROLL             DATE            30-Apr-91
2
3     No:    FIRST NAME      SURNAME         GRADE   BASIC   O/T    O/T     GROSS
4                                                          Hours  Amount    PAY
5     ---------------------------------------------------------------------------
6     165 Tony            Adams                1     400     0       0      400
7     290 Viv             Anderson             4     780    10   23.75   803.75
8     319 John            Barnes               2     480     2       4      484
9     208 Peter           Beardsley            1     400     0       0      400
10    107 George          Best                 4     780     5      10      790
11    170 Robert          Charlton             2     480     3       6      486
12    104 Jack            Charlton             3     530     2       4      534
13    135 Brian           Clough               5    1300     0       0     1300
14    101 Nigel           Clough               1     400    15    37.5    437.5
15    133 Glenn           Hoddle               1     400     8   18.25   418.25
16    181 Kevin           Keegan               5    1300     0       0     1300
17    109 Robert          Moore                3     530     4       8      538
18    180 Robert          Robson               2     480     0       0      480
19    113 Bryan           Robson               3     530     7    15.5    545.5
20    210 Kenny           Sansom               1     400   8.5  19.625  419.625
 LESSON8!B18              Text="Ro The total number of replacements was 3
Go  Range  Old-string  New-string  Case  Match  Prompt  Labels  Quit
 10>/Replace,
MENU  Start replacement
```

Fig 14.24

The **Replace** option can also be used on part-words, so select **Old-String** again and enter **Rob**, then enter **John** as the **New-String**. In order to make sure that all part words containing these characters are included select the **Match** option. This option can be used to match strings that begin, end, or contain the string at any point, or are exact matches. Select **Contains** (**Begins** is not always effective!) and then select **Go**.

This will replace not only the first names containing the phrase **Rob** but also those surnames that contain **Rob**. This demonstrates why the **Prompt** command has been included.

This concludes the lessons in this manual. Hopefully you should now be well versed in all of the attributes and commands available in SuperCalc 5, and should be capable of devising effective spreadsheets for your own applications.

Further exercises

Most of the examples in this final lesson have been condensed to save you having to type in large quantities of meaningless figures and formulae. Unfortunately, this does mean that the demonstrations of both **macros** and the **AUDIT** command are not shown to their full capabilities. In order to gain a better idea of the use of these commands you really need a larger spreadsheet file.

To save you creating a large file, as part of the further exercises you may find it more useful to examine the macro files supplied as demonstrations with SuperCalc 5, and also test them with the AUDIT command. There are a number of such files, but you may find that the following are particularly useful for demonstrating macros:

ANALYSIS	**AUDIT**	**CHARTS**	**COLORS**	**COMMODTY**
CONSOLDT	**CURRENCY**	**DATA**	**DEMOS**	**FNMAX**
FNPLOT	**GROWTH**	**HOUSING**	**USMAP**	

Load any of these files as normal and work through the demonstration so that you can see what it does, then press **Ctrl** and **Break** to examine the macro contents (NB: **BREAKOFF** will be on in some places); you will then have to search the spreadsheet to find where the macro is stored.

Appendix 1 *Summary of commands and functions*

This appendix includes: SuperCalc menu – level 1; SuperCalc menu – level 2; Function key assignments; Types of data; Types of graph; Types of formulae; Summary of functions; Financial function glossary; Graphics glossary.

Supercalc menu – Level one

/A	Arrange
/B	Blank
/C	Copy
/D	Delete
/E	Edit
/F	Format
/G	Global
/I	Insert
/J	Justify
/L	Load
/M	Move
/N	Name
/O	Output
/P	Protect
/Q	Quit
/S	Save
/T	Title
/U	Unprotect
/W	Window
/Z	Zap
/123	Lotus mode

Command summary

/Arrange

Sorts a block of cells into order, with or without cell reference adjustment. Allows up to three key sorts of columns and rows. Options include **Ascending** or **Descending** order.

eg: **ARRANGE A1.A5 , 1ST , ASCENDING GO**

/Blank

Erases the contents of the current cell, cells in a specified range, or unprotected cells.

Options include **Column/Row**, **Block**, **File** or **Page**.

eg: **BLANK A1.A5** deletes entries in range
BLANK ALL deletes all unprotected cells
BLANK A deletes all entries in column

/Copy

Duplicates cell contents and cell values. Duplicates cells from one spreadsheet to another. Does formula adjustment, copies values only, transports rows and columns, and adds, subtracts, multiplies, or divides the ource cell values by the destination cell values.

eg: COPY A1.A5 B1.D1
COPY A1.A5 B1 , TRANSPOSE
COPY A1.A5 B1 , VALUES

/Delete

Removes a row range, column range, block, or disk file. The remaining data is adjusted, including formulae.

eg: **DELETE COLUMN A**
DELETE FILE A:TEST

/Edit

Edits a source cell's contents, and puts it in a destination cell. The source cell may be in any spreadsheet in the computer memory; the destination cell must be in the current spreadsheet.

eg: **EDIT A1** edits contents of cell A1
EDIT A1 ,B1 edits A1 and makes entry in B1

/Format

Controls display formats (on screen) and the appearance of printed output. Defines numerical format, sets column width, determines appearance of dates and times, justifies values of text within cells.

Selects level as **Global**, **Column**, **Row**, **Entry** (**Block**), alters **User-defined** options or **Hide column**.

Options include **Integers**, **General**, **Exponential**, **£ ($)**, **Right**, **Left**, **Centre** (text and figures), simple **Graphics**, **User-defined** options, **Hide**, **Default**, or adjust **Width**.

eg: FORMAT COLUMN A.C WIDTH 12

FORMAT GLOBAL $
FORMAT USER-DEFINED NUMBER 3
FORMAT ROW 3 RIGHT

/Global

Establishes feature settings for the entire spreadsheet, including hardware and program default settings.

- ❒ **Optimum**
  changes settings for current or next session or adopts Lotus 1-2-3 mode. Setting options include memory allocation, manual recalculation, characters before and after figures, **Undo**, etc.

eg: **GLOBAL OPTIMUM PRESENT BEFORE £**

- ❒ **Keep**
  retains current settings for future use as defaults.
- ❒ **Graphics**
  alters graphic output device (printers), layout and size of graphs and graphics device interface.

eg: **GLOBAL GRAPHICS LAYOUT MANUAL WIDTH 6.5**

- ❒ **Spreadsheet**
  alters printers and other device options such as cartridges, printer fonts available, character translation tables.

eg: **GLOBAL SPREADSHEETS DEVICE B&W PRINTERS EPSON LX80**

- ❒ **Evaluation**
  alters order or method of calculation. Options include changing order of calculation, specifying when to carry out re-calculation, and iteration control.

eg: **GLOBAL EVALUATION ORDER ROW**

- ❒ **Values**
  displays current **Global** settings to show which **Global** options are currently **on**.

eg: **GLOBAL VALUES**

- ❒ **Formula**
  toggles between display of values and formulae.

eg: **GLOBAL FORMULA**

- ❒ **"**
  toggles between specifying text with the prefix " or simply typing in text.
- ❒ **Labels**
  toggles between **Name** display or **Cell** range display.
- ❒ **Protection**
  turns **Protection** on or off on all protected cells. Valid for current work session only.

eg: **GLOBAL PROTECTION**

- ❒ **Border**
  switches spreadsheet border display **on or off**.
- ❒ **Next**
  switches automatic cursor movement key on or off on pressing ENTER.
- ❒ **Tab**
  toggles between making cursor jump blank and protected cells.

eg: **GLOBAL TAB**

- ❒ **Unprotected**
  shields all cells explicitly **Protected** or only those not previously **Unprotected**.
- ❒ **Zoom**
  toggles between standard display and expanded display (works with VGA and EGA monitors only).
- ❒ **1-2-3**
  changes command menu to display Lotus 1-2-3 commands, allows Lotus commands to be entered which will then be translated into the relevant SuperCalc command.

/Insert

Inserts an empty row range, column range, or block, and adjusts formulas. Includes option to move block down or right.

eg: **INSERT BLOCK B1.B5 RIGHT**

/Justify

Wraps entered text around a specified range of columns and justifies text flush left, right, or center after entry; wraps text over a specified range of columns as you type. The **Single** option will justify a line down to the first blank cell in the range; the **Multiple** option will continue until there are two consecutive blank cells.

eg: **JUSTIFY SINGLE A1.C5 LEFT**

/Load

Loads all or part of a spreadsheet's contents, values, and format settings from a disk file. Loads Lotus 1-2-3 files.

Files can be added to existing files by use of the **Consolidate** option, or by loading only those values required.

eg: **LOAD A:TEST ALL**

LOAD A:TEST PART (from) A1.A5 (to) C1

LOAD A:TEST CONSOLIDATE

/Move

Moves a row range, column range, or block to new location and adjusts the formulae. Can also transport a block of data from rows to columns, and visa versa.

eg: **MOVE BLOCK (from) A1.C10 (to) D3 TRANSPOSE**

/Name

Establishes a name for a cell range to assist in easier identification of specific blocks; creates a table of range names. Use of the **Name** commands makes design of macros much simpler.

eg: **NAME CREATE SALES A1.A5**

NAME DELETE SALES

/Output

Sends all or part of a spreadsheet to a printer or disk file. Also enters **Grids, Lines** and **Shading** on reports (providing a suitable printer is in use).

Allows printing of multiple ranges on a single page, and lets you preview output on screen.

Printer options include titles, headers, footers, and margins on output, landscape or portrait orientation, selection of border character, condensed or normal printig and altering page width/length.

eg: **OUTPUT PRINTER RANGE ALL GO**

OUTPUT PRINTER RANGE ALL OPTIONS SETUP CTRL O

OUTPUT PRINTER OPTIONS TITLES AUTO

OUTPUT FILE A:TEST

/Protect

Prevents any changes to cells contents. Contents can only be altered by using **Unprotect** or **Global Protection**.

eg: **PROTECT A1.A5**

/Quit

Exits Supercalc or the current spreadsheet, and either returns you to the operating system, the next spreadsheet in memory, or begins another program.

eg: **QUIT DOS**

/Save

Saves all or part of a spreadsheet to a disk file. Has options to write calculated cell values only, or protected/unprotected cells only. Can save in formats compatible with SuperCalc3 and SuperCalc4, as well as Lotus 1-2-3.

eg: **SAVE A:TEST ALL**

SAVE A:TEST VALUES

SAVE A:TEST LEVEL 4 file can be read by SuperCalc 4

/Title

Locks columns, rows, or both on screen. Keeps reference labels in view while you scroll through the spreadsheet. Titles can be included in printouts by accepting the **Titles** option in the **Output** command.

eg: **TITLE HORIZONTAL**

TITLE BOTH

TITLE CLEAR

/Unprotect

Removes protection (applied with /Protect) from a specified protected range.

eg: **UNPROTECT A1.A5**

/Window

Splits the display window horizontally or vertically into two parts. Allows simultaneous or independent scrolling of the windows. There must be at least one column or row to the left/above the column/row selected for the window.

The F6 key will move the cursor from one window back into the other.

eg: **WINDOW VERTICAL**

WINDOW SYNCHRONIZE

/Zap

Erases a spreadsheet from memory, leaving a blank display window. The file on disk is not affected.

Includes an option to **Save** work before zapping.

eg: **ZAP YES**

ZAP SAVE A:TEST

/1-2-3

Executes a command via Lotus 1-2-3's menu structure. SuperCalc will then return to normal command structure.

eg: **1 WORKSHEET**

NB: The **Global** command has an optiron to toggle to **1-2-3** commands. This will show Lotus 1-2-3 commands, but they will be interpreted by the program as SuperCalc 5 commands. To return to the SuperCalc menu select WORKSHEET GLOBAL SC5.

Supercalc menu - Level two

//A	Add-in
//D	Data
//E	Export
//F	File
//G	Graphics
//I	Import
//M	Move
//N	Network
//R	Restrict
//S	Spreadsheets
//T	Test

Command summary

//Add-in

Attaches, invokes, and detaches compatible add-in programmes and functions for use in Supercalc. Allows linking of add-in programmes to function keys, and can establish automatic invocation of a single add-in.

eg: **ADD-IN ATTACH A:TEST 3** (for Function key 3)

ADD-IN INVOKE A:TEST

or SHIFT KEY and F3

//Data

Locates, extracts, or deletes selected data, computes frequency distributions and multi-variable regression analyses, performs matrix multiplication and inversion, solves simultaneous equations, generates data ranges, parses continuous data records into fields, calculatee one- and two-variable **what-if** tables.

eg: **DATA INPUT A1.C30**

DATA CRITERION D1.F20

DATA FIND

DATA BLOCK A1.B10 COLUMN NUMBER 100 10 999999

//Export

Saves a spreadsheet to disk in any of the following file formats: XDIF (exports formulae and values), DIF (exports values only), Comma Separated Values (for BASIC files), and DBase111. Use to save to a Lotus 1-2-3 file format. If a file is to be transferred to a Word-processor use the **Output** file command rather than **Export**.

eg: **EXPORT DBASE ALL**

//File

Allows creation of global and spreadsheet datapaths to guide automatic file searches. Displays the file list for the specified file type and changes the default directory.

eg: **FILE LIST 1-2-3** (displays Lotus files only)

FILE ALL (displays all files)

FILE DIRECTORY A:\SPREADSHEETS (sets default path)

//Graphics

Display spreadsheet data graphically in the following types of charts: bar, line, bar and line, pie, hilo, including three-dimensional and exploded charts.

eg: **GRAPHICS DATA A1.A4 B1.B4 C1.C4**

GRAPHICS LABELS AXIS A5.C5 BLACK STICK LEFT

GRAPHICS TYPE PIE

//Import

Loads files created by other programs. Imports the following file formats: XDIF, DIF, CSV, Numbers (and "text in quotes"), Text (ASC11 text files), VisiCalc, and DBase 111. Use **/Load** to load a Lotus 1-2-3 file.

eg: **IMPORT DIF DEMO COLWISE ALL**

IMPORT TEXT MEMO REPLACE YES

//Macro

Helps create and de-bug Supercalc macros; converts Lotus 1-2-3 macros to Supercalc format. Learn mode *captures* commands as entered, and **Write** stores macro on disk. **Analyze** and **Breakpoint** are used to check for errors, **Trace** can produce a printout for checking.

eg: **MACRO LEARN A1.A20**

MACRO WRITE DEMO ALL

MACRO EXECUTE DEMO

MACRO ANALYZE RANGE A1.A20 GO

//Network

Allows sharing of network resources in a supported network environment. **Lock** and **Unlock** can be used to prevent or allow other users to access files. **Output** will direct the printout to a specified printer port.

eg: **NETWORK DIRECTORY LINK b:\\SERVER\CALC1**

NETWORK LOCK

NETWORK OUTPUT 1

//Restrict

Restricts data input to a specified range. This command will cease to function in macros when the ENTER key is pressed.

eg: **RESTRICT A1.A20**

//Spreadsheets

Allows more than one spreadsheet at a time to be in memory; displays up to three spreadsheets on screen at once; lets you move among open spreadsheets, and hide them from view.

eg: **SPREADSHEET NEW** then load required file

SPREADSHEET DISPLAY 3 displays 3 spreadsheets

SPREADSHEET ZAP

SPREADSHEET HIDE DEMO

//Test

Offers commands for viewing your spreadsheets in formula and map view, highlighting related cells, tracing errors, identifying various cell relationships, and finding and replacing text and formulae.

eg: **TEST HIGHLIGHT CELLS FORMULA** Highlights all cells containing formulae

TEST FIND VALUE NUMBERS EQUAL

TEST SQUEEZE condenses formulae

TEST REPLACE OLDSTRING ERIC NEWSTRING JOHN GO

Function key assignments

In Supercalc the use of the function keys is context sensitive, i.e. the function changes depending on which menu is displayed. However, the function keys can be considered as having two main sets of value:

1) normal functions.
2) functions in graphics mode.

Note: The use of the function alters significantly in AUDIT mode, selected using the **//T** (Test command).

Normal function key usage

F1 Context sensitive help
F2 EDIT (invokes the **Edit** command)
F3 NAME (displays **Name** directory)
F4 ABSOLUTE (makes cell range absolute **A1**)
F5 GOTO (invokes **GoTo** command)
F6 WINDOW (moves cursor between windows)
F7 LABELS (shows range (a1.a20) or **Name**)
F8 STEP (executes each macro command separately)
F9 CALC (recalculates spreadsheet)
F10 VIEW (displays graph)

Graphics function key usage

If the **//Graphics** command is displayed on the prompt line then the function keys will perform the following operations:

F1 HELP (**Graphics** help menus)
F2 EDIT (invokes **Edit** command)
F3 NAME (displays chart **names**)
F4 POINT (for selecting cell ranges)
F5 ROW/COLUMN (toggles range row- or column-wise)
F6 COPY (copies attributes or defaults)
F10 VIEW (displays chart)

Types of data (cell contents)

- Numeric
  Integers decimals exponents and percentages.
- Date/Time
  Date and time are a single data type.
- String
  Any character string including the two types below.
- Repeating Text
  Characters preceded by a single quote causing them to repeat across the spreadsheet until a non blank cell is encountered.
- Control Text
  Special characters which are designed to be transmitted to a printer to turn on and off some functions such as batch print.
- Error Data
  Data type given to a cell that returns a value that cannot be calculated.

- ❒ N/A Data
  Data type given to a cell when data is not available.

Types of graph

- ❒ **Bar graphs**
  Simple bar
  Stacked bar
  Grouped bar
  100% bar
  Delta bar
- ❒ **Pie graph**
- ❒ **Dual graphs**
  Pie pie
  Bar pie
  Bar bar
- ❒ **Line graphs**
  Simple line
  Stacked line
- ❒ **Area graphs**
  Simple area
  Stacked area
- ❒ **Hi - lo graph**
- ❒ **X - Y graph**
- ❒ **Radar graph**
- ❒ **Word graph**

Types of formula

Logical
Calendar
Financial
Index
Statistical
Data Management
Arithmetic
Trigonometric
String
Special Purpose

Summary of formulae

There are ten categories of SuperCalc funtions. The following list summarizes each of the functions by category.

Logical functions

Function *Returns*

ISBLANK(expression)
True if expression is a blank cell.

ISBLANK(B2)

ISDATE(expression)
True if expression is date value type cell.

ISDATE(B2)

ISERROR(expression)
True if expression returns ERROR value.

ISERROR(B2)

ISNA(expression)
True if expression returns Not available.

ISNA(B2)

ISNUM(expression)
True if expression returns numeric value type.

ISNUM(B2)

ISPROT(cell)
True if cell is protected.

ISPROT(B2)

ISSTR(expression)
True if expression returns text or string

ISSTR(B2)

ISTIME(expression)
True if expression is a date value type cell with value <1.

ISTIME(B2)

ISVAL(expression)
True if expression returns numeric value.

ISVAL(B2)

ERROR or ERR
Displays ERROR.

FALSE
Displays 0 for logical value False.

NA
Displays N/A for Not Available.

TRUE
Displays 1 for logical value true.

Conditional logic

Function *Returns*

AND(value,value2)
True if value1 and value2 are true.

AND(A1=4,B2=6)

EXACT(string1,string2)
True if string1 and string2 match.

EXACT(A1,B2)

IF(CON,X,Y)
X IF Cond is True; Y if cond is false.

IF(A1>6,C1,C2)

NOT(value)
True if value is false.

NOT(A1=5)

OR(value1, value2)
True if any value is true.

OR(A1>4,B2>6)

Calendar functions

Function *Returns*

DATE(mm,dd,yy)
Date Value of specified date.

DATE(02,09,92)

EDAT(dd,mm,yy)
Same as DAT:European parameter order.

EDAT(09,02,92)

DVAL(value)
Date value of specified value.

DVAL(1) = March 1,1900

NOW
System date of specified value.

TODAY System date.

TIME(hh,mm,ss)
Time value of specified time.

TIME(14,23,50) = 2:23:50 PM

TIMEVALUE(time value or fractional string)
Converts string, time value, or portion of julian date/time into a formatted value

TIMEVALUE(.5) = 12:00:00

Date/time reference functions

Function *Returns*

DAY(VALUE)
Number of the day of the month of date value or integral portion of julian date/time.

DVAL(32311) = 8/16/88

JDATE(date value)
Julian date of date value.

JDATE(08,16,88) = 32311

JTIME(time value)
Julian time of time value.

MINUTE(value)
Minute corresponding to the minute portion of time value or fractional portion of julian date/time.

MONTH(value)
Number of the month of date.

SECOND(value)
Second corresponding to the minute portion of time value or fractional portion of julian date/time.

YEAR(value)
Number of the year of date value or integral portion of julian date/time.

WDAY(date value)
Julian number of day of week of date value

Financial functions

Function *Returns*

ANTERM(payment, rate, present value)
Number of payment periods.

PMT(present value, rate,term)
Equal periodic payment.

PV(payment, rate, term)
Present value of a series of payments.

BALANCE(present value,rate,term,period)
Remaining principal balance after period payments.

KINT(present value,rate,term,period)
Amount of interest paid in period.

KPRIN(present value,rate,term,period)
Amount of principal paid in period.

PAIDINT(present value,rate,term,period)
Total interest paid to period.

CTERM(rate,future value, present value)
Number of periods (terms).

COMPBAL(present value,rate,term)
Final balance in an account.

RATE(future value, present value,term)
Periodic interest rate.

FV(payment,rate,term)
Future value.

IRR(guess,row/col range)
Internal rate of return.

NPV(rate,row/col range)
Net Present Value of a group of cash returns

TERM(payment, rate, future value)
Number of periods.

DDB(cost, salvage, life, period)
Depreciation allowance using the double-declining balance method.

SLN(cost, salvage, life)
Straight-line depreciation for one period

SYD(cost, salvage, life, period)
Sum-of-the-years digits depreciation for specified period.

Index functions

Function *Returns*

ADDRESS(range)
Cell address of upper-left cell in range.

ADDRESS(SALES) = A1

BEGCOL(range)
Column number of upper-left cell in range.

BEGCOL(E4.F10) = 5

CHOOSE(x,vo,v1,...,vn)
The xth value from the list of values.

CHOOSE(1,4,5,6) = 5
NB: 4 is at the 0th position

COLCHARS(value)
Takes a number from 1 through 255 and returns the equivalent column string. A through IU.

COLS(range)
Number of columns in range.

COLS(A1.D20) = 4

CURADDRESS
Current cell address.

CURCOL
Column number of the current cell.

CURPAGE
Number of current spreadsheet page.

CURROW
Current row number.

CURSHEET
Name of current spreadsheet.

ENDCOL(range)
Column number of the lower right cell.

ENDCOL(A1.F35) = 6

ENDROW(range)
Row number of the lowest right cell.

ENDROW(A1.F35) = 35

HLOOKUP(x, range, row offset)
Content of the cell in the horizontal table.

HLOOKUP(23,SALES,2)

INDEX(range, column offset, row offset)
The value of the cell in range at column offset and row offset.

INDEX(SALES,1,2)

ITER
The current iteration count.

LASTCOL or LCOL
Right most column number containing data.

LASTROW or LROW
Row number of last cell containing data.

LOOKUP(value,range)
Last value in range that is less than or equal;

or LU(value, row/col range)
To value.

LOOKUP(A5,D1.D20)

N(cell)
Numeric value of cell.

N(A1) = 4

ROWS(range)
Number of rows in range.

S(cell)
String value of cell.

THISCOL or TCOL
Column number of the cell.

THISROW or TROW
Row number of the cell.

VLOOKUP(x,range,column offset)
Content of the cell in the vertical table specified by range, across row x, in the column defined by column offset

Statistical functions

Function *Returns*

AVERAGE(list)
The average (mean) of the list.

AVG(A1.A5)

COUNT(list)
The number value cells in list

COUNT(A1.A5)

MAX(list)
Maximum value in list.

MAX(A1.A5)

MIN(list)
Minimum value in list.

MIN(A1.A5)

RANDOM or RAND or RAN
Random number between 0 and 1.

STD(list)
Standard deviation of a population in list.

STD(A1.A5)

SUM(list)
Sum of the values in list

SUM(A1.A5)

VAR(list)
Population variance of the values in list.

VAR(A1.A5)

Data management statistical functions

Function *Returns*

DAVG(input, offset field, criterion)
Mean (average) of values in offset field of input range that meets criteria.

DAVG(SALES,3,JOHN)

DCOUNT(input, offset field, criterion)
Number of non-blank, non-zero cells in offset field of input range that meets criteria.

DCOUNT(SALES,3,JOHN)

DMAX(input, offset field, criterion)
Largest value in offset of input range that meets criteria.

DMAX(SALES,3,JOHN)

DMIN(input, offset field, criterion)
Smallest value in of input range that meets criteria.

DMIN(SALES,3,JOHN)

DSTD(input, offset field, criteria)
Standard deviation of population for values in offset field of input range that meets criteria.

DSTD(SALES,3,JOHN)
DSUM(input,offset field, criterion)
Sum of values in offset field of input range that meets criteria.

DSUM(SALES,3,JOHN)

DVAR(input, offset field, criteria)
Population variance for values in offset field of input range that meets criteria.

DVAR(SALES,3,JOHN)

Arithmetic functions

Function *Returns*

ABS(value)
Absolute value of value.

ABS(-3) = 3

EXP(value)
e to the power of value.

EXP(2) = 7.3890609

INT(value)
Integer of value

INT(4.589) = 4

LN(value)
Natural log.log base e, of value.

LN(5) = 1.6094371243

LOG10(value) or LOG (value)
log base 10 (common log) of value.

LOG10(12) = 1.07918124605

MOD(value1, value2)
Remainder from the division of value 1 by value 2.

MOD(15,4) = 11

ROUND(value, places)
Value rounded to number of places.

ROUND(4.589,1) = 4.6

ROUNDUP(value, places)
Value rounded up to number of places.

ROUND(4.336,1) = 4.4

SQRT(value)
Square root of value.

SQRT(4) = 2

TRUNC(value,places)
Value truncated to number of places.

TRUNC(4.336,1) = 4.3

Trigonometric functions

Function *Returns*

ACOS(value)
Arccosine of value.

ACOS(.5) = 1.04719755

ASIN(value)
Arscine of value.

ASIN(.5) = .5235987755

ATAN(value)
Arctangent of value.

ATAN2(x,y)
Arctangent of point.

COS(value)
Cosine of value.

PI
Value of pi.

SIN(value)
Sine of value.

TAN(value)
Tangent of value.

String functions

Function *Returns*

CHAR(N)
ASC11 value of n.

CHAR(65) = A

CODE(string)
ASC11 value of first character in string.

CODE("Adam") = 65

CONTENTS(cell)
The contents of cell as a string.

CONTENTS(A2) = "A1*5"

DISPLAY(value, format value or string, width)
String equal to value formatted according to format sting and displayed at width.

DISPLAY(12,$,5) = 12.00

FIND(searchstring)
Character position of searchstring in string.

FIND("a", "C and A",1) = 3

LEFT(string,n)
The first n characters of the string.

LEFT("C and A",4) = "C an"

LENGTH(string)
Length of string.

LENGTH("C and A") = 7

LOWER(string)
String converted to lower case.

LOWER("THE") = "the"

MID(string, startnumber, n)
Substring of length n beginning with the startnumber character position.

PROPER(string)
String converted to proper capitalization.

PROPER("t. jones") = "T. Jones"

REPEAT(string,n)
String repeated n times.

REPEAT("Hi",2) = Hi Hi

RIGHT(string, n)
Last n character of string.

STRING(x, n)
Converts x to string with n decimal places.

TRIM(string)
Removes excess spaces in front and end of string.

UPPER(string)
String converted to upper case.

Special purpose functions

Function *Returns*

FORMAT(cell)
Format value of cell.

TYPE(cell)
Character that represents cell type.

VALUE(string)
Numeric value of string.

WIDTH(range)
Width of column(s) where range is located.

Financial function glossary

- Rate
  The interest rate corresponding to a single period(10 % = 0. 10).
- Term
  The number of periods in the life of an investment.
- Period
  A single period between 1 and the term.
- Payment
  A periodic payment.
- Present Value
  Initial investment or amount borrowed.
- Future Value
  The value of an investment after TERM periods.

Graphics glossary

- Top Title
  Banner title at the top of the chart of up to three lines.

- Sub Title
  A further title of up to two lines already below the top title.
- Footnote
  A small title, which is left justified at the bottom of the charts, of up to three lines.
- X-Axis Title
  A heading below the X axis labels.
- Y1 Axis Title
  A heading along the left hand side on top of the chart defining the left Y axis.
- Y2 Axis Title
  A heading along the right hand side on top of the chart defining the right Y axis.
- Legend Title
  A heading at the top of the legend.
- X-Axis Labels
  Number of text which define the ticks along the X axis.
- Y1-Axis Labels
  Numbers or text which define the ticks along the X axis.
- Y2-Axis Labels
  Numbers or text which define the ticks along the Y axis (right-hand).
- Legend Labels
  Numbers of text that identify the series in a graph by matching colours or patterns.
- Data Labels
  Numbers of text that identify the value of each series.
- Ticks
  Small lines on axis charts that indicate the scaling units on the X and Y axes.
- Grids
  Horizontal and/or vertical lines that are displayed behind an axes chart.
- Series
  A user defined range of data to be displayed graphically.

Appendix 2 *Suggested answers* to further exercises

Exercise 1

```
     °   A   °°   B   °°   C   °°   D   °°   E   °°   F   °°   G   °°   H   °
1    SUGGESTED ANSWER: EXERCISE 1
2
3     230         SUM(A3:A8)
4     234         AVG(A3:A8)
5     410         COUNT(A3:A8)
6     75          MAX(A3:A8)
7     190         MIN(A3:A8)
8     89          A3+A7
9                 A4*A8
10                A5/A7
11                25%A4
12                110%A3
13                IF(A3>200,A5,A6)
14
15
16
17
18
19
20
 ANS1!A2
Width:  9  Memory:  186  Last Col/Row:B13
  1>
READY F1:Help  F3:Names  Ctrl-Backspace:Undo  Ctrl-Break:Cancel  CAPS NUM
```

Exercise 2

```
     °      A       °°   B   °°   C   °°   D   °°   E   °°   F   °°   G   °
14   SUGGESTED ANSWER: EXERCISE 2
15
16   SALES PER QUARTER:
17   -----------------
18   QUARTER                  1        2        3        4
19   -----------------------------------------------------------------------
20   MIDLANDS                 9      9.9    11.88   10.692
21   NORTH EAST              12     13.2    15.84   14.256
22   NORTH WEST              16     17.6    21.12   19.008
23   SOUTH EAST              19     20.9    25.08   22.572
24   SOUTH WEST               5      5.5      6.6     5.94
25
26
27
28
29
30
31
32
33
 ANS2!A15
Width: 15  Memory:  184  Last Col/Row:E24
  1>
READY F1:Help  F3:Names  Ctrl-Backspace:Undo  Ctrl-Break:Cancel  CAPS NUM
```

Exercise 3

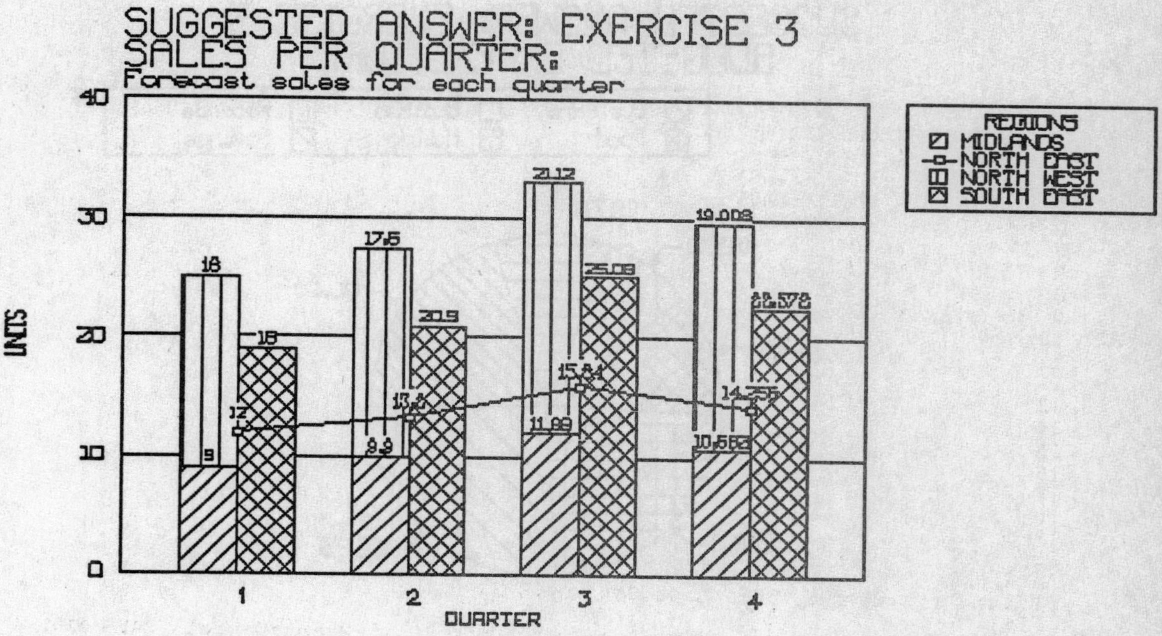

SUGGESTED ANSWER: EXERCISE 3
SALES PER QUARTER:
Forecast sales for each quarter
REGIONS
MIDLANDS
NORTH EAST
NORTH WEST
SOUTH EAST
UNITS
QUARTER

Exercise 4

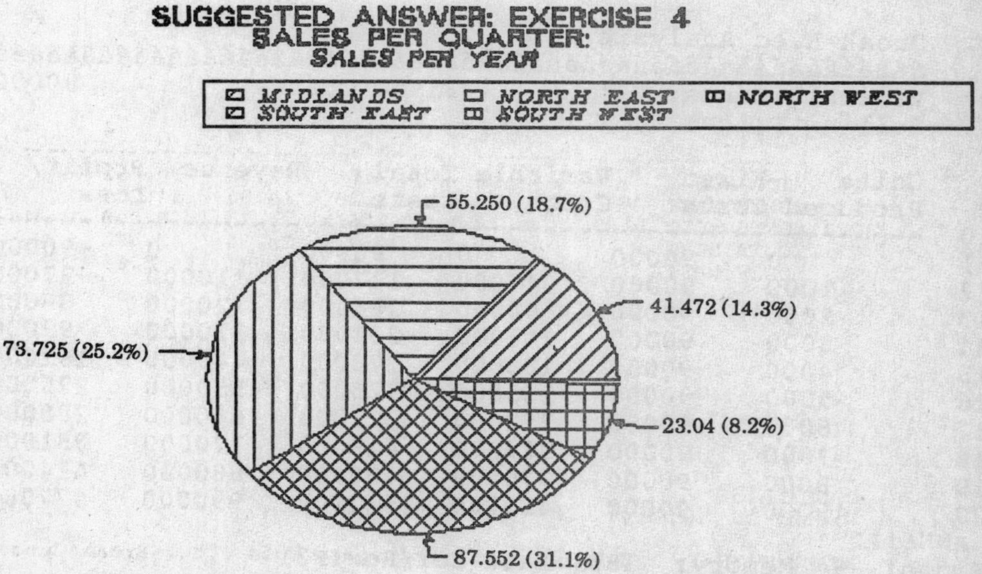

SUGGESTED ANSWER: EXERCISE 4
SALES PER QUARTER:
SALES PER YEAR
MIDLANDS
NORTH EAST
NORTH WEST
SOUTH EAST
SOUTH WEST
55.250 (18.7%)
41.472 (14.3%)
73.725 (25.2%)
23.04 (8.2%)
87.552 (31.1%)

Exercise 5

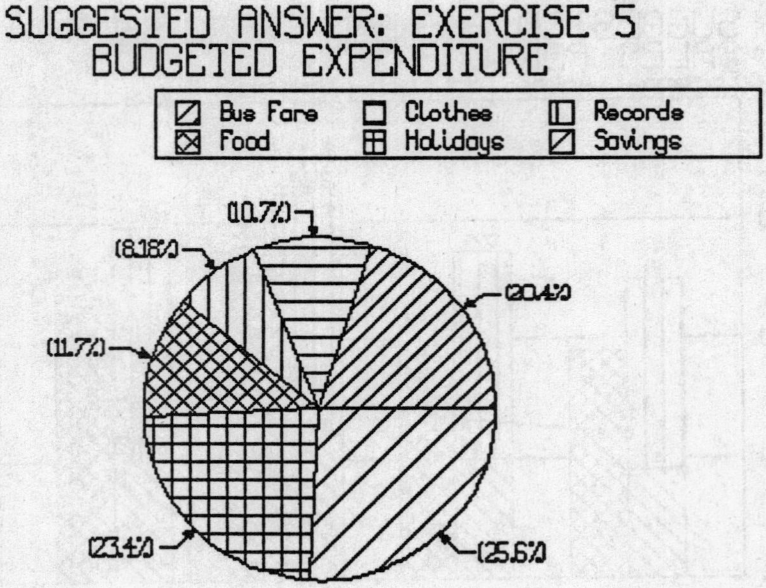

Exercise 6

```
      A       B       C       D       E       F       G       H
1   SUGGESTED ANSWER: EXERCISE 6
2
3   Break Even Analysis
4   áááááááááááááááááááááááááááááááááááááááááááááá
5   Variable Costs:          47Fixed Costs:            90000
6   Selling Price:          110
7
8   Units    Fixed    Variable Total    Revenue  Profit/
9   Produced Costs    Costs    Costs             Loss
10  ------------------------------------------------------------
11         0   90000        0   90000        0   -90000
12      1000   90000    47000  137000   110000   -27000
13      2000   90000    94000  184000   220000    36000
14      3000   90000   141000  231000   330000    99000
15      4000   90000   188000  278000   440000   162000
16      5000   90000   235000  325000   550000   225000
17      6000   90000   282000  372000   660000   288000
18      7000   90000   329000  419000   770000   351000
19      8000   90000   376000  466000   880000   414000
20      9000   90000   423000  513000   990000   477000
 ANS6!A2
Width:  9  Memory:  183  Last Col/Row:F31
  1>
READY F1:Help  F3:Names  Ctrl-Backspace:Undo  Ctrl-Break:Cancel  CAPS NUM
```

Exercise 7

```
     °     A      °° B  °°   C    °° D°°    E    °°    F   °°    G     °
1   SUGGESTED ANSWER: EXERCISE 7
2
3         ITEMS      CAT NO.    PRICE QTY      VALUE ORDER QTY RE-ORDER LVL
4   ----------------------------------------------------------------------
5   Desks                 123 180.75  13 2,349.75          7            10
6   Chairs                124  55.75  20 1,115.00         11            10
7   Typewriters           125  55.75   7   390.25          3             5
8   Filing Cabinets       126 120.35   5   601.75          5            10
9   Waste Bins            127   5.99  18   107.82          5            20
10                                   -------------
11                                    63 4,564.57
12
13
14
15
16
17
18
19
20
 ANS7!A2
Width: 16  Memory:  187  Last Col/Row:G11
  1>
READY F1:Help  F3:Names  Ctrl-Backspace:Undo  Ctrl-Break:Cancel  CAPS NUM
```

Exercise 8

```
     °  A  °°  B  °°         C          °°                D                     °
1   SUGGESTED ANSWER: EXERCISE 8 (SHOWING FORMULA)
2
3                  COMMISSION          BONUS
4   REP:    SALES: PAID                PAID
5   Joe"     12000  LOOKUP(A5,A16:A20) IF(B5>5000,250+((B5-5000)*3%),B5*5%)
6   Fred"    7600   LOOKUP(A6,A16:A20) IF(B6>5000,250+((B6-5000)*3%),B6*5%)
7   Anne"    4890   LOOKUP(A7,A16:A20) IF(B7>5000,250+((B7-5000)*3%),B7*5%)
8   Dalbir"  9020   LOOKUP(A8,A16:A20) IF(B8>5000,250+((B8-5000)*3%),B8*5%)
9   Ken"     2705   LOOKUP(A9,A16:A20) IF(B9>5000,250+((B9-5000)*3%),B9*5%)
10  Sue"     5400   LOOKUP(A10,A16:A20 IF(B10>5000,250+((B10-5000)*3%),B10*5
11
12
13
14          BASIC:
15  Joe"     200
16  Fred"    280
17  Anne"    220
18  Dalbir"  245
19  Ken"     170
20  Sue"     190
 ANS8!A1                 Text="SUGGESTED ANSWER: EXERCISE 8 (SHOWIN TEXT
Width:  7  Memory:  186  Last Col/Row:E20
  1>
READY F1:Help  F3:Names  Ctrl-Backspace:Undo  Ctrl-Break:Cancel  CAPS NUM
```

Exercise 9

```
   ° O °° P °° Q °° R °° S °° T °° U °° V °
1  SUGGESTED ANSWER: EXERCISE 9
2
3                                 \p      /LA:LESSON8.CAL~RY
4                                         /GB
5                                         {ENTRYOFF}
6                                         /PA1:O22~/UF6.F22~
7                                         /GT
8                                         {SUSPEND}
9                                         /UA1:O22~
10                                        /LA:PAY1~C/LA:TAX1~V
11
12
13
14
15
16
17
18
19
20
 ANS9!O1                 Text="SUGGESTED ANSWER: EXERCISE 9        TEXT
Width:  9  Memory:  188  Last Col/Row:T10
  1>
READY F1:Help  F3:Names  Ctrl-Backspace:Undo  Ctrl-Break:Cancel  CAPS NUM
```

Exercise 10

```
   ° E °°  F  °°  G  °°      H        °°      I       °°   J  °°   K  °
1  SUGGESTED ANSWER: EXERCISE 10
2
3  BASIC        No:     FIRST NAME     SURNAME        GRADE     BASIC
4    400                Bobby
5    780
6    480
7    400
8    780
9    480
10   530
11  1300
12   400
13   400          170   Bobby          Charlton           2       480
14  1300          109   Bobby          Moore              3       530
15   530          180   Bobby          Robson             2       480
16   480
17   530
18   400
19   780
20   480
 ANS10!E2
Width:  5  Memory:  185  Last Col/Row:K20
  1>
READY F1:Help  F3:Names  Ctrl-Backspace:Undo  Ctrl-Break:Cancel  CAPS NUM
```

Exercise 11

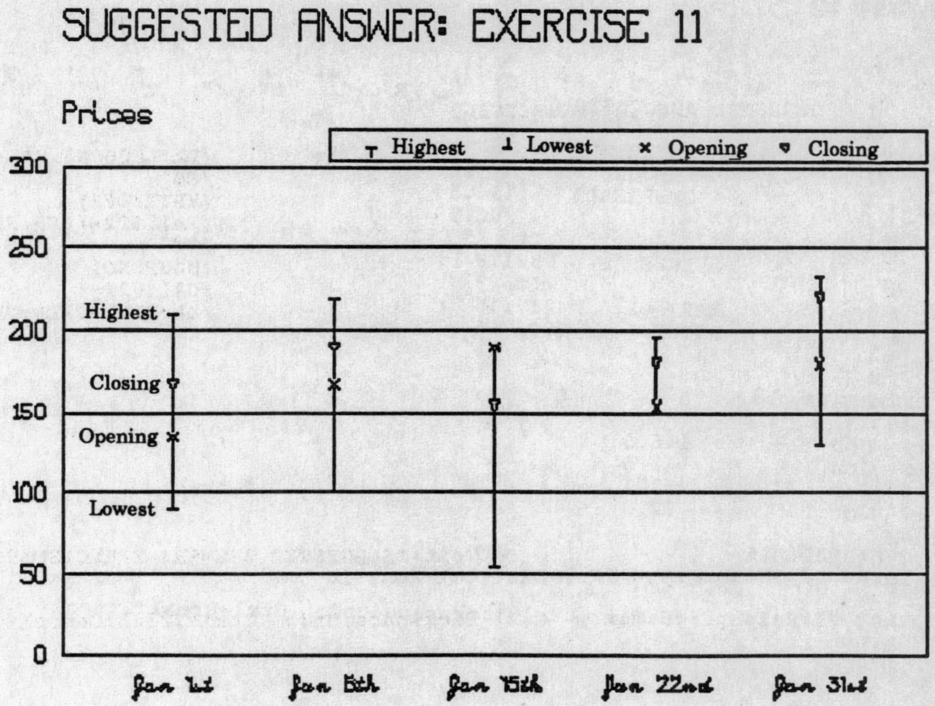

Exercise 12

	B	D	F	H	J
1	SUGGESTED ANSWER: EXERCISE 12				
2					
3	Proposed Projects				
4					
5	Summary of analysis of proposed projects using both Net Present				
6	Value and Internal Rate of Return techniques.				
7					
8					
9	+ --------------------	----------	----------	----------	---------- +
10		Project A	Project B	Project C	Project D
11	Investment	-100000	-100000	-100000	-100000
12	Year 1	12000	35000	60000	5000
13	Year 2	20000	50000	30000	5000
14	Year 3	28000	30000	30000	20000
15	Year 4	50000	20000	10000	60000
16	Year 5	40000	15000	10000	60000
17	+ --------------------	----------	----------	----------	---------- +
18	Net Present Value	7462.36	18654.03	14917.63	1940.07
19	IRR	12.3	18.4	18.1	10.5
20	+ --------------------	----------	----------	----------	----------

Exercise 13

```
      2°  A  °°  B  °°  C  °°  D  °°  E  °°  F  °°  G  °
   1           JOB COSTS        Job 123
   2
   3           MATERIALS          30
   4           LABOUR            120
   5           OVERHEADS       136.5
   6                           286.5
  JOB °  A  °°  B  °°  C  °°  D  °°  E  °°  F  °°  G  °°  H
  5           OVERHEADS     531.8
  6                        1085.8
  7           MARK-UP       217.16
  8           PRICE        1302.96
  9
  10
 OVERHEADA  °°  B  °°  C  °°  D  °°  E  °°  F  °°  G  °°  H  °
 13
 14  Job 123     136.5
 15  Job 124     111.5
 16  Job 125       201
 17  Job 126      82.8
 18
  OVERHEAD!B16                Form=201
 Width:  9  Memory:   12  Last Col/Row:E17
   1>
 READY F1:Help  F3:Names  Ctrl-Backspace:Undo  Ctrl-Break:Cancel       NUM
```

Exercise 14

```
SUGGESTED ANSWER: EXERCISE 14

Sample Charts
          This macro shows 19 sample charts.
\Autoexec{call Init}                        Sample charts macro.
          {let Check,""}
          {goto}Check~//gl{dn}
          {if Check=1}{branch Enable}        Graphics not enabled, inform
          {ready}{call Start}
Next      {call PickMenu}                   Select a chart, Show, or Quit
          {if ChartName=Quit}{quit}
          {if ChartName=Show}{goto}CMenu Hide~{for Num,1,ChartCount,1 Show
          {if ChartName<>Show}{Chartit 1e9}  Valid chart selection, always
          {Branch Next}                     Get next selection

Init      {onbreak Out}{entryoff}{windowsoff}Clear entire screen.
          {status ""}{indicator ""}{macroprompt ""}{message ""}{prompt ""}
          {return}
Start     {goto}Cmenu~{goto}Select~{windowson Go to first screen and place
          {return}
 ANS14!A2
Width:  9  Memory:  155  Last Col/Row:AW217
  1>
READY F1:Help  F3:Names  Ctrl-Backspace:Undo  Ctrl-Break:Cancel  CAPS NUM CAL
```

Index